THE DEVIL

IS

A WOMAN

© FRANK .J. PETERS

If you want to see the truth, close your eyes
to what appears to be true.
Jalal ud Din al-Rumi

1

In a darkened room, on a black-draped bed, somewhere in the
heart of the city, lies an old witch. Like an ancient spider, her
withered body seems lifeless. But inside that body, her mind
seethes as she reaches out like Death, scheming, controlling,
manipulating ...

Christmas in Paris.

A quiet time, at least ostensibly, a time of good-will, of peace
and love. Yet by the time dawn breaks next day, gloomy and
grey, one man has been hanged, and another, seemingly quite
unconnected with the first, has died the exotic Death by a
Thousand Cuts. Nor was the hanging any ordinary hanging, for
the man was hanged as he is supposed to be hanged according to
the tarocchi card: upside-down by the left foot, the right leg
crossed behind the left in an almost casual manner.

I learn of the Hanged Man only later.

The victim of the Death by a Thousand Cuts is the uncle of a
friend of mine. I hear all about that - and about my friend's arrest
- as soon as I enter the Lutetia.

'Mariana!' someone shouts. Raoul, the shy one.

'Ah! La voilà! Mariana!'

That is Evrard, who is not shy.

The tap-room is packed with people celebrating Christmas.
Someone by the door is playing a guitar, softly, sadly. No one is
listening. I put my hand on his head, ruffle his hair a little. He
reminds me of home, of Spain. He grins up at me.

Evrard makes his way over. He kisses me on both cheeks,
introduces me to the woman who is sitting with them. 'Mariana,
this is Mère Henriette, mother of Jaquet - you know? Jaquet le
Breton?'

'Of course I know Jaquet. But what - ?'

'And this, Mère Henriette, is Doña Mariana de la Mar - she's
actually half Scottish and half Spanish. But we call her La Belle
Marianne.'

Which was certainly better than Mariana la Puta, a name
which was beginning to haunt me.

'Mariana reads palms, and casts horoscopes,' Kateline, one of
the girls in our group, explains. 'She knows things.'

They pour me a drink and sit me opposite the woman. Then Evrard says, 'Now, Mère Henriette: tell Mariana the story. Start again, from the beginning.'

She is Jaquet's mother and she keeps the apothecary's shop at the sign of the Mortar & Pestle in the rue du Dragon, off the rue Saint-Denis. Jaquet is a friend of Marc's. Marc is a friend of Raoul's. He is sitting beside Raoul now. Marc's girlfriend, douce Kateline, is sitting next to him on the other side.

I like the Lutetia. It is in the rue des Carmes, on the university side of the river; it is clean, the food is good; and it is, they tell me, one of the few taverns anywhere in Paris with a welcoming attitude to women. In this, it contrasts markedly with the Sorbonne, where I am obliged to pursue my studies in theology clandestinely. I also sometimes attend lectures (again under false colours) at the School of Medicine, and at the College of Astrology, founded not long ago by the King, Charles V.

I met Jaquet through Evrard, but now, because we both attend courses on pharmacology and astrology, he is one of the few who know me, not just as a girl, but as the boy I seem to be when I am in the lecture hall, dressed in my long black gown, hood pulled over my eyes and thumbs hooked into the belt, the same as all the others.

But what is she saying? Jaquet has been arrested? Is being held in the Grand Châtelet on a charge of murder?

'Murder? Jaquet?'

'Tell her about it,' Evrard presses the woman. 'Tell her what happened. Tell her about Natalie. You remember Natalie, don't you, Mariana?'

Natalie? Yes. I'd seen the boys' eyes on her. Carroty hair. Freckles. Thin.

'Mariana, you're dreaming! Listen!!'

'I am listening! Don't tell me Jaquet is accused of killing her. He adores her.'

'Of killing who? What are you talking about?'

'Natalie. Didn't you say – ?'

'It is old Guillaume who is dead, not Natalie.'

'Guillaume?'

'Guillaume le Grec. Jaquet's uncle. The old man Natalie lived with.'

Ah, the miser. Now I understand. And I remember Evrard's jokes about Natalie's relationship with him.

'Now will you listen?'

I nod contritely.

Evrard thinks I am dreaming of him. I prefer someone less masterful. Someone like Raoul: he writes poems to me, or at least to various parts of me – my toes, my lips – and one to a rose I plucked and discarded. Or so he says. I remember no rose. I focus my gaze on the woman

'It was yesterday morning, early. Natalie came banging on our door. I was awake and working in the kitchen but Jaquet was still in bed. He gets tired, poor boy, with all this studying, though I buy him the very best candles. "What is it, ma fille?" I say. I do not like the girl, but there you are. What mother likes the girl who steals away the affections of her only son? So I try to be fair. "It's Maître Guillaume! He's dead!" she cries. "Dead? Cold?" I ask. "And stiff?" "Oh, no! No! Warm still …" How did she know her master was dead in his bed at that hour of the morning? Warm and dead? "And last night," she sobs, "he was fine. Happy and well. As happy as ever he is, sitting there with his things all around him." Counting his money, I'll be bound. I ask her in and sit her down, and give her a warm tisane to calm her, but what to do? She will tell me nothing more. She knows nothing more, or so she claims. "We'd better go and see," I say, "and take a physician with us in case he's not dead." "Oh, he is dead! Dead! Still warm, still bleeding a little, but – " Bleeding? I'd thought she meant he'd died. But if someone had killed him ... Had she killed him? No, whoever killed him would have taken the money and disappeared. Yet there was something … Beneath

all the drama, there was a – how shall I put it? While her hands
were to her eyes, wiping away her tears, she was peeping
between the fingers, trying to see the effect she was having. But
there, as I say, I am biased.'

And with that she comes to a stop at last.

Mais ça c'est vrai, I think to myself. That's true. She is as
biased by instinct and nature against the poor girl as Raoul (and
Evrard?) would be biased in her favour. No, perhaps not Evrard,
but Raoul would have wanted to wipe away those tears, comfort
and stroke her; Mère Henriette clearly just wanted to put the girl
over her knee and spank her.

'So what did you do? Let her go up to Jaquet's room?'

'No! Nor did I go up to call the boy. He needs his sleep. I went
to Maître Guillaume's house with her. And it was true. It was
horrible. He had been stabbed many times, many, many. There
was blood on the bed, on the floor, in the corridor, in the
laboratoire, blood on the chair, the table, the floor again. So I
went to find the sergeants of the watch, and she came with me,
she wouldn't stay with him alone …'

The laboratoire? Had he been an alchemist? A magician?

'The sergeant came, and two of his men, and they looked.
They looked at poor Maître Guillaume, they looked round the
house, and I knew what they were looking for, they were looking
for the gold. Everyone knew him, you see, knew that although he
seemed so ordinary he was as rich as Solomon.'

'And there was no sign of this treasure?'

'No. So they seized the girl, Natalie, and started hitting her,
and she told them Jaquet – my Jaquet – had been there the
previous evening.'

'And had he?'

'Well, I denied it at first, of course, but when we all marched
back to my house, the sergeant and his men dragging along the
sobbing Natalie, followed now by a procession of urchins and
good-for-nothings and a couple of putains who seemed to know

Natalie — and it wouldn't surprise me if they did, she has the
walk of a putain … '
   She pauses, obviously thinking about that walk, and gives me
a long look.
   As well she might, though how people like her can tell is a
mystery to me.
   'It turns out he had been there. He was the last to see the old
miser, poor Maître Guillaume, alive. If we are to believe the girl.
And they decide they do, if only because it was her who found
the body and raised the alarm. If she'd had the money, she would
have taken off with it during the night and no one would ever
have seen her again.'
   'So they arrested Jaquet?'
   'Oui, dem'selle.'
   'When was Jaquet born? Exactly, I mean. The year, month,
day, time …'
   'Mariana knows astrology, Mère Henriette. It will help her to
understand him, to understand what happened,' Evrard explains.
   'He was born on the last day of February in the year 1359.
Under the Sign of the Fish.'
   Pisces, yes, she is right. An unlikely murderer. 'At what time
exactly, madame?'
   'In the early evening. The bells were ringing for vespers.'
   I must look that up in my almageste.
   'And Natalie? Do you happen to — ?'
   'I know nothing of Natalie.'
   'Maître Guillaume was not your brother, I take it?'
   'My brother?' She seems amazed at the suggestion.
   'I understood that Jaquet was Maître Guillaume's nephew, yet
your name, Jaquet's name, le Breton, is not the name of the
murdered man, so …'
   'My poor husband, Hugues le Breton, was Maître Guillaume's
brother. And for that, I understood, Maître Guillaume came and
settled in this district — when? — seventeen, eighteen years ago.

Soon after my poor Jaquet was born. He was using this new
name, le Grec, but his name was le Breton, same as my Hugues.
Then poor Hugues died and after that we had little contact. He
had no wish to help us. I sent Jaquet round from time to time, of
course, to keep in touch … I must get back to Le Châtelet to see
if he needs anything!'

What will they do to him, I wonder. I don't know Paris. 'Will
they put him to the question?'

Mère Henriette lets out a loud wail and covers her face with
her hands, while Marc, who is a student at the school of law,
explains that they will, yes, of course, eventually, but not till the
commissaires-examinateurs have completed their enquiries and
gathered all the evidence.

'So we have a few days.'

'A few hours, a few weeks – who knows?'

I turn back to the weeping woman. 'What time did Jaquet
come home last night?'

She peers at me. She is going to lie.

'I want the truth, madame.'

Marc glances at me, at her. 'Don't lie to anyone about
anything, Mère Henriette. If the commissaires suspect us of
lying, they will put Jaquet to the question immediately.'

'Oh – oh – oh,' she sobs. 'He was late, I don't know when, I
was asleep. I, who always wait up for him, I fell asleep! I do not
know what time he came in! I do not know what state he was in!
I do not know if he was carrying anything! I do not know …!'

She totters out of the bar, an old woman suddenly. One of the
boys goes with her. The others at our table turn to me.

'Mariana? What do you think?'

'I need to speak to Jaquet. And to Natalie, of course. But first
… One of you, run after them and ask her where Maître
Guillaume came back from eighteen years ago, will you?'

'I'll go,' Raoul volunteers.

'But can we say anything now?' Evrard insists.

'Like had naughty Natalie been sleeping in her master's bed,' I
laugh. 'The fact that he was warm when she found him could
mean simply that, recovering consciousness, he rang for her, then
died before she arrived.'
      'She would take quite a long time, yes, if she was asleep.'
      'We can also assume that Mère Henriette's main interest is le
butin, the treasure,' Marc points out. 'That's why she kept sending
Jaquet round all these years. He's the old man's natural heir.'
      'So the idea of him stealing the money is ridiculous.'
      'Yes, it's all his anyway.'
      'But he might kill the old man. Then steal the money to
mislead enquirers.'
      'That doesn't sound like Jaquet,' says Evrard.
      'No, but I have to talk to him. Before I talk to Natalie. Ah,
Raoul. Did she know?'
      'Yes, he'd been living on an island called Ibiza.'
      Ibiza. Well, well. 'Then I - but I'm taking the lead too much
here ... '
      'No, please, Mariana,' Kateline begs, 'you must help us save
Jaquet.'
      'All right, I'll try. But remember I don't know Paris well, and
you will have to help me.'
      They nod and promise, raising their cups and drinking to
Jaquet and to me. Like children.
      'Then I have another job for you, and whatever friends you
can enlist. I'll need to talk to anyone who was living or working
on Ibiza at that time - seventeen, eighteen - oh, up to twenty
years ago.'
      'What shall we ask them?' Evrard wants to know.
      'Nothing.'
      'We bring them to you?'
      'No, no, nothing like that. Just come and tell me who they are
and where I can find them.'
      'Shall I come to the Châtelet with you?'

'No, you join in the search, Evrard. I'll do better alone. Especially if I go home and make myself presentable first.'

'Gilding the lily,' he smiles.

Evrard's words are just words. It is Raoul's eyes that are glued to me.

2

The sergeant at the gate of the Grand Châtelet seems unimpressed by my décolletage. He shouts something to one of the guards, then carries on with what he was doing.

I wait patiently.

When I do finally get his attention, it is not the kind of attention I want. He is wondering, and not without reason, whether I am simply a well-spoken whore.

'Sergeant,' I say, all sweet and innocent, 'there's no need to look at me like that. In my country, this is the way ladies dress.' (At least inside the harems of Granada.)

'It must be a very warm country. You'll catch your death dressing like that here in the middle of winter.'

'It's how you feel inside that counts, sergeant. In my country,' (Scotland now, my father's country, where I have never been) 'we swim when the beaches are thick with snow and the sea is frozen over so that we have to smash a hole in the ice to slip in.'

'I've heard of holes in the ice for fishing, but for swimming? What might your country be? You speak very good French.'

Too good for a putain, he is thinking. 'Too good for une française?' I say.

His face relaxes slightly. Is that a smile?

'I am Lady Marian MacElpin, of the County of Ross, in the Kingdom of Scotland.'

He allows himself a brief glance. 'If all the ladies in the Kingdom of Scotland look like you, it's time I went on my travels.'

'Only in the County of Ross.' I beam. Then turn pensive. 'I have a friend – I do not have many friends in Paris, you understand – and this friend, a student, has been brought to the Châtelet, no doubt through some mistake. I would like to speak to him, see if there is anything I can do to help.'

'But if this friend is a student, he shouldn't be here. The students of the university have their own system of justice, under the King. They're not held in the Châtelet.'

'Then?'

'Where is he from? Is he also from Scotland?'

'Oh no, he's from here, he's Parisian.'

'Ah well, then, my lady, he's a citizen, that's why they put him in here. His name?'

'Jaquet le Breton.'

'Ah. Oui. But that's a case of murder. He killed his uncle.'

'No! That's not possible!'

'It seems it is. He was the last to see him, and the uncle's money has disappeared.'

'I didn't know …'

'Still, there's no reason why you shouldn't see him for a few minutes once a day. And you can send your maid round with food for him, as well.'

'Can I see him now? Find out what's happening, what he needs?'

'Oui, d'accord. And come back at this same time every day, come to me: that way you won't have any difficulty getting in to see him.'

'Sergeant, you are very sweet, very understanding! If only everyone was like you!'

I give him an unexpected kiss on his harsh stubbly cheek as he calls a guard over. He pretends not to notice. The guard, a young man, grins.

'Take Dem'selle Mariana to the prisoner Jacques le Breton. Wait at the door of the cell while she's with him, then escort her back here.'

Outside, the Châtelet is elegant enough and the entrance is tall and imposing, but once you turn the corner and start down the stairs to the cells and dungeons below ground level, everything is black and gloomy and cold, though not wet like some prisons I've heard about; and as you can't see very much you are more aware of the smells: smoke and urine, rotting food and flesh, ordure.

The young guard carries a torch, the only illumination in that corridor. He stops outside one of the doors, slides aside a heavy bolt, pushes the door open and stands back for me to go in.

The stench is overwhelming.

The rushes on the floor look as though they've been there for years. They must be crawling with vermin. The slop bucket hasn't been emptied in - how long? How long would it take a normal person to - ?

'Mariana? You? Here?'

'You haven't seen your mother?'

'No! She sent in some food, but - '

'Ah. Maybe because she knew I was coming.'

He is trying to clean with his hand and sleeve the surface of the wooden bench that is the only furniture in the cell.

'That's all right, don't worry.' Still holding my skirt well clear of the floor, I sit down on the part he has cleaned.

'She asked me - us - to help you.' I indicate that he should sit beside me.

'How can you help me? They believe I killed my uncle.'

'I don't know yet, but I'm sure we can. Listen, we need to know everything.'

'They'll torture me, and I'll say I killed him, I'll say I took the money! I'll say whatever they want me to say!'

'Shh.' I take his hand to comfort him, and he lifts mine unexpectedly to his lips and kisses it passionately, hungrily. It is – I am – his lifeline, I realise: although we attend the same courses at the École de Médecin, he is still only a boy, and is dependent on me to save him from torture and a horrible death.

My hand is wet with his tears when he lowers it to his lap, then, embarrassed, gives it back to me. I hold onto his hand now, in my lap, and say: 'Let's try, shall we?'

He nods gratefully, and I press his hand.

'First, tell me about the evening: why you were at your uncle's house, what time you arrived there, what you did there, what time you left …'

'I arrived at sunset. I'd arranged to meet Natalie to go for a walk. She was waiting for me, and – oh, I don't know – we were out for about two hours. Then we went back. She can't stay out long. If my uncle needs her for anything and she isn't there, he gets angry.'

'And shouts? Hits her? What?'

'I don't know. I've never seen him angry. I can't imagine him angry. But she says – '

'What is her position in the house, exactly?'

'She … You mustn't listen to what Evrard says, and those others, they think they're funny, but she doesn't, she never has. She wouldn't. I mean – you know – '

'Jaquet, you're the one I'm listening to. You're the one who knows her.'

More tears fall and he gives a convulsive sob. I squeeze his hand again. 'Tell me about her. I only have a few minutes.'

He stares at me through his tears. 'You will come back?'

Somewhere, deep down, he had believed, like a child, that I would be here for ever now, holding his hand.

I nod, and promise. 'Every day, at this time … So, she is, was, your uncle's housekeeper, in effect?'

'Yes. Her mother did everything for my uncle, and as Natalie grew up she helped her mother; but her mother died and since then Natalie has done everything.'

'Your uncle didn't employ any other servants?'

'No. He wouldn't. He's a miser. You must have heard.'

'You mean he wouldn't want to pay someone? But what about her? Doesn't he pay her?'

'No. She has nothing.'

'Well, I'll ask her about that. Go on with what happened that night.'

'We stayed down in the kitchen, talking and laughing together. He never bothers us. She took him a drink and said he was busy in his laboratory. When it was time to leave, I went up to see him.'

'Why?'

'My mother always tells me to be polite to him. He peered out round the door, asked how I was, and said "Tell your mother you've done your duty."'

'Sarcastic?'

'Yes. About that.'

'What was he like, your uncle? I never met him. Was he tall? Short?'

'Short. A little man with thin grey hair and pale blue eyes.'

'I see … And then, you left? Went home?'

He nodded.

'And did you see Natalie again before you left?'

'She was waiting. She took me to the front door to see me out.'

'Where does your uncle keep all his money?'

'I don't know. No one knows.'

'You've seen him take it out or put it away?'

'Oh no.'

'Who is your uncle's heir?'

He looks at me.

'I am, I suppose.'

'Give me your hands. Both of them. I want to read them.'

I hold them in mine, examine the backs briefly, then turn them over and study the fingers and palms. Nowadays, I simply hold the hands and glance at them from time to time while I gaze into the person's eyes in silence or talk about astrology, but then, in Paris, when I was young, and was studying chiromancy, and was always in search of a chance to practise it in a real situation (as opposed to doing it to entertain), I kept it pure and took it very seriously.

The only mount which could be called protuberant was the Mount of Mercury, at the base of the little finger, but it was not overdeveloped, and all it indicated was that he thought quickly and would be good at his trade of apothecary. The Mount of Venus (the big base of the thumb that occupies a third of the hand) was also well-developed: he would be loving, affectionate, a good husband.

'Dem'selle? The time ... '

It is the young guard. 'Wait!'

The Line of Life, round the Mount of Venus, is correspondingly long, strong, and well developed, and is joined to the Head Line at its root, indicating a certain amount of caution. Another not unexpected feature is that the Line of Heart begins on the Mount of Jupiter: he will tend to place people (Natalie, for instance) on a pedestal.

Most interestingly, he has the out-turned thumb of the generous-minded.

Now I let my eyes grow cold: snake-eyes – like the snake-arms in belly-dancing – something you learn if you have a good teacher. He blinks, but holds up valiantly.

He has those soft brown forest eyes, the eyes of a furry creature among the trees waiting to be spotted by someone who likes wearing furs, or who knows someone who likes wearing furs. Someone like me.

This boy never hurt anyone. Never will hurt anyone, except perhaps a woman who - no, not goads him beyond all endurance but disappoints him beyond all endurance.

'Jaquet, I need to know more about the relationship between your father and his brother, your Uncle Guillaume, and how your mother fitted in.'

'Dem'selle? We must go now. Really. I - '

'All right, all right, I'm coming. Tomorrow, Jaquet.'

'I'll be waiting.'

He would indeed. My visits promise to be the only bright moments in some very bad, very long days.

'Can I bring you anything?'

'Maman sends in food. Perhaps Natalie ... or some news of her, if she can't come in?'

'I'm going there now. I'll give her your love.' I kiss him, and follow the guard back up and out.

3

It was an unimposing house in the rue Saint-Pol; two floors, and a small pointed attic where Natalie slept and kept her few personal possessions. We started there because she didn't like being in the house now, whereas in the attic she felt safe: it had always been her place.

'And your mother? When she was alive?'

'She was Maître Guillaume's - like his wife - not his wife, because they weren't married, but - you know …'

I nodded. Yes, I knew.

We sat on the narrow bed in the narrow attic with the roof coming down to the floor on both sides of us, and it was true, yes, it was homely: cosy and safe. She had impressed her personality upon it, and there was no hint of her master here, living or dead.

'What was her name, your mother?'

'Lule.'

'Where was she from?'

'Albania.'

'Albania? How did she come to be in Paris?'

'He brought her here. Maître Guillaume.'

'I see.'

Back in the middle of the century, when so many people died during the first two onslaughts of the Great Mortality that whole villages, whole towns, were wiped out, peasants moved into the empty manor houses and bondservants into their masters' deserted mansions, and there was no one to do the work. One of the areas which was not badly hit by the pestilence was Serbia-Albania, or so Ferchard (my father's old friend, Sir Farquhar) told me, and he should know because he's been there. According to him, it's a place that has always served as a source of slaves, with Albanian brigands raiding Serbian villages and Serbian brigands raiding Albanian villages, each nominally doing it in revenge for previous raids but all actually interested only in procuring as many slaves as possible for shipment to the markets of Africa and the Levant, where a beautiful girl with carrot-coloured hair, green eyes and white skin like this Natalie is worth a fortune. In the wake of the plague, though, everything changed. The slavers realised that the rich northern Mediterranean was open to them once more. Soon the slave-markets of Thessalonika, Crete and Ibiza were full of Serbian and Albanian peasants, with labourers and serving-women being sold by the score before being shipped up into mainland Europe.

'Where did your master obtain your mother?'

'I don't know. I heard things, but no one ever told me the whole story properly.'

'On Ibiza?'

She stared at me. 'How do you know? I mean, know that they were there?'

I gazed back. 'Knowing things is what I'm good at. Which is why I may be able to help you and poor Jaquet.'

I knew something else, too. I couldn't put my finger on it, but I'd been here before, in this house. In my dreams?In a previous life?

'I don't need any help.'

'Oh yes, you do. You have no home, no money, nothing. You don't think they'll let you stay here and pretend nothing has happened, do you?'

'It will be Jaquet's house now.'

'Jaquet is in the Grand Châtelet, and will be tortured and hanged - or worse - if I don't find out what really happened.'

There was a pause while she digested this. Then: 'Anyway, it wasn't on Ibiza that he actually bought her, it was somewhere called Thessa - Thessaloniki - '

Thessalonika. 'You can tell me about that another time.'

'There's nothing to tell. He bought her there, then took her with him to Ibiza.'

'Intending to re-sell her?'

'I don't know. I don't think so. Then they came to live here, in Paris.'

I wanted to know about Natalie's parentage. Was she already a babe in arms when Old Guillaume bought her mother? In which case she belonged to him just as her mother had. Belonged to Jaquet now. Or had her mother, Lule, been pregnant when he bought her? In which case, the same would apply. Or had she been conceived later, after Lule had become Guillaume's property? She could easily be his daughter.

She would lie to me. You could tell she'd grown up without much regard for anything so unprofitable as the truth: she told her master - and everyone else - only what she thought good for them to hear, which meant good for her that they should hear.

I would ask Mère Henriette, get some idea first before continuing on that subject with Natalie.

'Tell me about your master. Describe him to me. Remember I've never seen him.'

'He was small, with blue eyes and grey hair, but for the last few months - few years - I don't know - he was like his clothes, he was as though he'd been washed and washed and washed and now was all washed out, faded, shrunk.'

'Did you not see your master again that night after Jaquet left?'

'No.'

I stared at her.

This girl was no shrinking furry creature; she was another snake, caught out in a lie.

'Ah, yes, I remember now, I did see him once more: he came down to the kitchen to take some blood.'

'Blood?'

'Yes. He used to take a few drops of my blood. He needed it for his work.'

Did he indeed ...

When I was a child, in Spain, my Uncle Yacoub used to take a few drops of my blood sometimes for scrying - a few drops in a syrup of various herbs in a shallow silver basin … We saw my father in it, when he was in another room, simple things like that - I did it myself sometimes - and occasionally scenes that Yacoub said came out of history, out of the distant past of that little corner of Spain where we lived; but not much else. Certainly we never managed to trace my brother in the years after he disappeared - or died.

But was it for scrying that Guillaume had wanted the blood?
He must have been a magician, no one else would have wanted
those drops of blood "for his work": but for scrying, or for
something else?

She had been gazing at me while I sat there remembering, no
doubt wondering how much she should tell me; or rather, how
little she could get away with. What I needed now was an
unexpected question, an intelligent question if I could manage it,
to put me ahead again.

'Did he ask whether - check whether - you were still a
virgin?'

She gasped, changed colour like the sunset, as people with
hair the colour of peaches so easily do. 'How - ?'

'I don't mean usually - I assume he did usually - but that
night, did he ask you when he took the blood that night?'

She nodded.

'And did he check?'

'Yes, while he was taking the blood.'

'While he was taking the blood?'

'He always took the blood from my left hand; I held the stone
in my right hand.'

'Stone?'

She stared at me, blushed again, laughed, and said, 'You
thought - you meant - oh no, he could never have, he was a very
private man, very shy …'

'Tell me about this stone.' There's a lot to be said for not trying
to look clever.

'I had to hold it tight, clench my hand, make it warm. If it
changed colour, went red, I wasn't a virgin.'

'Did it - ever?'

'No, of course not.'

So she was a virgin: not because I believed in the stone but
because she believed in the stone.

'What is the stone like?'

'About this size,' (the ball of her thumb) 'and yellowish.'
'And how do you know it works?'
'He said so. I believed him. And because once when Maman
was still alive he gave it to her to hold, in front of me. It turned
deep, deep red, blood red. He wanted me to be sure.'
'He took your blood even then? When you were a child?'
'He's always taken it. When I was little I used to cry …'
I never cried. But then I loved, and trusted, Uncle Yacoub.
And if I had cried, my father might have noticed. What could I
have told him? If he had learnt about the blood, he would have
killed Yacoub.
'How did he do it exactly?'
'He pricked one of my finger-tips, squeezed a few drops out.
Sometimes, when he needed more than that, he bled me with
leeches, then used the leeches in whatever he was doing. Once or
twice, when he needed a lot of blood quickly, he cut my palm –
here – then made me clench my fist, squeeze the blood out for
him into a bowl.'
There were two recent scars across her left hand, and one or
two older ones, less distinct.
Yacoub had never, would never have, done anything like that.
But what could Guillaume have wanted so much blood for? Not
for scrying – or not by any method I'd ever heard of.
Distracted by the scars on her left hand, it was only now that I
concentrated on her right hand and noticed the distinctive Line of
Head, long, firm, and tilting gently from its commencement at a
link with the Line of Life right across to a point below the little
finger: a sure indication of brightness, of memory and of
foresight, of powers of concentration, of individuality and
potential for success in life. I also noticed that the Mercury Line
(the Line of Death, as some say) was well-formed, stretching
right up to the Mount of Mercury below the little finger, a sign of
intuition, and that her Great Triangle was spacious and large: this
girl had enormous potential, and was only being held back by her

circumstances and upbringing; a situation that, with her character, she should certainly succeed in overcoming.

'You're reading my hands!' she cried suddenly, and snatched them away from me, before I could confirm my reading in the other features of her hands.

I smiled at her. 'It's nothing.'

'You know that? Palm-reading?'

I nodded. 'And astrology. When were you born?'

'I'm not telling you. I don't have to. I don't have to do anything.'

'Of course you don't. It just makes it easier for me to understand. And I have to understand if I'm to help Jaquet — and you … You were telling me that you hated it when he cut your palms, that it hurt. What did you do? Did you fight and scream? I know I would have.'

'When I was little I did, at first, but Maman used to beat me …'

'And that hurt more than Maître Guillaume's knife.'

'Much more,' she smiled.

'And since your mother died? Does Maître Guillaume beat you?'

'No, I told you, he's — he was — a very shy man. He would never have touched me in any way.'

'But he took your blood.'

'That was different. He needed it, so I let him.'

'You mean you went on letting him even after your mother died.'

'She made me promise not to run away, to stay with Maître Guillaume and look after the house for him so he would never need another woman — working here, I mean. And always to do exactly what he said.'

'And the blood?'

'I was used to it.'

'No, I mean did you have any idea what he needed it for?
What his work was?'

'No. But the abbé who comes here with the Sire de Montrouge
asked me once if I knew anything about my father's alchemical
practices. I said, "He's not my father, and he doesn't have
alchemical practices, whatever they may be." The abbé smiled
and patted me and said, "He may not be your father, but he
certainly does practise alchemy, my child." The Sire de
Montrouge just smiled and stared at me, you know, the way a
dog stares at a piece of meat.'

I could imagine. But who were this Sire de Montrouge and
this abbé?

'How old were you then?'

'Oh, this was not long ago. They've been calling here every
week for the last three or four months.'

'Always together?'

'Yes, or the abbé on his own.'

'And did you ever tell them about your master using your
blood?'

'No! No one knows about that but me and Maman – and now
you.'

'Grace à Dieu. If they ever learn that, you may be in great
danger.'

'Why? You mean …? But I didn't do anything.'

'They believe your master was practising alchemy. You will
only be safe for as long as they think you know nothing – in fact,
for as long as it does not occur to them that you might possibly
know something … When was the last time you saw either of
them?'

She hesitated. She could be a good liar when she felt she
needed to be, I already knew that from her hands. But she was
clever, too, and she knew I knew. The question was, why would
she want to lie?

Suddenly, I understood. One or both of them had been there that night.

Her master had been tortured to death.

And she was terrified.

I was terrified just thinking about it.

She couldn't stay here.

Time for a change of subject. 'Show me your master's rooms.'

'I can't.'

'You must. I need to see the rooms where he worked, where he slept. Mère Henriette told me there was blood in two rooms and along a corridor. How did that happen? Do you know?'

'How can I know? He must have staggered - crawled - from the laboratory to his bedroom before he died ...'

'Show me.'

The laboratory was wood-panelled, but a tall casement window overlooking the courtyard behind the house meant it was not dark. Under the window, and running right round the corner and along the adjacent wall was a wide workbench, with a variety of phials and retorts and flasks and burners on it, some empty, many containing bright-coloured liquids. On one side, a beautiful astrolabe. Some time, I would like to examine that more carefully.

'It's the world,' she said, suddenly. 'And the heavens. He believed the world was round.'

'You don't laugh?'

'Why should I laugh? He was a very clever man.'

Oh, that Head Line of hers! But I'd seen one of these before. Ibn Khaldoun, my master when I was in Granada, had owned one. Uncle Yacoub, too, had told me that many of the greatest philosophers and masters even in ancient times had believed the world was round. He'd shown me why and I'd been convinced, but hadn't thought much about it since. It wasn't necessary for astrology.

It wasn't astrology that concerned me now. It was alchemy.

Against the wall opposite the window was a table, and on the table a large box.

Natalie opened a drawer, took out a small leather bag. Inside the bag were two stones, one a clear, beautiful green, the other almost colourless. She held the colourless one tightly in her hand.

'The virgin-stone,' she said, and carried on holding it.

She opened her hand. Nothing had changed.

She gave it to me. Smiled.

I held it. Felt it growing warm. Strange: it had been cool - not cold, but definitely cool - when it left her hand.

She nodded. I opened my hand. The stone was dark red, blood red.

She took it back. 'But I know a woman who can control it.'

'Really?'

She nodded, and put it away. As she did so, I glanced at the big box on the table. Something had moved.

'What's that?' I tried not to sound frightened.

She looked round. 'In the box? That's Chuvar.'

'Chuvar?'

'A snake.'

I peered in. A rat snake, nearly six foot in length, but slender, brownish, paler than the ones I'd seen in Spain.

Well, most magicians kept an animal of one sort or another.

There were some stuffed animals on the shelves, some animals in jars, but no other live animals. Not even a spider.

'Who cleans in here, Natalie? You?'

She shook her head. 'I'm not permitted in here, usually. Even Maman wasn't permitted in here.'

'You mean she never was but you sometimes are?'

She blushed again. 'Yes, but not often now. When I was little. He used to explain things to me. He introduced me to Chuvar. He showed - '

'So Chuvar knows you.'

She nodded.

'Who fed him, you or your master?'

'Me.'

'What does he eat?'

'Mice.'

'Mice?'

'There are mouse-traps down in the cellar, those traps like cages that catch them live.'

'And how do you give them to the snake?' As soon as I asked the question, I knew, and wished I hadn't asked.

'Like this, holding them by the tail. Chuvar opens his mouth and you … ' She mimed letting go of the tail.

'Ugh. Well, you can't stay here on your own, so you'd better feed him and do anything else that needs doing – '

'I can stay up in the attic. I don't mind.'

'It's not your feelings that concern me. They're going to break in, looking for your master's money, and they're going to search everywhere. They'll find you, and then – '

'The gold isn't here.'

'That's not the point. People think it's here. You get on with the jobs that need doing and I'll have a look round.'

'I told you, the gold's not – '

'I'm not looking for the gold. Or not particularly. I'm looking for anything that will help me understand what happened that night.'

She didn't want to let me, but didn't know how to stop me.

'Anyway, how do you know the gold's not here?' I challenged her.

Another sunset blush. 'I don't, but …'

'Go and get ready. Leave me alone up here for a while.'

She did so, reluctantly.

I found nothing strange in the bedroom save a portrait of a woman who looked like Natalie, the same high cheek-bones, the same chin, though the hair was fairer and the eyes were blue.

And it was odd that the portrait was not on display, but hidden away in the back of a closet.

   Nothing else. I wanted to search here again slowly, in my own time. And I wanted to do so before they broke in and smashed everything. Which could be tonight.

   I went through to the laboratory and found Natalie there, feeding live mice to the snake, one at a time, head first, down the snake's gullet.

   There were no doubt worse deaths for a mouse.

   'Natalie, that painting in the bedroom. Is it of your mother?'

   She nodded.

   'She was beautiful,' I said.

   She knew that. And she looked very like her mother.

   'She was Maître Guillaume's concubine? I mean openly so?'

   A nod.

   'Then why did he keep the picture of her hidden?'

   'Hidden?'

   'In the closet.'

   'The picture was in the closet? But no, it was never in the closet.'

   'It was when I found it.'

   'He must have put it there …'

   'It wasn't kept there usually?'

   'No.'

   'Natalie, he can't have wanted the Sire de Montrouge to see it. Or the abbé. Or someone else. And that could only be because he wanted to keep you in the background, invisible. He was trying to protect you.'

   She was nodding and tears were running down her cheeks.

She put the cover back over the box that housed the snake and turned to look at me.

   'We shall hide you.'

   'Hide me? Where?'

'First, though, you must come with me to the Châtelet and make a statement that you saw Maître Guillaume still alive, and spoke to him, after poor Jaquet had gone home. And that later you – what? – heard the voice of the Sire de Montrouge? Or saw him?'

'No! I can't!'

'We'll hide you … Is it the abbé or Montrouge?'

She hesitated. Then: 'The abbé. When I feel his eyes on me, I – I feel naked – but all through, inside, as well. He reads me, you know, like one reads a book. Can you read?'

I nodded. She was deliberately changing the subject. But she was gazing at me, too. I realised this was the first thing she had envied; not my money, my clothes, but this: being able to read. She was living up to her Line of Head all right.

'Maître Guillaume was going to teach me when I was small, but Maman said it was not for women to know how to read.'

'And you listened to her? Or did he?'

'He did. She caught me looking at a book once, you know, wishing I could read. She took the book from me, carefully, laid it down, carefully, then grabbed me by the hair – not at all carefully! – and hauled me out to the kitchen, where she kept the stick she used on me. I never picked up a book again.'

I wanted to say, Your maman sounds awful; instead I said, 'And later? Couldn't you have learnt later?'

'After Maman died I had so much work to do, cleaning and cooking, washing and mending that I had no more time for dreams … I did say to Maître Guillaume when he came and sat beside me once when I was ill in bed, and read me a story from a book, a story about a girl who had to climb a glass mountain to save the boy – the prince – she loved – I said: "Would you have loved Maman as much if she'd known how to read?" He gazed at me and smiled, and said: "Your maman was perfect just as she was."'

'Did he often do things like that? Sit by you? Read you stories?'

'No, that was almost the only time. Perhaps two or three other times, when I was small. He only spoke if he wanted something done, something cleaned, something special to eat. Or if he was angry: you know, I hadn't done something properly, or I'd been out of the house when he rang for me.'

'But he would never hit you.'

'Oh no. He didn't even shout, he just spoke coldly, without any smile. Me, I was just a child and all I wanted to do was please him, make him smile again.'

'And now? Now you're no longer a child?'

'He no longer gets angry.'

'Not ever?'

'Not ever. Now he's like a child. Was,' she added, remembering he was dead.

Time for some direct questions.

'Did you ever wonder if you were his daughter?'

She looked at me. 'Of course I did. I asked Maman once. She told me not to be silly, and gave me a slap.'

'But she didn't say No.'

'She didn't have to.'

'Did you ever ask him?'

'I didn't have to. Is that how you treat a daughter? Like a servant? A slave?'

We sat in silence and thought about that for a minute.

Finally, I said: 'It could be. If she was illegitimate, the daughter of a maid-servant … Or if you didn't want anyone to realise that she was your daughter.'

She made no response.

I said, 'How long had he known those two men? The abbé, and the Sire de Montrouge?'

'I don't know. A long time. But it's only recently that they began to visit him here.'

'Both of them, you said?'

'Sometimes. Sometimes just the abbé.'

'And last night?'

She held my gaze, then said, 'I heard only the voice of Montrouge.'

Now we were getting somewhere.

'Did Maître Guillaume often open the door to visitors himself?'

Another long look. And a slight smile. Then, 'No, he never did.'

'So you let the Sire de Montrouge in.'

She nodded.

'How did he seem?'

'Seem?'

'Calm? Well-dressed? Upset? In disarray? Had he been drinking?'

'He's always been drinking ... He seemed calm. His touch was calm. He always touches my neck, my throat - here - but sometimes I think that beneath the calm smile he is desperate.'

'Desperate? For what?'

'Who knows?'

'What are men ever desperate for? Money. A woman: not just any woman, some particular woman. Power. In his case, I should think it must have been money.'

'But why? He was rich, wasn't he?'

'I will find out,' I said.

'How?'

Good question.

'Now what are we going to do with you? Would you like to come with me, to my house? I live on the left bank, in the rue Alexandre l'anglois. You know it? Off the rue Saint-Victor.'

She shook her head.

I persisted. 'I'm not alone. There's a woman who will look after you. And a wonderful Scottish soldier, Sir Farquhar de

Dyngvale, who will protect you.' I didn't mention that Big
Ferchard was a rather old Scottish soldier, having been born
about seventy years ago: he was still big, still strong, still very
brave. She looked intrigued. 'And there is a huge, completely
hairless, Moor, a eunuch, called Yahia, who would protect you
with his life.'

Now she really was curious. What girl wouldn't be? But she
shook her head again.

'You can't stay here.'

'I have ... a friend. An Albanian.'

'An Albanian? Tell me about him.'

'No, I can't. But I'll be safe with him.'

'Where does he live?'

'I can't tell you.'

'All right. Go to him. But ask him about going to the Châtelet
to help poor Jaquet, see what he says. I'll meet you here again
tomorrow – when? At the same time as today?'

'All right. Are you going now then? Shall we go together? I
want to leave now too.

4

When we parted in the rue Saint-Antoine, I gave a sou to one of
the gamins who hang about there, a boy with a dirty face and
bright blue eyes, and told him to follow Natalie, see where she
went, then come to me in the rue Alexandre l'anglois.

I wanted to know what Raoul and the others had found out
about life on Ibiza eighteen years ago. I wanted to get back to the
house of Maître Guillaume le Breton, alias le Grec, and give it a
thorough search before anyone else did. But I also wanted –
needed – to go home for a while.

Ferchard was out. Only Khadija was there, and Yahia. Yahia is always there, always waiting. He's like a big dog. If he had a tail, it would certainly wag madly when he saw me coming. They cut the tails off dogs, sometimes. How must it feel for a dog to be with no tail?

I tell him I will need him with me that evening, I am going into a house and I will be in danger. What do I want him to do? Stand outside the door, keep guard? No, they may come in from the back or through a window or – who knows? I want him inside, near me, so that wherever they come at me from I won't have to face them alone.

He nods gleefully and goes to prepare himself, which means exercising and oiling his body ready for combat.

Khadija nods too, but not gleefully. 'You are never on time for your dinner, oh no, or for anything else serious or important, but a rendez-vous with danger, with death, that is not to be missed!'

'Yahia will be there. You heard me.'

'And is Yahia to save you from two, three – who knows? – six, eight, vicious Nazranis?'

Nazranis are Christians.

'There won't be six or eight. Two or three we can handle. I'll be helping.'

'You! A child still! Take Sidi Farquhar with you. He may be old but he's brave, and he knows the world – this world – better than poor Yahia. Or you.'

'Where is Ferchard?'

'He went to a funeral. So he can't go with you. So you can't go.'

'What funeral?'

But just then the boy with blue eyes arrived and informed me that la fille had gone into the cour des miracles of the Porte Saint-Antoine.

'And then?' I asked, as Khadija, eyeing the street urchin suspiciously, gave him a large crust of bread and a dish of tajine, a Moorish stew.

The boy eyed the tajine as suspiciously as Khadija had eyed him, but when she made as though to take it back, he dipped his filthy finger in it and cautiously licked the finger. His eyes lit up. 'Mais c'est bon!'

Then Khadija insisted that he should wash his hands before he ate. He caught my eye when her back was turned and touched the offending finger to his temple. I laughed, and when he had finally settled down with his dinner, I repeated: 'Et alors?'

'Et alors quoi?'

'The girl! Where did she go? What did she do?'

He shrugged, mouth full.

'Did she meet anyone? Speak to anyone?'

'I lost her. I didn't see.'

'You lost her?'

'I can't go in there. I don't belong to that court. The Albanian would kill me. They say he spits boys like me, serves them up as gamin des rues … ' He was busy eating ... 'Alongside the porcs des rues, the pigs, his men come across wandering unattended through the streets when the pig-monks are distracted for a moment … and the sheep, the moutons de campagne, he liberates from Les Halles.'

I smiled.

'Only the boys?'

'He has other uses for girls.' He grinned.

Natalie! What are you doing?

'So he's not all bad, this Albanian,' I said, teasing him. 'I mean disinfesting Paris of its plague of street-pigs and street-urchins seems praiseworthy enough – '

'You're not one of the urchins, dem'selle.'

Not now, no.

'And it's not just him,' the boy went on. 'The Church, too - the real monks - they "save" us from the streets, and take us to work on their estates in the country. They're very kind.'

'Is that true?'

'My friend Mâchefer escaped from a monastery and made his way back.'

'And the Albanian? What else do you know about him?'

'He masquerades as a beggar. An old soldier who has lost his sword arm. It's true he has no right arm, but he fights with his left better than any other man with his right. He owns a bordel - the Adriatica. And he runs an assassination business: you know they used to say "If you want someone not to see next year, contact Le Cardinal"? Now they say "If you want someone not to see next week, contact L'Albanien".'

'Ah. But should you be talking like that?'

'I trust you, dem'selle.'

I looked at him.

'I trust you, too - what do they call you?'

'Le Cafard.'

'I trust you, too, le Cafard. Listen, watch the miser's house. You know it? Ask for it. It's in the rue Saint-Pol. The miser, Maître Guillaume le Grec, has been murdered. The girl you followed is a maid-servant there. You'll be able to find it?'

'Oh yes. She didn't do it, did she? She's pretty.'

'No, she didn't do it. But she's in danger.'

'They're going to do her next?'

'Yes.'

'Not the Albanian?'

'No, not the Albanian.' Or not as far as I know. 'Find that house and watch it. Remember anyone who comes and goes, including me. But don't leave your post. Only leave to follow Dem'selle Natalie. If you see her come out of the house, follow her, see where she goes. Otherwise, stay put. Here.' I gave him a half dozen sous to keep him going.

'How shall I contact you, dem'selle – Dem'selle – ?'

'Maryam,' I said without thinking. Then left it at that. After all, he'd probably heard Khadija call me Maryam.

'Dem'selle Maryam.'

'If you see me stand outside the house, and look this way, then that, then this again, follow me to the corner. At the corner I'll stop. There you can approach me.'

'D'accord.'

'Give him some more bread to take with him,' I told Khadija, in Arabic.

She did so, and he ran off, happy with his new-found responsibility, his new-found source of food and money, and his new-found friends. He knew as well as I did that from now on he would always be able to call in for a crust or whatever was going, and Khadija would never turn him away.

I washed and sat down to have dinner. I was still eating when Raoul and Evrard arrived with a list of names of people who had been on Ibiza.

Khadija gave them food and I told them about my meeting with Natalie; and watched Raoul's eyes light up at the mention of her name. A very attractive girl, obviously. But could that have been what was bothering the Sire de Montrouge? Evrard didn't think so. He had heard that Montrouge was a gambler and in debt: and anyway, if Montrouge had wanted Natalie he would simply have taken her.

'But Mariana, you haven't heard the news.'

'What news?'

Evrard was infuriating sometimes, especially when he knew, or thought he knew, something I didn't.

'Tell me, Raoul.'

'Montrouge is dead.'

'Dead?'

Evrard cut in. 'Apparently his bailiff found him. He was hanging by one leg.'

'By one leg? But that … Do you know when?'

'This morning. He must have died last night, the same as old Maître Guillaume.'

'I must talk to that bailiff. And anyone else who might have some idea how it happened.' Or why. Why would be the most important question. 'The new Sire de Montrouge, for a start. Who is the new Sire de Montrouge? Do you know?'

'Yes, his half-brother, Jean. And according to my informant, if you think no one could be worse than Pierre de Montrouge, you haven't met P'tit-Jean.'

Khadija, whose Spanish was fluent if idiosyncratic, could sometimes get the jist of a conversation in French and surprise us all – and she could always pick out names she knew. 'Montrouge?' she said. 'That's the man whose funeral Sidi Farquhar went to.'

Was it? Then I would wait and talk to him first.

'Raoul, give me that list. Is there anything special about them? Anything I should know?'

'The first one – '

'Pietri, the money-changer?'

'Yes – '

'For money-changer read money-lender,' Evrard put in.

'He remembers Old Guillaume.'

'Yes?'

'Yes. But as Guillaume le Breton, not Guillaume le Grec.'

'So he probably took the name le Grec after he returned to Paris. And when you change your name, you're usually hiding something – or hiding from someone.'

'This one, Madame Gauberte, remembers him too,' said Evrard. 'As a fortune teller and astrologer. She also remembers his woman – Lule – and she says Lule used to tell people's fortune with something called Tarocchi. Apparently Lule was right about Madame Gauberte becoming a widow quite soon.'

'Tarocchi. Interesting.' Does Natalie know how to read
tarocchi cards, I wonder?

'Why interesting? What is it?'

'It's fortune-telling with a set of special picture cards – used
by travellers – jongleurs and troubadours. But not only
travellers.'

Evrard sighed. 'Don't tell me you learned that, too, when you
were a studious little chica back home in Spain?'

'No, I didn't. My uncle Yacoub's views on Tarocchi would
have been much the same as yours seem to be, Evrard.'

'There you are then.'

'But he did tell me that in scrying – fore-seeing, anyway, if
not for far-seeing – it's not the tool, the system, you use that
matters, it's the mind. A good scryer can use almost anything, or
nothing at all; just hold the person's hands, gaze into his eyes.'

'You haven't answered my question, and I have to go.'

'Why am I interested? Your Sire de Montrouge was hanged in
a very special way. One of the cards is called the Hanged Man. It
bears the image of a man hanging by one foot, the left foot, with
the right leg crossed casually behind the left knee. From his
purse or pockets, money spills.'

'But what does it mean?' asked Raoul.

'So far as I know, it signifies self-sacrifice, the willing
abandonment of a life of self-indulgence. But the point may be
rather what people think it means.'

Evrard wasn't interested. 'I'll see you tomorrow, chérie, at the
Lutetia.' He went for my lips but I turned slightly, catching
Raoul's eye as Evrard gave my cheek a quick peck and smiled
and left.

Raoul and I gazed at each other, aware that this was the first
time we had ever been in any real sense alone together.

He smiled. Spoke. 'Were you serious about the Tarocchi
connection, Maryam?' I had taught him to call me Maryam, at
any rate when we were alone together – as Khadija and Yahia

did, of course. My Arabic name - Maryam al Qartayanni. I'd always rather liked using it.

'A Tarocchi connection? Yes. And this murder - these two murders, for Montrouge didn't hang himself like that - must be the last link in a long chain of events that stretches back into the past.'

'Ibiza, eighteen years ago.'

'At least. And not the last link, either, I'm afraid. They are but the latest links. It isn't finished.'

'Maryam, you're not placing yourself in danger here, are you?'

'No. Listen, I have to go, I have to get ready.'

'Wait. This woman here,' he pointed at his list, 'she's known as La Mireille, and - '

'La Mireille?'

He laughed. 'You will see for yourself. I just want to tell you she knew Pierre de Montrouge, there, on Ibiza.'

'At about the same time?'

He nodded. 'Yes. And these two - '

'Raoul! I have to go! Leave me the list, I'll look at it in the morning.'

'Yes.' He took me in his arms. Held me. Kissed me. This was more like it. 'Don't go out with your - '

'I know. It's very cold.'

'I wasn't thinking of the cold, I like the cold. I was thinking of the way the men will cluster round you and you may end up in the arms of - '

'Raoul, men do not cluster round me - especially when I'm dressed as a boy.'

'You're going as a boy? Oh, well, that's all right then. But be careful of the women! You don't have my experience of fending off women.'

'Raoul, you cannot possibly begin to imagine some of the experiences I have had.'

He looked shocked. Then curious.

'I'll tell you about them – the ones I think suitable for your ears. But not now. Ah, Yahia.'

Raoul stared. 'You're not taking him with you dressed like that?'

Yahia was naked apart from a loin-cloth, and hairless, and oiled all over. He had a sheath at his hip, hanging from a broad band that crossed his chest and passed over the opposite shoulder. It contained a long curved dagger.

'You don't think he'll be good protection?'

'I … He'll be perfect.'

'And you needn't worry about his clothes any more than you need worry about mine. He'll wear a burnous – a cloak – in the street and will take it off and be as you see him now while he's guarding me inside the house.'

'What house?'

'The house he and I are about to visit … Well? Are you going? Or does Yahia have to ...?'

'I'm going.'

'Good. I'll see you in the tavern at midday tomorrow.'

'Don't forget the Emperor's arriving in the city tomorrow. There may be some difficulty moving about.'

'Ah. Yes.' I'd forgotten.

The Holy Roman Emperor, Charles IV of Bohemia, and his son and heir Prince Wenceslas, were visiting their cousin Charles V of France. The Emperor was something special. I should have loved to be able to meet him.

'The grande rue Saint-Denis will be closed off.'

'You mean we won't be able to cross it at all?'

'There'll be barriers, and sergeants. I expect they'll let people cross at various points when nothing is happening. And the river might be frozen by then.'

That great river? Frozen? I'd heard of it, but I couldn't believe it. 'You mean solid?'

'People will be able to walk across it. We'll have fun. But you have to be careful, especially at night: starving wolves come up it and – '

'Raoul! I must go!'

'Why don't we watch the procession together?'

'We'll see.' I let him kiss me once more, briefly, on my lips, then headed up the narrow staircase to my bedroom followed closely by Yahia.

'My boy's clothes, Yahia. The brown outfit Evrard got me; it's inconspicuous.'

He was surprised. Since we'd arrived in Paris I'd worn boy's clothes only for the university, under my gown. But Yahia never argues. And for such an enormous man he has astonishingly sensitive fingers and can do the most delicate jobs. I'd much rather be dressed by him than by Khadija.

When he has me ready, with my hair tucked up out of the way inside a fashionable hat, we set out for the little road by the Palais Saint-Pol.

I leave Yahia in the doorway and look back out at the street, look left, right, left again, then saunter up to the corner.

Nothing.

I wait. Shivering.

Then a little voice behind me says, 'Excusez-moi, chef … Don't misunderstand me, but … are you a woman?'

'Of course, I'm a woman!' I hiss, rounding on him. 'You don't think I changed in the last two hours, do you?'

'You changed your clothes!'

'Ah. Oh. Yes. Listen, it's freezing and I'm in a hurry. Have you anything to report?'

'Two men came and peered in about half an hour ago.'

'What kind of men?'

'Retainers. Armed. The Church, I think. They stayed about five minutes, then went.'

The abbé's men? 'All right. I'm going in now. You wait at
your post. If you see anyone come in, don't try to warn me. Just
keep out of sight.'
    'Oui, dem'selle Maryam.'

5

Inside the house, I led Yahia first to the laboratory. I wanted to
start with the most important rooms in case we were interrupted
and had no chance to complete our search. I looked. He stood
guard.
    I turned out all the cupboards. Nothing. For some reason, I'd
expected everything to be old and dirty, but no, apart from the
splashes of blood, everything was clean and shiny. Guillaume
had been working.
    I reopened the drawer where he kept the virgin-stone.
Curious, I took it out of its bag once more, examined it. It was
clear, almost colourless, with just a hint of yellow, and felt very
smooth, very cool. I closed my hand around it, held it tight, felt it
getting warm … opened my hand: the stone was scarlet.
    'What's that? A blood-stone?' Yahia held out his hand for it.
    'No, a virgin-stone.' We looked at each other. 'Hold it,' I told
him.
    He closed his great hand around it. Held it. Opened his hand
again.
    The stone was colourless.
    He grinned, passed it back to me. I held it. After a moment, I
opened my hand. The stone was pulsing with fresh warm blood
again.
    I grinned back at him.
    We were not here to play games.

I put the stone away and closed the drawer.

Alchemy.

I wished I knew more. Who could I turn to? Who could I ask? Could I go to the top? Consult Thomas of Pizan, for instance? Alchemists are very secretive. Understandably so, for in the eyes of the Inquisition they are the same as wizards and sorcerers. Thomas of Pizan, who was a Doctor of Astrology of the University of Bologna, and who sometimes lectured here at our university (I had heard him, and I was impressed) was Court Astrologer to Charles V of France. He was also known to be an expert on, and sympathetic to, alchemy. With the King's protection, he had little to fear … for the moment.

Could I get to him?

Chuvar the snake was asleep.

Chuvar. Strange name.

There was nowhere else anything could be hidden.

'How do you feel about snakes, Yahia?'

He touched the top of its nose with just one finger tip, then, oh so lightly, so gently, began to stroke it with that one finger tip, then two, then three, gradually stroking further and further back along the neck until finally he ran his hand all the way down to its tail. He smiled.

'Can you lift it out?'

He did so. It went on sleeping in his arms.

The base of its box was hollow: another box. I pushed down on the bottom and simultaneously pressed the right hand side of the box outwards. Nothing. Then the left hand side. Then each end. Then both ends at the same time while pressing still on the bottom with my middle and index fingers. The bottom fell away, revealing a large cavity full of papers. On top was the one I wanted. I knew it immediately, and knew also that I must not touch the others. I took it, and closed the lid so that it formed once again the bottom of the upper compartment.

Yahia gently laid the snake back down while I peered at the paper. It was folded, but not closed, sealed only beneath the signature.

It was the Last Will & Testament of Guillaume le Breton, known as Guillaume le Grec.

I refolded it and tucked it away inside my shirt.

We went through to Guillaume's bedroom. There, Yahia found something and gestured excitedly: some robes covered in astrological symbols. With a grin, he tried one on. It was far too small, but he liked himself in it, and struck a pose.

We heard a sound.

I snuffed our candle, wet-fingered to prevent any smell.

The door opened – inwards, into the bedroom from the landing – and a very superior monk came in: Natalie's abbé. He was short and plump, with jowels running to fat and little hair. He was followed by two retainers in black livery, presumably the men who had cased the building not an hour before.

One of the men had a lantern, but they didn't notice us in the shadows. Then the man used it to illuminate each part of the room in turn while the abbé took it all in.

'Stop there,' he said, calmly.

I was caught in the beam of the lantern.

'What in heaven's name are you doing here, boy?'

'The same as you, I imagine, mon père.'

'And what is that?'

'Seeking something, mon père.'

'I am not sure I like your attitude, boy. And I am not sure I like your accent, either. Where are you from?'

My usual nom d'étudiant, that of my twin brother Magnus, would not do here: it might very well be known to the Church already. I needed a whole new identity, something quite untraceable.

'From England, mon père. From London.'

'Where in London?'

What did I know of London? Yes, the city was on the north bank. 'The South Bank, mon père.'

'Ah, by the Church of St Mary Overie.'

Merde! He knows London! 'Oui, mon père. And the bear pit.' I was improvising now.

But he smiled. 'I know it, yes. Know of it, that is. But for a young man like you … And your name?'

'Jack, mon père.' I knew an English Jack, a stranded soldier missing a leg who begged his bread in the rue Pierre-à-Poisson. I sometimes gave him something when I crossed the river by the Pont-au-Change. I wouldn't like to be a soldier left behind in enemy territory by a retreating army. Left behind for dead, but not dead, just buried – under a pile of the dead and dying of both sides. An old woman, a corpse-stripper, had tossed a coin for him, let her ancient gods decide, and her gods had given him back his life. She had cared for him, then put him on the road north, and he, by feigning dumb, had got a lift in a cart of pigs to Paris, to Les Halles – and there, he told me, laughing, had nearly ended up with the rest of the pigs lined up waiting for the butcher's knife when the driver went off for his breakfast and forgot he had him in there. 'There are worse ways to die, lad.'

'Jack what?'

'Jack Cutting.'

'Cutting? Strange name.'

'My forebears cut purses, mon père. So they say. Or maybe throats.'

And so was born that alter ego of mine, later to become notorious in the back-streets – and not just the back-streets – of London and Paris: Jack Cutting, spy.

'And what is it you imagine I seek here?'

'Gold, mon père. Or the means to make gold.'

'Seize him!' he snapped, waving his arms towards me, but even as his men moved they were themselves seized from behind by two mighty arms, their heads were cracked together, and they dropped to the floor unconscious.

'You seem little better at choosing your bodyguards than at choosing you words, mon père.'

'My — my words?'

'"Seize him!" Not diplomatic. And nor were all the questions. What made you suppose that you were in a position to question me? You hadn't even looked round. Careless. Arrogant. Hardly the way to make cardinal … Perhaps now you will tell me, not what you seek here this evening, for that I know, but what happened here yesterday evening, twenty-four hours ago.'

'I know nothing of what happened.'

'A man was murdered. Tortured to death — the Death by a Thousand Cuts.'

'I know nothing of that.'

'Then I must be mistaken, mon père. Perhaps you simply wandered in by chance, knowing nothing of whose house this is … Do you often do that when your two men have reported that a house seems empty? If I didn't know better, I might take you for a common burglar.'

'That's enough, boy. Have you any idea who I am?'

'Yes, I have. A certain abbé, not unknown to the Sire de Montrouge, now deceased, and his half-brother, the new Sire de Montrouge. And also not unknown to the owner of this house, one Guillaume le Breton, known as Guillaume le Grec, also deceased. Deceased, like the Sire de Montrouge, yesterday evening. If your superiors heard of your involvement in this …'

'I have no involvement in this!'

'Tell me. J'écoute, mon père.'

'I will tell you nothing! You will release me instantly, and you will — '

'Did I introduce my bodyguard? His name is Hercule. Unlike Hercule, though, the original Hercule, my Hercule is a eunuch. This makes him very angry when he sees men behaving as you behaved when you thought you were three men against one boy. He thinks they do not deserve to be men. Do not deserve their cojones. He comes from Spain. In Spain, they eat cojones, I understand. They believe – the men, that is, believe – that cojones contain something they need. Certainly, he does look very manly for a eunuch, does he not?'

It was fortunate that Yahia understood nothing of this. He is desperately shy in front of men – when he is not attacking them.

But the abbé wasn't finished yet. 'In France, too, men eat les couilles. But of course, being young, ignorant and English, you know nothing of the customs of our great country.'

'I am learning, mon père. Perhaps Englishmen do not need to. Now, though, a lesson for you. Yahia, your knife.'

He removed the wizard's robe, laid it carefully back where he had found it, then removed his curved dagger from the shoulder-strap sheath hanging at his hip.

'Non! For the love of God, keep him away from me!'

I shrugged.

Yahia stepped forward, his huge naked bulk gleaming in the lantern-light.

The abbé dropped to his knees. He crossed himself with one hand, clutched his cojones with the other. 'Stop him! Keep him off me!'

I gestured to Yahia to pause …

'I will tell you what I know, but it is nothing, nothing,' he sobbed. 'You have heard of Pierre de Montrouge and his brother P'tit-Jean. Pierre had learnt, somewhere, that Maître Guillaume was an alchemist. A successful alchemist.'

'Where had he learnt this? On Ibiza?'

'You know about Ibiza?'

'You may assume I know everything.'

'Then you do not need me.'

'I said you may assume that I know everything, mon père. My teacher used to say, "Assume that you know nothing. Assume that your enemy knows everything."'

'You are my enemy, boy?'

'I would much rather not be, mon père, but … we shall see.'

He gazed up at me, calculating.

'The truth, mon père. Ibiza.'

'I was, still am, engaged in charitable work on behalf of the Church. My mission at that time was to save poor Christian souls who had fallen into bondage, obtain their release, and ship them back to France.'

'How did you do that?'

'We bought them, boy. Which cost a very great deal of money. However, the great monasteries of France were charitable, and put huge sums in gold at our disposal on Crete and Ibiza.'

'I assume the great monasteries of France were also at that time desperately short of labour.'

He smiled at me, still on his knees but clutching his cross now, and regaining his equanimity. 'Of course, boy. There is always a reason. If you want to get something done, find a good reason why someone else might want it done, might do it for you.'

'So you bought hundreds of Christian slaves and shipped them to France to work on land belonging to the Church.'

'With a view to liberating them – indeed a commitment to liberate them. But, in a word, yes. I came to Ibiza from Marseille, where my overseer and I had recently delivered a consignment of six hundred slaves from Candia – '

'Candia?'

'On the island of Crete. Candia is the biggest slave market in the Mediterranean.'

'Apart from those on the coast of Africa, mon père.'

'Ah, well, yes, of course, as you say. And possibly Constantinople. I took the same ship and the same overseer with me to Ibiza, where there were now many Christian slaves to be saved at not too great a cost.'

'Would this overseer's name have been, by any chance, Pierre de Montrouge?'

'It would, my son. But on Ibiza we had a disagreement and went our separate ways. I hired a new – '

'What did you disagree over, mon père?'

'The purchase of women. The monasteries, of course, wanted only men, but those men needed women. Most monasteries agreed, unofficially, to a quota of four women for every hundred men, as a means of protecting the local peasant women and avoiding conflict with their menfolk. Pierre wanted to import young women, on the side and in large numbers, for the bordels of the cities of the south – not Marseilles itself, Marseilles is well provided for, but Toulouse, Avignon, Narbonne … '

I laughed. 'Shipping costs covered by the great monasteries of France.' I was beginning to understand Pierre de Montrouge. 'And Maître Guillaume was on Ibiza at that time.'

'That is not a question.'

'No. But can you confirm that he was, mon père?'

'Yes. Listen. I wanted to know the situation in Thessalonika. I was sent to Maître Guillaume, who had recently returned from there. When I enquired as to his profession – was he a slaver? – they laughed at me, said he was a wizard. A wizard? I could not do business with a wizard! But when I met him, he turned out to be a modest, self-effacing, little man with an exceptionally beautiful Albanian slave-woman, Lule. He was an astrologer. She read tarocchi cards. Not much harm in that. He had bought her in Thessalonika just weeks before; and it was over her, in effect, that our disagreement began, for Pierre argued that if he could import a hundred, fifty even, like her … I told him he was dreaming, there were not fifty women like her in the whole of

Albania, and that if there were, I would not, could not, go along
with it ... He asked for a tarocchi card reading, just to sit before
her, talk to her, gaze at her: she drew the Hanged Man for him.
In a fury, he flounced off, leaving her unpaid and me to my own
devices. Well, as I say, with a new overseer, I returned to France
with my cargo of slaves. I did not meet Pierre de Montrouge
again until last summer.'

'Where had he gone from Ibiza? Do you know?'

'He went to Thessalonika. Later I heard a story of him
meeting Maître Guillaume and Lule once more on the road
somewhere. I do not know what happened.'

'Did Lule have a baby with her at that time on Ibiza?'

'Yes.'

'A boy or a girl.'

'A girl, of course.'

'Why "of course"?'

'You know her – that slut Natalie – '

'There is no "of course" about it, mon père. Did you know,
then, that the baby was a girl?'

'No.'

I gazed at him.

He read my mind. 'It is difficult to think clearly in this
position.'

'You mean, on your knees? I would have thought a man like
you would be used to that, er, pose. However, if you prefer to sit
… Hercule, help the abbé up, sit him on that chair.'

Yahia went behind him, picked him up gently, one hand under
each armpit, and set him down on the chair, while the abbé's face
moved from terror to bewilderment, and finally amusement.

'If you ever think of selling him ...'

'He was bred for the harem, mon père. He is only really happy
working with women. Actually, he belongs to my sister,' I added
quickly, catching the slip.

He hadn't noticed, of course - why should he? - but the idea that I had a sister caught his attention. 'Sister?'

I gazed into his eyes. Easy to read: a sister might be vulnerable. Looked down at his hands. I have a professional interest in hands. They were small and white - too small for a man - much smaller than mine - with thin fingers and pale, bloodless nails.

I would hate to be my sister if she ever fell into those hands, ever found herself at the mercy of whatever lurked behind those eyes.

Be my sister? I am my sister!

'Sister?' he repeated, looking up at me curiously.

'Lady Jane Cutting,' I improvised, pulling myself together. 'She is no concern of yours. Now, what happened when you met Montrouge again last summer? How did the meeting come about?'

'He had learnt somewhere that Maître Guillaume was an alchemist. He wanted my help. I agreed.'

'Why?'

'If he was a successful alchemist, he was indeed a wizard and beyond the pale of the Church. I wished to put him to the question.'

'You wished to find his gold, mon père.'

'Non! Bien, oui, mon fils. But not for myself. Myself, I have no interest in gold, but the Church always has need of gold to enable it to carry out its charitable works.'

'And then?'

'Then we came here, he and I. Guillaume claimed at first that he had never succeeded, then he claimed that though he had succeeded a few times that was many years ago and he no longer had the means and had himself run out of gold. I - '

'Shh …' It was Yahia. He has much better ears than any normal man.

The abbé looked at him, looked at me, froze.

The door was open. We heard soft footsteps approaching. A lady appeared in the doorway, cloaked, but the hood was down and I knew that hair. Natalie.

As she opened her mouth to scream, Yahia placed an enormous hand over it, and with the other he lifted her, carried her over to me, held her in front of me. The abbé couldn't see her face, I realised; she couldn't speak. He needn't find out that I was not all I seemed. I winked at her. She stared at me in horror.

Didn't she recognise me?

I winked again.

This wasn't working.

'Would you excuse us for a moment, mon père?' I said over her shoulder. 'I wish to speak to this lady. Alone.'

At first he thought I was going outside, then he realised I wanted him to go out. He stood up, nervously.

'He'll flee,' said Yahia, in Arabic.

'I know.'

He went, with a furtive, backward glance, like a fox not believing that it is being freed.

I closed the door behind him, checked the two men on the ground: they were alive, but unconscious still. I said to Yahia, 'Let her be.'

He took both hands away.

She thought about screaming. Changed her mind. Said, 'You!'

'Yes,' I said, 'but I didn't wish him to know.'

'The abbé?'

I nodded. 'You said he reads you like a book. Let this be one time, the first of many I hope, when he does not.'

She hesitated, then nodded. And smiled.

'Why did you come back?' I asked her.

'This is my home. Why did you come back?'

'There were things … This is Yahia, the eunuch I – '

'You said he would protect me!'

'He will from now on, if you are going to be on our side.'

'I think …' She looked him up and down, then glanced at the
two unconscious men on the floor. 'Did he do that?'
　　I nodded.
　　'I think I prefer to be on your side.'
　　'Good, because we are on yours.'
　　'I've never known a girl who dressed up as a boy before.'
　　'You like that?'
　　'Oh yes!'
　　'Listen, Natalie. This is not your home any longer. This is a
house where an alchemist once lived and where dangerous
people believe gold to be hidden, and even perhaps the recipe for
turning base metals into gold, or for the elixir of immortality.
They will stop at nothing.'
　　'It isn't dangerous for me.'
　　'It is dangerous for anyone – as Monsignor l'Abbé and his
men discovered. If I hadn't had Yahia with me, I'd be the abbé's
prisoner now and he'd be questioning me, and he wouldn't be
doing it gently.'
　　'But – '
　　'You're the one they want, not me. And they'll be no more
merciful to you than they were to your master.'
　　'But I don't know anything!'
　　'They won't believe that until you are dead, and they won't let
you die. Did you ever meet Pierre's younger brother, P'tit-Jean,
the new Sire de Montrouge?'
　　'Then you know – '
　　'I know. How do you know?'
　　'The Albanian told me.'
　　'Did he know who had done it?'
　　She shrugged. 'It must have been P'tit-Jean. He's worse than
his brother, they say. Pierre was a gambler and a fool, but P'tit-
Jean … P'tit-Jean …'
　　'What would have happened to you if I hadn't come here this
evening, or if I'd come here on my own, without Yahia?'

She thought about it. 'The Abbé would have taken me to –
somewhere. And then P'tit-Jean would have come, tonight or
tomorrow, and questioned me.'

'Let's go, while we still can. If P'tit-Jean arrives now with a
dozen men, even Yahia won't be able to protect us.'

She was convinced.

'Yahia,' I said in Arabic, 'drop these two off in the street
somewhere as we leave, will you?'

I went ahead with Natalie. Yahia, having donned his burnous,
followed with the two retainers, one under each arm. It was a
mistake that almost cost us very dear.

When we got to the street door, I opened it and peered out.
Nothing. I went first, I was the gentleman, and – they were upon
me, one from above crashing onto my shoulders, knocking me
down, banging my face on the ground, others from the corner –
then the one on top of me gurgled horribly and fell off, and the
others fled.

All over.

Everyone came out of it with honours. Except me. I came out
of it with badly bruised and grazed hands and knees and, yes,
nose! – which was bleeding down my front and felt twice its
normal size.

Natalie, it turned out, carried a small, razor-sharp stiletto the
Albanian had given her and shown her how to use; she had used
it, instantly, between the ribs of my attacker, saving me and
giving Yahia a chance to get to the others.

'I think I'm very glad we're on the thame thide,' I snuffled,
through the blood that was pouring from my nose..

She laughed. 'Just because you're wearing boy's clothes
doesn't mean – '

'Natalie, ma chère,' I said, leaning forward, trying to keep the
blood off my clothes and examining my poor palms, 'you can
wear the long hothe from now on, I'll thtick to thkirtth and
petticoatth!'

They took me home, one each side, grinning conspiratorially, the beautiful girl and the huge eunuch. And when we were there, I stripped off my boy's outfit, let Yahia bathe my nose and my knees, and smooth soothing unguent over them. His touch is, as I say, much gentler than Khadija's. Then he put a silk kaftan on me – he likes me in kaftans – and I went down to talk to Natalie, who was in the kitchen with Khadija.

I took her through to the parlour, where I wouldn't have to endure Khadija's eyes on my nose.

I wanted to ask her what had happened to the astrolabe, which, I had suddenly realised, wasn't there on my second visit.

At first, she didn't believe it. Then she couldn't explain it.

I didn't want to tell her le Cafard was watching the front door. I simply said: 'Is there a back way in?'

She nodded.

'Then ... '

But she shook her head and held up a key. 'There's a door that opens into a narrow alley from the back garden of our house. It's a small, arched door, set in a high wall made of red brick.'

She handed me the key. 'I came in that way this evening.'

I took it. Did she mean me to keep it? I changed the subject. 'What do you know about Tarocchi, Natalie?'

She shrugged. 'Not much. Just what I remember of things Maman showed me. There's old Mère Bórbala in the Cour who knows …'

'The Cour?'

'Le Cour des Miracles that the Albanian rules. The one between the Porte Saint-Antoine and the Palais des Tournelles.'

'And Mère Bórbala? Strange name. Where is she from?'

'I don't know. Somewhere – there.' She waved her hand vaguely in what I guessed was intended to be a south-easterly direction: "there" beyond the borders of France in the direction

of Albania and Serbia. 'She offered to teach me, as my own
mother can't.'

'Teach you Tarocchi?'

'Yes.'

'And Maître Guillaume?'

'He didn't take Tarocchi very seriously.'

'What can you tell me about the Hanged Man?'

'He's the greedy one whose life is overset and who loses all
his money, everything.'

'The greedy one? The miser?'

She looked at me. 'Yes. No. I don't know. Not necessarily a
miser, but a greedy man, like Messire Pierre.'

'I see. So it doesn't necessarily mean death.'

'Oh, no.'

'Did you accept Mère Bórbala's offer?'

She smiled. 'No. It's a way of making money, and it can give
you prestige, but it can also make you enemies. Or so Maman
said. It can make you hard, too, and proud, knowing things that
others do not. Maman was beautiful, but I – well, I didn't like her
very much.'

'Because she beat you?'

'No, not that. Not just that,' she smiled. 'Though I know now
she beat me much more than she needed to … Maître Guillaume
was good to her, always. He adored her. He even adores her
memory. She didn't need to have men visit her …' Tears were
running down her face.

'He was a miser. Perhaps she needed money.'

'She could always get what she needed from him. And
anyway, it was only after she died that he shut himself up like
that, became known as a miser.'

'And you fear that one of those men may have been your
father.'

'One of those men, yes! When I asked her who my father was,
she beat me! Why? Because she didn't know!'

'And Maître Guillaume could not possibly have been your father, in your view.'

'No, I told you. He wouldn't even look at me. Look me in the eye, I mean. He used to avoid my eyes.'

'Because you reminded him too painfully of your mother, perhaps? You're very like her.'

'I'm not very like her. Her eyes were blue, her hair much fairer.'

'You have the same features. If you closed your eyes and wore a cap, you would be her.'

'I know ... '

'Who your parents are is not important, Natalie. It's who and what you are that matters.'

I needed to know more about Natalie's mother, Lule, l'Albanienne; and that, it seemed, meant learning more about this other Albanian, who took such an interest in Natalie. He must be a very powerful man indeed in the Paris underworld if he ruled his own Court of Miracles, as not only Natalie but also le Cafard claimed.

Alone in my room, at last, I open Maître Guillaume's will and skim through it. He says the Albanian, "a rich man, I understand," has been a father to the boy Charles le Grec. Who is Charles le Grec? Anyway, Charles gets nothing. And Jaquet? … To his nephew Jaquet le Breton, he leaves Natalie, "if she will have him". And Natalie? "Natalie has been more than a daughter to me all these years … All the gold that remains to me I bequeath to her and to her mother, Lule."

Lule? This must be an old will.

I collapse onto the bed and fall asleep.

6

Next morning, I leave Natalie asleep with Yahia on guard, while
I go in search of some of the more likely people on Raoul's list.

I start at the baby-shop, which is nearby.

Their name is Spanish, so I decide to be a great lady from
Spain. Intimidate them. So long as they don't see my nose. I'm
dressed for the part and such a lady would be unlikely to remove
her veil.

The shop is in the cellar of a dilapidated building in rue de la
Harpe, almost next door to the Mouton, a seedy tavern that is the
boys' favourite because they serve the best lentil soup in Paris.
The building looks as though it is shored up by those on either
side of it. They all do. If one fell, they would all fall, like a pack
of cards. Like the people involved in this mystery? I feel a
premonition. How long will P'tit-Jean last?

I must find out who the next heir is. Perhaps Ferchard will
know, when he returns from the funeral.

I go carefully down some icy, chipped stone steps. The door
hangs open.

A baby wails, setting off another. Soon there are half-a-dozen
crying for their mothers, for the breast, for milk. Well, they will
get milk here, and the lucky ones will find, somewhere, another
mother.

Inside, it is almost dark. There is a sweet smell of baby caca
and stale milk – and on a bench, a large blonde woman suckling
two babies at once.

'Señora Dolores de los Niños?'

She nods towards a door at the back.

How do they find enough wet-nurses?

I knock – but imperiously – on the narrow door. 'Señora de
los Niños?'

The door opens. 'Sí?'

'I am Doña Mariana de la Mar. I am in search of information concerning a baby.'

'Come in, Doña Mariana. Come in, sit down.'

I find myself in a small room, as dark as the first and almost as smelly. There are benches along three walls and a low table in the middle. On one of the benches, on a straw pallet, lies a baby. It is awake and gazing at us. I cannot tell whether it is a boy or a girl: it is wearing a long, grubby smock. The woman has been shaving its head.

'Why do you shave its head, señora? So that no one will recognise it?'

'Please, sit down.'

'I prefer to stand. Where is your husband?'

'Mi hombre? He's out. He goes in search of babies. When he finds one, he brings it back and – '

'"Finds" one?'

'Doña Mariana, our babies are all abandoned. We save their lives.'

'One or two, maybe, girls, but for the most part, no, I don't believe that.'

'And beggars sell us their babies.'

'"Their" babies?'

'One can't always be sure where they got them, it's true, but …'

'With you they at least have some chance of finding a good home.'

Her eyes light up at this unexpected concession on my part. 'Oh yes! That's it! And the shaving is mostly for lice.'

'So,' I say. 'I am interested in a baby ... '

'What kind of baby?'

'A baby that will now be grown up.'

She looks at me, the fear back in her eyes. Then says, brightly, 'Oh, we keep no records.'

'I am sure you should.'

'We should, yes, but mi hombre can't read or write, so …'

'This baby was on the island of Ibiza, seventeen or eighteen years ago.'

'Oh, we have never visited Ibiza.'

'I happen to know that you have. That you were there then, at that time.'

'Ah. Yes. That girl who was here yesterday, wheedling things out of mi hombre. Was she from you?'

'She may have been. I asked some students and their friends to help me in my search.'

'What kind of baby?'

'A girl. She would have been with a French astrologer, Maître Guillaume le Breton, though he was not her father, and an Albanian slave-woman who was the mother.'

'And what might my contact with them have been, Doña Mariana?'

'Who knows? But I would pay you well for anything you do remember. And I would forget the babies with the shaven heads.'

'What I told you was true. We have never visited Ibiza. We were born there, both of us. We came to Paris because the trade in babies on Ibiza was so small, apart from … Mi hombre wanted to go into slaving – not grown-ups, but dealing in children, you know, rather than babies as we had been doing.'

I know.

'He met a Frenchman, an aristo, who was interested in young slaves of either sex for the child bordels here in France. I didn't like it, but we did sell him a few older ones – seven, eight-year-olds ... Then when he disappeared, we came to France ourselves with a dozen children, and we stayed.'

'You sold them, and set up here.'

She nods.

'And Maître Guillaume and the girl-child?'

'Mi hombre met the astrologer while he was going about with
the French aristo. Mi hombre was very proud to be with him, to
be in his company, you understand. Me, I was not so proud …
The astrologer has a girl-child, he told me, a beauty. He is not
interested in it. It cries. It is an inconvenience. It is his? No! It is
his slave-woman's brat. She already had it when he purchased
her. Her previous master's, no doubt. So. So? So would I go and
talk to this slave-woman, arrange to relieve her of it. All right, I
would. I did. But we had no language in common, and when she
asked her husband to interpret for us and he realised what I
wanted, he told me to clear out and never come back. Mi hombre
had got that one wrong.'

He sounded like a man who got most things wrong. 'And the
baby? This is the baby I'm interested in. Tell me about it.'

'Some money, Doña Mariana. You promised me some
money.'

I took my small purse out and gave her a silver sou.

'It was a girl, Doña Mariana. A beauty, as mi hombre said.'

'Describe her. Her hair, her eyes, anything. How old was she?'

'Oh, less than a year. And she had thick dark-brown hair and
brown eyes.'

'B- ' I stopped myself, showed no reaction. 'You're quite sure
of that, señora? For if I find out later that the baby had, say,
green eyes, you and your husband will be in the pillory for days.
Then hanged, if you're still alive. Or is the penalty for
kidnapping here in Paris being boiled alive? The people don't
like baby-snatchers. '

'But it is true, Doña Mariana! Everything I told you is true! I
remember them all! And I've seen him here, in Paris, the maître,
though I've never seen her or the child. There is a girl lives with
the maître, I know, I've seen her, but that is not her. Her I have
never seen again. And that is God's truth, Doña Mariana.'

'Could I be her?'

'You? Is that what this – ?'

'Could I?'

'No, Doña Mariana! Your eyes are - are bluey-green. Hers were brown, I told you. And your hair is more - more Andalusian, than hers was.'

No changes there.

I am ready to leave, but then her husband arrives. A man's voice, the door opens, and he comes in with a bag over his shoulder. The bag moves, as though it contains an animal, then it lets out a wail.

'Give your wife that baby, señor.'

He looks at her, for guidance.

She nods.

He hands her the bag and she takes out a tiny baby, no more than a few hours old.

I say, 'Señora, concern yourself with that poor child. Say nothing. I have a question for your husband, and I want his answer, not yours. Now, señor. At one time, on the island of Ibiza, you were in some sort of partnership for a while with Pierre de Montrouge.'

Shocked, for she has deliberately avoided giving me the name, the woman opens her mouth to speak.

'Say nothing, señora!'

She closes it again.

'At that time, señor, you met a man, an astrologer, by the name of Guillaume le Breton. You remember him. That is not a question. You also remember his woman, an Albanian slave named Lule. Now listen carefully. Lule had a baby. It was a beautiful baby, was it not?'

He glances at his wife.

'Señor! Keep your eyes on me! Good. Now answer the question.'

'Sí, señora. She was beautiful - would become more beautiful. She would have been worth, oh - '

'I am not interested in what she was worth, only in the colour of her hair and eyes.'

'Her hair? It was thick and dark and - and her eyes were brown, too.'

'Like her mother's.'

'Her mother's? What - ?'

'Answer me, señor.'

'No, not like her mother's at all. Her mother was blonde.'

'Gracias, señor.'

I turn to go, turn back. 'Did you ever see that girl again? Or her mother?'

'No, señora.'

I was close to the river so I took a boat across to the jetty below the Grand Châtelet. Next on my list was La Mireille, the "abbess" of La Fille d'Or, a bordel situated just off the Place au Chats, near Les Halles.

She was a stranger to winter, a rose, and in full bloom, her glorious hair bright yellow, red lips and nipples - the breasts at least whitened and the nipples rouged.

'Are you looking for work, chérie? Let's see your face. Fais voir.' She leant forward, released the veil. Stared. 'Po-po-po … Did he do that to you?'

'I was in a fight.'

'Ça se voit. Bien. First, you'll need to learn how to handle men without upsetting them. Though husbands can be difficult for the best of us.'

'He was not my husband.'

'Non? Take the cloak off.'

I took it off, and twirled as she twirled her finger at me.

'Mais tu es belle!'

I sat down, laughing despite my nose.

'Madame, I do not seek work. Truly. I seek only information.'

She was on her guard again immediately.

'There are two things you can help me with, Madame Mireille. First, La Adriatica.'

She raised one practised eyebrow.

'It is owned apparently by the Albanian, but I need to know who actually runs it.'

'Why? You prefer to work there?'

'And where it is. I don't even know where it is.'

'I said "Why?".'

'Well, that has to do with my other question, and the reason I came to see you in particular. When you were very young, you spent some time — a summer? — a year? — on Ibiza. Yes?'

She considered. Then nodded. 'Yes.'

'And while you were there, you knew a man called Pierre. A man who later became the Sire de Montrouge. A man who was found yesterday morning hanging upside down, by one foot, in the posture of the Hanged Man in the tarocchi card.'

'I heard last night that he was dead, that he had been hanged, though I didn't know about the — about him being upside down … But what has this to do with me? Or you?'

'For now, Madame Mireille, you must trust me. I am trying to help a friend in trouble — terrible trouble. And in order to help him I need to know certain things.'

She considered me again. 'Pity you're not looking for work. You are young, sweet, and persuasive. And you'd be beautiful if you looked after your nose. Get a man to do your fighting for you,' she laughed. 'I always do.' Then she said, 'Your name?'

'I am Lady Marian MacElpin, of the County of Ross, in Scotland.'

'Ah.'

Not what she'd been expecting.

'That is a Scottish accent?'

'My French sounds better when my nose is not so swollen!'

'Lady Marian, I will tell you what you want to know.' There was a knock on the door. 'Oui?'

A girl of thirteen or fourteen came hurrying in, wearing very little, and whispered in Madame's ear. Madame shook her head. 'No, you may not. Listen, he's very eccentric, that Don Francisco. Tell Jasmine to see to him.' She gave the girl's bottom a slap. 'Go!'

The girl ran out and Madame turned back to me. 'The young wish always to bite off more than they can chew – or at least swallow. And you are very young still, Lady Marian … My sister and I were on Ibiza with Pierre de Montrouge in the summer of 1360. He was rich, comparatively, and young and aristocratic. We had fun, when he was sober.'

'Was it he who set you up here?'

'It was, yes. Clever of you. At first we had only very young girls – and we still do have some, as you saw. Our youngest now though is twelve, thirteen, not ten or even less as it was then. I didn't like that.'

'And you haven't seen him recently?'

'Not for a while, no. The last time was when he turned up here, suddenly, with a little girl, gave her to me, and after sampling a couple of my older girls – sixteen, seventeen, the age he prefers – rode off into the night.'

'That girl? The one who came – '

'Eh? Oh, no. Prettier than that. And much younger. Would you like to see her?'

She pulled a bell-cord and the same girl came running in.

'Marie, tell Isabeau I wish to speak to her.'

'Oui, Mère Mireille. The other, he is with Jasmine. Can I watch through the peep-hole?'

'Very well. But if you giggle and he hears you, Seraphina will beat your bottom so hard it'll be months before you giggle again.'

'Oui, Mère Mireille! Merci!'

Marie ran back out again.

'La Adriatica is in la rue de l'Enfer, by the way. It is run by a certain Mère Véronique. Véronique is old now, but she is not stupid. Ah, Isabeau, ma fleur.'

Isabeau was certainly no more than six. She was pretty, yes, but she was still a baby.

Madame Mireille said, 'She is not abused, Lady Marian. I do not run that kind of house. She is treated as a pet, a baby. She goes everywhere, sees everything; she watches and she learns. She is very astute.'

'But who is she?'

'Who? You think she is somebody?'

'Why else would Montrouge ...?'

'Montrouge ...' repeated the child.

'Isabeau, little girls are to be seen and not heard.'

The child held her tongue but to judge from the dancing green eyes was not in the least intimidated.

'Isabeau, I am Lady Marian. Will you answer a question for me?' She nodded, and I went on: 'What do you remember of your life before you came here? Your maman, your home, your ...'

'I remember Maman ... and Fernand.'

'Who is Fernand?'

'My dog!' As though I should have known.

'Have you any brothers or sisters?'

She shook her head, uncertainly.

'Did you have servants? Did a maid-servant wash you and dress you in the morning?'

'Like Seraphina does?'

Madame Mireille interrupted: 'Seraphina does that? She's supposed to be training you, not treating you like a princess!'

'Please, madame, let her answer. Well, Isabeau? Who did that for you when you were at home? Your maman? A maid-servant?'

Suddenly her eyes lit up. 'Jeanne! Jeanne used to dress me and brush my hair and sometimes she pulled and it hurt, but not like when Seraphina does it. And she didn't use to beat me, either, like Seraphina does; only Maman was allowed to beat me.'

'And the man who brought you here, Isabeau? Did you know him before that day?'

'No. He – I don't know, I don't remember.'

'All right, you can go now,' said Madame Mireille. 'Say "adieu" to Lady Marian.'

'Adieu, Lady Marian.'

'Isabeau, may I see your hands for a moment?'

She held them out to me and I took them in mine.

There seemed little doubt that she would be reunited with her family. Everything pointed to happiness and success in life: for instance, the Sun Line started on the Mount of Venus, a sure indication of early success based, at least at first, on family position or inherited wealth.

'Adieu, ma petite. Here, let me give you a kiss.'

I pulled her to me and kissed her, and hugged her for a moment, then let her go.

She backed out of the room, gazing at me.

When the door had closed, I said, 'Madame, would you let her go if I found her family?'

She smiled, but the smile did not extend to her eyes. I should have taken that little warning more seriously. 'Of course. Why? Do you expect to?'

'I consider it possible. I shall be digging deep into the lives of les Sires de Montrouge during the next few days. Who knows what may turn up? She's not just some urchin he found in the street.'

'Be careful, ma fille. They are dangerous men, and from what I hear the step-brother is the worst of the brood.'

'I will be. This nose of mine was the result of no personal quarrel.'

'So battle has already been joined. I see. Farewell, Lady Marian. I should be delighted if you were to call again. I hear many things – and, too, learn much from others like myself, such as Mère Véronique. We can exchange news.'

We kissed on both cheeks.

'I shall do so, madame. I look forward to it.'

I put up my veil and walked to the Pont-au-Change, lined on both sides, right across, with three and four-storey houses and the shops of the goldsmiths and money-changers. I approached the guards at the gate. 'Maître Pietri?'

'Fourth on the right, dem'selle.'

I thanked the man and walked towards the shop he had indicated. I rather wished I could become "Jack Cutting" for this next interview, but I couldn't, not without wasting a lot of time – and anyway, if I did my nose would be on show. Well, I would follow my Uncle Yacoub's advice and take it as I found it, one step at a time.

7

Maître Pietri was not a Jew – he was from Corsica, and there are no Jews left on Corsica – but he looked very Jewish and I decided on the spur of the moment to adopt a quite different identity. For years I had been to all intents and purposes a Muslim in Andalucía, but I could also pass as Jewish, had done so for a while once when I was with ibn Khaldoun in Granada. I say "pass as", but in a sense, I was – I am – Jewish.

I should explain at this point that my mother, Doña Maria de la Mar, was Spanish. She was the daughter of Sebah of Cordoba, and Sebah, as you can tell by the name, came of a Moorish family. She had been given in marriage to my grandfather, Don Joaquín de la Mar, the Alcalde of Los Alcazares, a man of peace and a childless widower, as a mark of respect and affection at a time when such mixed marriages, once common in the Maghreb and Andalucía, were becoming rare. And my great-grandmother, Sebah's mother, had been Rebbekah of Salé, the fourth wife of a rich Moor who brought her with him when he was appointed by the Sultan of Morocco to be his official representative in Andalucía. Now Rebbekah was Jewish; and as descent among Jews is reckoned through the maternal line, and I am the daughter of the daughter of the daughter of a Jewess, namely Rebbekah of Salé, I am, in a sense, Jewish myself. Also, my teacher throughout my childhood, Yacoub ben Amar, a distant relative of my mother's, was a Jew: I grew up immersed in Jewish culture, including the Kabbalah (he was a true mystic) and both Hebrew and Djudezmo. So:

'Maître Pietri?'

He glanced up.

'Shalóm,' I murmured. Greetings. Peace.

He peered at me. The way I was dressed, he could see very little.

'Shalóm, demoiselle ... You are Jewish?'

I nodded.

'And your name?'

I ignored his use of French, carried on in Hebrew. 'My name does not concern us. I am here only in search of information.'

He stared at me. 'I am not a Jew and do not speak the Jewish tongue.'

He was frightened, as he had every right to be. Jews, especially Jewish money-lenders, had been slaughtered by the score all over Europe in the aftermath of the Great Mortality, and it had not been forgotten. Would never be forgotten.

Whose side had he been on?

It didn't matter.

I went into French. 'Maître Pietri, the language we speak is of no importance. Nor is your religion, though as a Jew I would naturally have found it easier to do business with a Jew … I need to know what happened to certain people on the island of Ibiza eighteen years ago. That is all. If you can help me, I shall be grateful.'

He looked at me guardedly, but said nothing.

'When you were on the island, did you have any dealings with either Pierre de Montrouge or Guillaume le Breton, known as Guillaume le Grec?'

'And why should I answer these questions, dem'selle, when you do not even do me the courtesy of introducing yourself?'

'You are right, maître. I am Miriam ben Amar, daughter of Yacoub ben Amar.' Uncle Yacoub would forgive me that: in fact, he would love it. 'The veil is not a mask of secrecy, nor is it worn out of modesty, nor even because it is the custom among my people: it is not. I am wearing it because I have injured my nose,' I lowered the veil, 'and I am embarrassed.' I smiled.

And he smiled too.

'So, Dem'selle Miriam, you may ask your questions. And to answer the first: yes, I was on Ibiza from 1353 to 1363. I made my money in the slave trade, then after ten years I'd had enough. I came to Paris, and set up here on the bridge where you see me now. I had no dealings with Montrouge. He was working with the Church, but on the side he was dealing in children for the child prostitute market and, well, though there is no morality in business, I didn't - still don't - like that. I have children of my own, you understand. Grandchildren now.'

'How many?'

'Grandchildren? Five, alive and well.'

'That's wonderful!' How my father would have loved to have grandchildren around him. But his other children died in the pestilence long before Magnus and I were born, and I was the only one left, and hardly more than a child still, when he himself died.

'Are they here in Paris?'

He looked at me.

He was right. Who could you trust, these days?

'I am sorry. Those are not the questions I came here to ask. But I wish them health, and happiness – and you too, joy of them.'

'Thank you, Dem'selle Miriam. The other man you asked about, Maître Guillaume, I also remember, yes. With his idiot brother.'

Idiot? Jaquet's father?

'Maître Guillaume,' he went on, 'le Breton, then, not le Grec, as you say, was an astrologer and fortune-teller. The brother, Charlot, the simpleton, was apparently necessary to him in his work in some sense. I don't know. I never consulted him. I have no time for such nonsense.' He smiled. 'That is not entirely true, for I drank with him on several occasions before he left for Thessalonika, and though he never used to talk about his work, he did once try to explain astrology to me, to persuade me that it made sense. And he succeeded, a little.' He looked at me. 'Are you an astrologer?'

I was not the only perceptive one here.

'Yes.'

'Then tell me my star sign. That was what he did that made me begin to wonder.'

I considered him. I never like doing this. 'May I hold your hands? I also read hands and it would help me …'

He looked at me. Smiled. Shrugged. Held out both hands, palms upwards.

There was no time for a detailed reading, just for what was distinctive, anything that made him special. The skin of the hands was firm, indicating a firm, healthy character. The tops of the thumbs were very square, showing a strong will, someone decisive, but reliable rather than obstinate. None of the mounts stood out particularly. The Great Triangle was wide and clear. All good signs. I held his hands and gazed into his eyes. Though he was a lover of gold, he was no miser; he was finely dressed, his hands were cared for, his face and eyes were cared for … His planet was probably the Sun …

'Do you tend to want to control your household, to take over even the kitchen, when you are at home,' I asked him, 'or do you happily leave all that to your wife?'

'I do tend to want things done my way, yes.'

'Do you have many friends? Any friends?'

'I have had, but … I seem to fall out with them, lose them.'

He met my eyes unwaveringly.

He was born under the sign of Leo.

'You are un Leon,' I told him.

He smiled. 'Yes, you are right, dem'selle. I was born at the end of July. And that means?'

'It doesn't mean much unless you tell me exactly when you were born and where, and I look you up in my almageste.'

But he was a surprisingly good man for a slaver and money-lender.

'Is that about organising the household really a characteristic of Leos?'

'Oh yes. That's why it's so difficult for two people born under the sign of Leo to live together.' Or one of the reasons.

'I see. Yes. I have a sister who is also a Leo and … well, you are right.' He smiled.

I laughed, and changed the subject. 'Can you tell me any more about this brother, Charlot?'

'He was thin, and very tall. He smiled all the time, smiled and whistled and talked, talked to himself if no one else would listen. I think if he'd been able to write he would have been a writer, a poet – he could entertain people, children especially – make them laugh – but in a practical sense he was helpless, completely dependent upon his brother.'

'Was he like his brother in appearance?'

'No, except that they both had blue eyes. Charlot's were bigger, though, and brighter, more full of laughter – and sadness too, His hair was darker than Guillaume's, and thick. And he was a lot taller. Did you ever meet Maître Guillaume? No? He would have come up to your shoulder. You, who are tall, would have come up to Charlot's shoulder. It was said that when he was young, his body grew and went on growing at the expense of his brain.'

'You have no idea how exactly Charlot used to help his brother in his work.'

'None.'

'And do you know what happened to them?'

'They sailed for Thessalonika, where Maître Guillaume bought himself a beautiful woman; and then they all crossed over to mainland Spain, but – '

'Spain? Where would that be? Coming from Ibiza? Valencia?'

'If he was going straight back up to France, then he might make for Barcelona.'

'If he was going straight back up to France, why would he go to Spain at all?'

'Right. Unless he knew he was being pursued.'

'That's a thought.' I studied his face. 'Do you know they were being pursued?'

'I never lost touch with him – we've been doing business together for years – but we never really talked again, after Ibiza. I don't know what happened then or what's been happening since. And nor can I tell you the nature of our business, which was always confidential.'

'Of course not. But you do know that Maître Guillaume was murdered the night before last?'

He nodded. 'I do, yes.'

We gazed at each other for a moment. Then I rose to my feet. 'You've been very helpful. Thank you, Maître Pietri.'

He stood up. 'I was born in Ajaccio on the 29th of July, 1329. Sometime in the evening, for I remember my mother saying she'd been in labour all through a very hot day.'

I smiled. 'I'll look you up, let you know if I find anything interesting!'

'Do that. Au revoir, dem'selle.'

'Shalóm, Maître Pietri.' I put my veil back up as I stood on his door step.

'You have remarkably un-Jewish eyes,' he said.

'You have remarkably Jewish ones.'

He smiled and turned back into his shop, and was gone.

I had a lot of things to think about, to sort out in my mind. I needed to talk to someone.

Natalie? She was too involved.

Raoul, perhaps.

But first, the Châtelet was close by, and it was time to visit poor Jaquet.

'A veil is a very good idea in there, my lady,' was my sergeant's only comment, and he nodded to a guard to take me through.

Jaquet kissed my hands (I couldn't stop him) begging for news and for someone to listen to him. He was full of ideas and had no one to talk to. 'All I do is sit here imagining the worst. And the worst is bad.' He grinned.

He would be all right. It was probably the first time he'd grinned since it all began.

I told him I was beginning to think the Montrouge brothers, one or both, were responsible for the murder of his uncle, and then something of what I'd found out about them and the abbé, and about Natalie's mother, Lule.

He was speechless. Natalie had mentioned something to him at some point about someone called Montrouge visiting his uncle, but he hadn't been listening, hadn't been interested.

'You were only interested in Natalie, I know. Listen, I have one or two questions that you can answer: such as, what was your father's Christian name?'

'My father? Hugues. Hugues le Breton, apothecary. It's still up outside the shop.'

'Then who is Charlot?'

'Charlot?'

I told him the story.

'But I've never had, have never heard of, another uncle. There were just two brothers, Hugues and Guillaume. Ask Maman, though. She may not have told me, may not have wanted to, if he was dead. I can't ask her because they don't let her through, they just bring me the food she leaves at the gate.'

'Has anyone come to speak to you? Anyone official?'

He shook his head. 'But the Emperor's here now, isn't he? Nothing will happen for a few days.'

'That's very good news for us. We need those few days, Jaquet.'

'But what will you do? Isn't Natalie in danger? That's what I think about most - if anything happens to her while I'm shut up in here, unable to protect her!'

'She is in danger, yes, but I have her at my house, where a huge Moorish eunuch called Yahia guards her night and day.'

'A eunuch?'

'Mm. He belongs to me.'

'Hou la! She will like that. She might even insist on having one of her own when … when this is all over.'

I laughed.

The guard called. 'Lady Marian?'

'Oui, j'arrive. I'll see you again tomorrow, Jaquet. Try to think of anything that might help. Anything your mother may have told you about when your Uncle Guillaume returned to Paris. Anything you might have seen or heard in your uncle's house in the last few months that struck you, or strikes you now, as not normal. As unexpected.'

8

By the time I got to the Lutetia, only Raoul was still waiting. The
others had gone to watch the procession, and now who knew
where they were?

I pulled down my veil.

'Maryam! Your nose! It's – '

'Don't tell me.'

'But your face! What happened?'

'I was jumped on. From above. I forgot all that Ferchard – Sir
Farquhar, you know – had taught me about defending myself. I
landed flat on my face – and on my hands, look ...'

He held them, kissed them gently. Which was what he had
wanted to do with my face.

'And my knees …'

But he was still working on my hands. He had little choice,
here, in this public place.

'Till I was splayed out like a flattened frog.'

'Oh, Maryam.'

'I want to talk, Raoul.' I needed comfort, I needed love.

'Shall we go to your house?'

'Too many people. Let's go to yours.'

'Mine? But – '

'You haven't tidied up. I don't care, so long as there's a bed
and a cup of something, preferably clean water. And you read me
one of those poems.'

Raoul was a student at the College of Navarre. He lived outside
now that he'd finished his Bachelor's degree and was studying
theology, but he still had to wear the black gown, the soutane,
which (along with good Latin) was all it took to be able to pass
in and out. His lodgings were in a small alley quite close to the

Sorbonne, off the rue Saint-Jacques, and predictably at the very
top of the building. Five flights – five! – of very rickety stairs, a
rickety door, a rickety floor, a rickety bed. But somehow warm,
despite the lack of heating.

I sat down on the bed.

He pulled his hood back off his head and stood and gazed at
me. I had the distinct feeling that a dream was coming true
before his eyes. I had no wish to spoil it.

'Er – would you – that is – this water is clean, Maryam.'

I nodded, eyes sparkling. Then remembered my nose. That
had not been in his dreams.

He gave me a cup of water, which he watched me drink, his
eyes on my throat, adoration on his face. He refilled the cup. I sat
there, holding it, sipping.

He watched me, shyly. He was obviously very inexperienced
with women.

I waited.

Suddenly he said – or rather croaked, and had to start again:
'So what did you discover, Maryam?'

I told him. While I was speaking, he took my empty cup
away, then held my hands, oh so gently …

When I finished, he went on gazing at me. I wondered if he'd
heard anything at all. 'Sum it up for me, Raoul. Draw me one or
two conclusions.'

'What? Oh – yes. Right. So … We know about Ibiza in 1359.
That the miser was there then, and so was Pierre de Montrouge.
That the miser was an astrologer and fortune-teller. He may also
have been an alchemist. However, nobody knows that for sure.
He has an idiot brother he uses in his scrying or his alchemy,
perhaps both. This brother disappears from the scene, as does a
brown-haired, brown-eyed baby girl, both last heard of crossing
over to Spain. Certainly they seem never to have reached Paris,
though that needs to be checked with Mère Henriette. Later, the
abbé and Pierre began to press the miser for gold. He would not

or could not satisfy them, so they killed him. Who was the fool who killed the goose that laid the golden eggs?'

'Of the three, the abbé, Pierre and P'tit-Jean, the one who best qualifies for the role of fool – though not the Tarocchi Fool – is Pierre. Anyway, he is already the Hanged Man.'

'He may not have been already hanged when the miser died ...'

'No, he was at Maître Guillaume's house that night. Natalie let him in. By the time he left, Guillaume was dead … Or was he?'

'He could have gone home. His brother could have killed him.'

'Killed Pierre, you mean? Then come to try his powers of persuasion on poor Guillaume? Possible. Yet it was Pierre who was desperate, I believe, and desperate men do foolish things.'

He was stroking my palms, the touch of a butterfly. I could hardly feel it, despite the grazes.

'But we need to know more about alchemy, and what might require the blood of a virgin in occasional large quantities. For that, I'll go to Maître Thomas of Pizan. We also need to know what, if anything, happened between, say, Valencia and Paris. Could you ask Mère Henriette what she remembers? Was Charlot with them still? Did they have any babies with them? If so, how many, and what colour were their hair and eyes? I am sure you'll get on better with her than I seem to.'

'Yes, leave her to me.'

'We need to know who the Albanian is, and what his connection with all this might be. He could be a relation of Lule's – and therefore of Natalie's.'

'He could be Natalie's father.'

I looked at him. 'You know, you're really very clever. I shall have to talk to you more often.'

'Oh, yes. Please.'

My next job would be to approach Thomas of Pizan. 'I want you to take me to the university. I will go as Doña Mariana, your Spanish friend, not as a student. You must get me as close as possible to Thomas of Pizan – then leave me.'

He looked at me so sadly that, remembering his dream, I said,
'But first, that poem.'
He read me one.

As I rode out one morning
I saw a white rose in bloom.
I leant down and plucked that white, white rose,
And carried it with me home.

I gave it to my Lady
Where she sat in the Garden of Love
With a unicorn beside her
And on her wrist a dove.

As I rode back that evening
I saw a rose red as blood.
I left that red rose to bloom and die
Where it grew, in the garden of God.

I kissed him. 'That's beautiful,' I said. 'Especially the image of
the poet riding away from the red rose at the end. But is it a
happy ending, or a sad one?'
'Roses always have a sad ending.'
'That's because the rose is the woman ... '
He gazed at me. 'It is, isn't it. But a butterfly is a very
masculine symbol, surely. Yet that too is ephemeral.'
He was right.
'So let's enjoy today.'
'Yes, let's. You said you hurt your knees.'
'That's right, I did.' I lifted my skirts. Both knees were bruised
and grazed.
'But that's awful! You must let me wash them for you.'
'They've been washed, and treated with an unguent.'
'What unguent? Are you sure you - ?'

'A salve of ivy and bistort - yes, yes, I'm sure! - they are both plants that come under the rule of Saturn, the planet that also rules Capricorn, to which the knees belong. And I also had stonecrop mixed into the unguent: stonecrop is ruled by Mars, which is the ruling planet for those born in the Night House of Scorpio, which means me; and stonecrop does indeed always work well for me except when Mars happens to be adversely positioned.'

'And it isn't now?'

'No, chéri, it isn't.'

'Then - '

'Then the best thing you can do is kiss them better. Gently. Just as you did to my hands.'

'Your hands?' Croaking again. 'Your hands are better?'

'Oh yes. So now, my knees. I thought that's what we came up here for?'

'Oh. Oh, yes - it was.' Softly, softly, he kissed my left knee, the one nearest him - the touch of a butterfly wing again, but this time with his lips.

I waited.

His confidence grew.

Soon he was gently licking. And when he had finished both knees to his satisfaction, he began to work down my right leg.

I let him.

I let him remove my boot and ankle-sock and kiss my foot, then bare my other foot and kiss the top of each toe, then lick along beneath them, his strong, wet tongue sliding down between each pair of toes. I stretched, relaxed, enjoying it ... Realised that the next move was up to me: took his head in my hands, drew it up, taught him what and where.

Then, having shown him how to pleasure a woman, set about showing how a woman pleasures a man ...

At last we lay back, him like a dying deer at the end of the hunt,

me smiling contentedly. 'Where – where did you learn all that?'
he panted.

I decided not to mention the bordels, one in Spain, one in the
south of France, where I had really learnt my trade. I'd promised
Ferchard to comport myself (his phrase) like the Lady I was here
in Paris; the less everyone knew about my past, the easier it
would be for me to keep that promise. 'My master was ibn
Khaldoun.'

'Your "master"? You mean teacher?'

I thought about that.

'My teacher, yes. But also my master, in a literal sense. He
owned me. Like the rose in your poem, the white rose, I grew in
the garden of God, but was plucked and carried off; then was
planted out in a Garden of Love, and became a red, red rose …'
Which reminded me of the virgin-stone, so I told him about it,
but he wasn't really listening.

'You were a slave?'

'Yes. I think that must be one of the reasons why I'm getting
so involved in this mystery of the murdered miser. Parts of it
might almost be my story.'

He caressed my belly, my groin. 'A slave … Was it there,
among the Moors, that you were – depilated?'

'You don't like it?'

'I adore it – I think. I just couldn't believe it, at first. I mean,
here in Paris it is … '

'It is what?'

'It's the mark of a whore.'

I knew, of course. It was the same in Avignon. You can't win.

'Didn't you know?'

'They plucked all the hair from my body before I ever went to
ibn Khaldoun. Then, when he liked it, I kept it that way, and
have kept it that way ever since.'

He kissed and licked me for a few more moments, then said,
'Ibn Khaldoun ... Tell me your story, Maryam. You're not going

anywhere until you tell me.'

He was learning. Well - we didn't have much time but, oui, d'accord, I would tell him a simplified version of one small part of my story.

'You know a little of my background - my mixed descent, my uncle-teacher Yacoub, the Kabbalist.'

He was gazing at me.

'In the autumn of 1372, my father died. I was fourteen - my birthday is at the end of October, as you know - '

'I did not know! I'm only just beginning to know anything about you at all! So you're a Scorpio. I shall write a poem - '

'You asked for the story. Listen. Yacoub was not there. No one was there. My grandfather, the Spanish one, had died when I was eleven. There was only Khadija, and although she's so bossy and seems so sure of herself - like me, you are thinking, I know -'

'No!'

'Unlike me, she is also ignorant, illiterate, and a slave. Well, ignorance is relative, and I too have been a slave, but faced with creditors demanding what my father owed them, she could do nothing. They took many valuable things from the house - my grandfather's things - and they took me. When I arrived back, four years later, I discovered that my father owed nothing, that my grandfather had been very rich and that everything was now mine.'

'Which is why you are now so ... '

'Which is one of the reasons why I am now so, as you say. But then I knew nothing of this. I was a penniless orphan being sold into slavery to pay her father's debts.'

'But that is awful! I shall write a long story-poem about you being dragged off screaming to some unknown future: the beautiful Christian slave-girl.'

I smiled. 'The ones who took me were Christians. And I don't scream. Oh, that's nice. Down a bit. Yes, there … Where was I?

Yes – in Cartagena, a house there where I was held with another girl. Then, one night, bags were put over our heads, our ankles were tied so that we could only shuffle, and we were loaded onto a cart and taken down to the sea. There they put us in boats and rowed us out to a ship that was collecting cargo along the coast before crossing to Oran, in Algeria – or such was the rumour. For a few more days we stood off the coast each day while the sun was high then went in under cover of darkness to pick up other captives.

'One night, when we were close to the shore near Almería, someone said it was our last night in Spain.'

'And you could still see Spain? It must have been – '

'We could see the beach, the houses, the people.'

'You must have been in despair.'

'Yes, but – gently on my knees. Yes, like that, that's wonderful. Your tongue is soft now, like your lips, not hard and stiff, as it was before … Despair? No, it just seemed impossible to escape while we were at sea. Suddenly, though, we heard shouting, then a great bang as the ship hit something or something hit the ship. We all fell over. There were sounds of fighting. We were being attacked! We were saved! But then we heard Arabic! We peeped out. They were Barbary Pirates! You know? Like Corsairs, only worse. Much worse than the Spanish slave-traders we were already with. "Let's jump!" I screamed. In a moment our chance would be gone. I saw a dead man not far from the hatch and slid out and over to him. He had a knife, a big one. Suddenly he opened his eyes – he wasn't dead! – and grabbed my wrist! But my left wrist. My right hand closed on the knife. I cut his throat.'

'You what?'

'I had to! I just slashed it straight across as I had seen them do with sheep and goats. The blood spurted up into my eyes. I screamed, and retched, then leapt over the side, but some man grabbed me, got hold of my leg – I felt his hand slip as I hung

over the sea, head down, still screaming, then slip again, then I
was in the water,

'I swam as far as I could, swimming, swimming, swimming,
until I had to surface in order to breathe. I saw the boats in the
distance. One was on fire. Ours, I supposed. The dark line of the
coast was over to my right. Then I heard something behind me.
An arm came round my neck, forcing up my chin, squeezing my
throat! I struggled and fought, but I couldn't breathe! I was
fourteen, and he was a grown man.

'I stopped struggling, and he released his hold on my throat a
little, let me turn in his arms and gaze at him with big, wide eyes
and cling to him till he relaxed. What else could I do? I couldn't
fight him. I relaxed in his arms. Let him take me in to shore.'

'Halfway, he got cramp, let go of me, and began to drown.
"Help me!" he pleaded, "Help me, as I have helped you!" and
went under again. What could I do? I pulled him up to the
surface and towed him the rest of the way to the beach I could
now see in the distance. I held him by his long dark hair and
whispered "Now you relax!" Fortunately, he did. I could not have
managed him if he had struggled. If he had fought me, we would
both have drowned. I think he knew that, too. And how did he
thank me, this Pedro, after we had lain on the beach for several
hours and the sun had come up and warmed us? He took me to a
monastery – Las Hermanas de la Reconquista in the mountains
above Mojacar, right on the border between Christian Spain and
the Emirate of Granada – and left me there! An act of contrition,
he said. And a vow he had made to the Holy Virgin when he'd
thought he was drowning. And an act of gratitude to me.'

'But this is good, not bad.'

'Good? I didn't realise what he was doing until I was in there!
"I would rather have gone to a harem!" I screamed at him as the
great door swung closed. No, it didn't, it was a small door set in
the great door. Anyway, this did not endear me to the Reverend
Mothers, who spent the next year trying to beat the Devil out of

me: they only succeeded in confirming me in my opinion. Oh, there was one I got on with, Sister María Teresa her name was. She was a kind of mother to me, unlike the Mothers … Listen, I have things to do!'

'But – !'

'No, seriously. Think of poor Jaquet.'

'All right. Yes. But how did you come to be in Paris? And rich?'

'Another time! After many other adventures (and misadventures) I ended up with a historian, a Moor, the one I told you about, Abd-el-rahman ibn Khaldoun.'

'Your "master"?'

'Yes. I saved his life. In return, he gave me my freedom and a purse of gold and the eunuch Yahia to be my bodyguard, and sent me back across Andalucía to my home. I was eighteen.'

'You saved his life, yes, I remember. As now you are trying to save Jaquet's.'

'At the moment, it is your life that is in danger! I have to go! Stop stroking me … And when I got home, I found my father's old friend, Sir Farquhar de Dyngvale, who had been to Granada and even Tangiers searching for me in vain. I found, as I say, that I was rich, that I could stay there, live the life of a lady … But the atmosphere of reconquista in the south of Spain was bad, and getting worse. It was no place for me, with my mixed blood, and my little "family" – my Moorish slave-mother Khadija and my Moorish eunuch and bodyguard Yahia. I discussed it with Ferchard (Sir Farquhar) who has been everywhere, and he suggested moving slowly north, to France, and then to Paris, and then we would see.'

'And you will stay here?'

I smiled. 'As I say, we will see. Now I must go.'

'You said you were screaming as you hung over the side of the boat – '

'Yes. Ah. All right, I have been known to scream.'

With a loud laugh, he pushed me down and began kissing me
again. It does a man good to be right occasionally.

9

Raoul took me to the house of Philippe de Saint-Helier, a lecturer
he knew, one who was close to Thomas of Pizan. As soon as I
saw Philippe, I realised I knew him; and he knew me – but in my
student persona, as my brother Magnus of Orkney. As Mariana
de la Mar, I had not met him.

We all sat down by the fire. He fetched us wine.

I said: 'Saint Helier?' as to a stranger.

He gazed at me. He had no idea we had ever met before. 'On
Jersey. One of Les Îles Normandes.' But though he was gazing at
me, he seemed to be talking to Raoul. 'Off the coast of Brittany.'

'I didn't know there were any islands between France and
England.'

'Oh yes. Beautiful green islands with low hills and huge sandy
bays. We had a house that looked out over the bay of Saint
Aubin … So what is it exactly that I can do for you, Raoul?'

'Doña Mariana needs to meet, to speak to, Maître Thomas, as
soon as possible. I thought you might be able to help her.'

Philippe's eyes moved from Raoul to me … back to Raoul …
then finally rested on me. He would speak to me. But no. His
eyes on me, he addressed Raoul.

'Doña Mariana is very beautiful.'

I laughed. 'Apart from the nose!'

'Apart from her nose, as she says. Though that will mend in
time. It is a basic principle of philosophy' (he was still gazing at
me, talking to Raoul) 'that things alter, adapt, adjust, so as to

harmonise with their surroundings. An ugly nose cannot go on
being ugly on such a beautiful face.'

I had heard that argument before. How long can a boy go on
being a boy living all his life surrounded by girls? 'That is one of
the principles of alchemy.'

'Is it? Yes, I should think it probably is. You are interested in
alchemy?'

I nodded; smiled a little shyly.

He said, 'I may be able to help her if you don't mind leaving
her here alone with me, Raoul.'

'He doesn't,' I said, holding his gaze. 'But he would like to
know when he can come and collect me.'

'Ah that. We shan't be staying here. Maître Thomas is at the
Palais Saint-Pol. He and his charming lady have been summoned
to meet the Emperor. So you see, she may be anywhere.'

I did not see. 'I'm afraid I - '

'He has no charming lady. His mistress left Paris in the
company of a student last week. He has told nobody. He is
embarrassed.'

'I see. And you are suggesting ...?'

'Not only will Maître Thomas be indebted to you, but you will
meet the Emperor face to face and may well get a chance to
discuss philosophy and alchemy with him.'

My dream! He was an enthusiast, though of course he had to
remain circumspect in public.

'But how could I impersonate her?'

'You would not be asked to. You would be yourself. Faced
with you, who would recall that there had been another woman -
indeed, that there are other women?'

'Are you by any chance a poet, sir?'

'I am. Philippe de Saint-Helier at your service. As a matter of
fact, I too, like Maître Thomas, am in the throes of losing my
muse. If you were to consider - not at once, but - when your
nose resumes its former glory - '

I interrupted him. 'Raoul, I think I will be all right here.'
'But - '
'And Philippe will make sure I get home safely.'
'I - oui, d'accord, Mariana. I will see you tomorrow.'
Philippe showed him out, then returned to me.
'What keeps you here, in Paris?' I asked him, testing.
'My great-grandmother. She came here years ago with me and
my mother, and now she is too old to move, to travel. Indeed,
she is hardly able to get to the privy, let alone the coast.'
'You sounded so nostalgic when you spoke of that bay - Saint
Aubin, I think you said. And I know how you feel. Some days
the city grows too much for me and I would give anything to be
back by the sea.'
'In Spain?'
'The south-east corner of Spain, the Mar Menor. It must be
very different from your island, but …'
'The sea is the sea, and home is home,' he smiled.
There seemed to be no servants. Apart from the bed-ridden
great-grandmother, we were quite alone. And the mother …?
'Mariana, shall we spend an hour celebrating your advent in
an act of love before - ?'
'No, I don't think so, Philippe.' He was too old for me, thirty,
at least, though he had a smile that … What was I talking about?
Abd-el-rahman ibn Khaldoun had been forty-two when I'd been
sixteen. And in the bordels in Cuenca and Avignon I'd had men
of all ages, of course. I was getting spoilt.
'Is your mother at home?'
'Avice?'
Strange question. 'I don't know. I assume you have only one
mother, and if her name is Avice, then - '
'No. No, she is not.'
There was something not quite right about Philippe de Saint-
Helier: he was all charm and sophistication on the surface, but he
had problems, problems he could not handle. I should read his

hand, find out his date of birth, but - not now. 'Philippe, I understood poor Maître Thomas was already at the palace, and embarrassingly alone. Don't you think we should …?'

'I am Maître Philippe de Saint-Helier and this lady is Doña Mariana de la Mar, companion to Maître Thomas of Pizan, who is expecting her - indeed awaiting her, impatiently.'

This formula took us into the outer courtyard, took us from there through to the inner courtyard, and from there to a hall where various people were standing about, waiting. Most of them in vain, as they were beginning to realise.

Philippe took me to a man a little older than himself, though certainly no more than fifty, with long, straight, greying hair tied back in a pony-tail, a short grey beard, and a gold earring in his left ear.

'Thomas, this is Doña Mariana. She is Spanish, but speaks French, of course. She wished to meet you.'

'Did she, indeed?'

'And I thought that here, now, might be an appropriate moment.'

'Oh indeed, yes. Most appropriate. Your servant, Doña Mariana.'

He raised my hand to his lips, brushed it with his beard. Nice. Polite. Interested. But distant at the same time. Worried. Philippe had not kissed my hand in front of Raoul, but if he had he would have kissed it as Raoul kisses … hungrily.

'And you would like to spend the evening with me, here, waiting, Doña Mariana?'

'I should adore to spend the evening with you, maître, here or anywhere; but I do not enjoy waiting.'

'No more do I. Let us see whether we can expedite matters. Philippe, I shall not forget this favour, old friend. To whom shall I have her delivered when the night is done? To you?'

Here we go again.

'Oui - ' he began.

'Non,' I interrupted, firmly. 'You will have me delivered to my home in the rue Alexandre l'anglois.'

'You know her home, Philippe?'

'Oui, oui, in the rue Alexandre l'anglois.'

I smiled at him, but he avoided my eye.

'Then you will see her there - tomorrow, no doubt. Au revoir, Philippe, et merci.'

So Philippe took his leave, and Thomas led me away from where the mass of supplicants were clustered and over to another smaller door which was also closed and guarded.

He whispered something to the elder of the two guards. The man turned and looked at me, then he whispered something to the other guard, who opened the door, passed through it, and closed it again behind him.

'Why did you wish to meet me, Doña Mariana?'

'You are the foremost authority on astrology and alchemy in the whole Kingdom of France.' With the possible exception of Blanche d'Evreux, whom I had met in Avignon and would rather not meet again. Anyway, she was presumably either in Avignon or at her Château de Neuphle, both far away from Paris.

'Usually, yes, that may be so, señorita. But can you be unaware of the Emperor's interest in these and kindred matters?'

'No, I am not unaware of it, dottore.'

'You are an astrologer? An alchemist?'

'An astrologer, and chiromancer. Of alchemy, I am almost completely ignorant.'

'That is best.'

'Yes, but I have one or two questions you might - '

'Come, he is calling us. May I address you as Mariana?'

'Of course, dottore. I was hoping you would.'

We went along another corridor, narrower but much grander, then attendants opened a double door for us and we were in the presence of the King. Two Kings. I curtsied, Maître Thomas bowing low at my side. I kept my head down. Where I came from, we would both have been flat on our faces, foreheads pressed to the floor. Not here, however.

'Ah, Thomas,' cried a voice, 'have you been presented to my uncle the Emperor?'

'Yes, yes, we are old friends.' Another voice. This must be the Emperor Charles IV, the other King Charles V of France.

I kept my head down.

'You are very kind, messire. It is a great honour to be in your presence once more.'

'And your charming lady, Thomas?' This was the King again. 'It is always a pleasure to see her.'

'This – this is a different charming lady, messire.'

'Ah, Thomas, Thomas.'

'May I present Doña Mariana de la Mar ... Mariana?'

I raised my eyes, my head.

'This is King Charles of France, long may he reign.'

'Votre Majesté.' I bowed my head again.

This was becoming quite a strain. There was something to be said after all for the prone position. At least it was restful.

'And this is the Holy Roman Emperor, Charles IV of Bohemia.'

I looked up, looked at him. 'Your – your – ' I appealed to him with my eyes.

'Majesty will do,' he smiled. 'Only the Pope is entitled to the attribute Holiness. This is my son and heir, Wenceslas, King of the Romans.'

Three kings …

'His Royal Highness.' The Emperor was still helping me.

'Your Royal Highness.' I bowed my head again.

'And this is Prince Sigismund, and this Princess Anna. Please, stand up now. In fact, sit down. This is an informal gathering.'

One would have to be very fit to survive a formal one.

'There, Thomas,' said the King. 'Sit Doña Mariana beside you.

Good. Thomas, you may converse with my uncle. For the
moment, I prefer simply to listen.'

'Thomas, I wish to consult you on certain matters.'

'I am at your service, messire.'

'Then tell me, if you will, how you foresee the rest of this
century; the next twenty-three years.'

'On a large scale, messire.'

'In large terms, yes.'

'Then first, the recurring pestilence known as the Great
Mortality. I do not foresee any further major outbreak, though
there may be minor ones, especially thirteen years from now, in
1390, affecting mostly children and horses.'

'So the population will begin to increase again? Now there are
not people enough over most of Europe even to till the fields.'

'I do not foresee that, messire. The harvests will continue to
fail in France, as elsewhere.'

'And the war, Thomas? This terrible ongoing war between –
ah – us and the English which makes the bad so much worse?'

'Again, I foresee little change. But I confess, I do not know.
Unlike the pestilence and the weather, this is open, unfixed – '

'Open, maître?' asked Prince Sigismund.

Thomas smiled at him. 'A good question, your Highness.
Some matters are open to human intervention – may even result
from human folly – others are not. If I say a man is going to die
before the end of next month, then he is going to die. But if I say
he will be in great danger for the next month, then he may die,
but he may not. He will not if he takes the appropriate
precautions.'

'So the Great Pestilence we could do little or nothing about.'
This was Sigismund again, a bright boy obviously – and a
beautiful one, with straight yellow hair the same as that of his
sister Anna, sitting beside him. 'But war we can do something
about.'

'Exactly, your Highness – at least for the most part.'

'For the most part?'

'If you wish to participate in the discussion,' drawled the dark Wenceslas, the elder brother, who was perhaps eighteen, almost my age, 'then think before you speak. Maître Thomas means that a life here, a life there, may be saved during the pestilence, but for the most part nothing can be done, it is out of our hands. Whereas the war is for the most part of our making, in the sense that it was brought about by people, and will continue for just so long as those people in a position to do so do not take steps to bring it to an end.'

'I was – '

'Be quiet, Sigismund,' said his father, the Emperor – but gently. 'I wish you, Thomas, to cast a horoscope for the new young King of England, Richard – '

'I have, messire.'

'And for my daughter here, my beloved Anna, as Queen of England. I wish to know whether such a marriage would be conducive to peace between these two countries, and whether it would benefit the people of the two countries in general. Let me have them before I leave France.'

'Oui, messire. Doña Mariana is also an astrologer. Would you like her to – ?'

'No.' He turned to me. 'No, I don't think so. You do not know King Richard, señorita, nor are you fully acquainted with the situation, as Thomas is.'

'She is a chiromancer, too, messire. May I suggest that you let her read Princess Anna's hands, and cast Princess Anna's horoscope, on just that understanding – that she is unacquainted with any of the details of Princess Anna's life and prospects.'

'I see. Yes. And that would help you, too, Thomas?'

'Very much, messire.'

'Then you come and sit here, señorita.' He pointed to a stool by his daughter's feet. 'Anna, Doña Mariana is going to read your hands. While she does so, she will ask you questions. I should like you to answer them.'

'Yes, Father.'

I sat on the stool and took both her hands in mine. Small, soft, well-cared-for hands, of course. I looked up into her eyes - blue eyes, the colour of cornflowers, eyelashes almost as fair as her hair.

She was shy, but she held my gaze. Smiled.

I said, 'While we are doing this, just for now, may I call you Anna, your Highness?'

She looked round. No one was listening to us except Sigismund. He grinned.

'Yes,' she said, 'if I may call you Mariana.'

'Of course.' I looked back down at her hands.

'But not just for now,' objected Sigismund. 'I don't like such arrangements. I had this problem with my friends. Either you are Mariana to us, or you are Doña Mariana.'

'But in public?' protested Anna.

'Oh, in public, of course, we have to be formal. But in private, it will be like with other friends.'

'Yes, I agree,' said Anna.

I looked up at the two beautiful children, so like young angels.

'What happened to your nose, Mariana?'

'Sigismund!' Anna was shocked.

I laughed. 'I fell over. I landed on my face. And hands.' I showed him my grazed palms. 'And knees.'

'How did you come to do that?' he asked.

'Someone jumped on me, from above, as I came out through a doorway. It was totally unexpected.'

'What happened to him?'

'He died.'

They both gazed at me.

'Sigismund! Be quiet! Mariana is trying to read Anna's hands!'

Mariana? The Emperor may have been taking part in another conversation but he had not missed much of ours.

'If I had a penny for every time he says "Sigismund, be quiet", I'd be richer than the Pope,' muttered Sigismund.

'Hush!' Anna wanted me to concentrate.

'Splay your fingers, Anna. Like that, yes.'

The gap between the index finger and the middle finger was narrow: there was not much capacity for individual thought. She would follow where she was led on all major issues. However, the thumb was long, and that indicated intelligence and the ability to influence other people's opinions.

Time to tell her something. 'You allow yourself to be led on major issues – by your father, brothers – ' I glanced at Sigismund.

'Not by her brothers,' he laughed. 'Not even Wenceslas.'

'Prince Wenceslas,' his father put in. 'He has no part in this agreement of yours. But go on, Mariana.'

'And by your husband.'

'But that is right,' said Anna. 'That is how it should be.'

'Yes, but I am not talking about what should be, I am describing what is. And by contrast, you have the ability to influence others' opinions, and do so, though on what you may consider less important issues.'

There was no very prominent mount, but the Mount of Venus was firm and large, meaning that she would be well-formed, graceful, seductive. Was already.

'You love beautiful things, whether they be clothes and jewels or sunsets over mountains. You love peace and harmony. You hate to cause suffering … When were you born, Anna?'

'I was born on the 28th of September, the Day of St Wenceslas, after whom my brother is named. The sun was in Libra, of course, and the moon was in Cancer.'

'So. You know all about that.'

'A little, that others have told me.'

'It matches your hand. You will be protective, and sensitive, as I said before, to human suffering. Too sensitive, it may be.'

'Can you tell me any details?'

'From your hands? Yes, but I cannot tell you everything here, now.' An early marriage, an early death. At least the marriage would be happy, though it would produce no children. 'But, for instance, these two crosses on the Line of Head here, are not a good sign, and nor is the narrowness of the space – look – between the Line of Head and the Line of Heart. They indicate a certain weakness, a tendency to palpitations and fainting.'

She just gazed back at me. It was a gaze of trust, almost as though I who had made the diagnosis would also be able to effect a cure.

I said, 'Like you, I should wish to be able to put an end to all the suffering I see around me, but I cannot.'

She smiled.

Her father, the Emperor, still listening with one ear, said, 'Of course not. And if you could, that would be – what would it be, Thomas?'

'If it worked but rarely and partially, messire, it would be called medicine. If it was truly effective, miraculous in effect, it would be labelled magic, and condemned – '

'Precisely so. In this day and age, Mariana, be thankful you have no such gift. Anna, tell Mariana the precise time and place of your birth for her to consult her almageste when she gets home. And then I should like you two little ones to leave us.'

'Little ones,' Sigismund muttered, but stood up as Anna said, 'I was born in Prague on, as I say, the 28th of September, in the year of our Lord 1367, at the hour of Matins. Goodnight, Mariana. We shall meet again.'

I too felt that. I stood up as she did, smiled, and made a half-curtsy. 'Goodnight, Anna. Goodnight, Sigismund.'

'Goodnight, Mariana.'

They went, through another, smaller door, accompanied by two attendants.

I turned, confused now, to the others.

'Sit, Mariana. Stay as you are. That's it. You were right in all you said about my daughter, and no doubt in most or all of what you did not say … Now tell me, would you like to read my hands?'

'Your majesty?'

'I have here, on this paper, Thomas' prognosis regarding my future. Understand that I, that my son, Prince Wenceslas, that the King here, and many others need to know. I have also my own prognosis, on this other paper. Mariana, you may read my hands, you may gaze into my eyes, you may ask me questions, but leave astrology out of it. I want an independent prognosis. How long do I have to live – at the least, at the most?'

'Messire, I – '

'Do it, Mariana,' said the King of France.

I did it.

His right leg (he suffered from gout, I remembered) was propped up on a stool. He beckoned, and I moved my stool closer to that one and sat beside his leg.

I took his hands. Compared them. There was little difference between them, though he was naturally left-handed and had been trained from an early age to use his right hand. They were well-formed, the backs were hairy but not excessively so, and the fingers, though long, were not so long as the very long palm, indicative of a quick mind, sometimes too quick.

I looked up into his eyes. Black, bright still, yet there was pain in them. He had been a handsome man once, despite the slightly hunched back. His thumb, I had already noticed, was wide open and formed a right angle with the palm, an exceptional feature which meant that he was a fighter for causes and would, had, contributed to the advancement of mankind. 'What are you proudest of, messire? Your proudest acccomplishments.'

'That I helped to conserve human knowledge during the dark days of the Great Mortality. I founded the University of Prague and five other universities during those years. I was also instrumental in bringing to an end the massacre of the Jews that occurred all over Europe when ignorant people - and many who should have known better! - foolishly blamed them for the outbreak of plague.'

I gazed at him. This was a man.

Then, shy suddenly, I looked back down at his hand.

The Mount of the Sun was prominent, indicating that he was fast, ambitious, successful, never a plodder, adaptable, versatile, loved fame, tended towards the sin of pride. Well, who wouldn't? But the flesh of the palm was no longer firm; it was flaccid. On the Line of Heart there was a circle, and three islands: a heart condition. Apart from that, few problems. It was enough.

Now, and only now, did I allow myself to check his Line of Life.

He was not going to live beyond sixty.

'How old are you, messire?'

'Sixty-one, Mariana.'

'And how bad is that heart condition?'

'You tell me.'

'You have had at least one heart attack, messire.'

'Two.'

I wasn't allowed to use astrology, but … He was a Libra, like his daughter. He hadn't long to live - the gout, the heart disease - the interest. He would probably die within the year. Which was such a shame. His body failing him while his mind was still active, his soul still full of fire.

Next year, all year so far as I could remember, Librans would be safe, relatively, until, in the autumn, the sun had passed through Libra once more. Then, when the sun was in Scorpio, things would be much less favourable.

I would have to risk it. But first … 'You have had four wives, messire.'

'And one mistress. She was French too, like my first wife. Do I have time for another one?'

'Wife, messire? Or mistress?'

'Oh, mistress.'

'Then yes, you do. But must she be French?'

'No. No, I don't think so. Variety - '

Wenceslas' cold eyes lashed us both. 'Father, please. Doña Mariana, if you have any kind of serious prognosis to put to us, then please do so.'

The King of France joined Wenceslas. 'Yes, please, do tell us any conclusions you may have drawn, Doña Mariana.'

I looked at each of them, the French King, the German King/Emperor, the other German "King of the Romans", and the Italian astrologer, Thomas, my companion. I said, 'Then it is my view that Wenceslas, King of the Romans, should prepare himself to assume full responsibility for the Empire within the year, and more specifically, next November … I am so sorry, messire.' I kissed the hands I now found myself still holding, and let them go. Old men, dying men, were so much less proud, so much more human, than middle-aged men - even when they were the most important men in the world.

'Shall I read these now?' asked Wenceslas.

'Read them to yourself, my son, then tell us what they say. Spare us the details. I am tired suddenly.'

'Yes, Father.'

We waited while he perused the first. He looked up. 'This is your own, Father. You too specify next November.' He read the other. 'Maître Thomas is not so specific. He expects you, though, to die within the next twelve months.'

'Then I should like to thank you, Maître Thomas, and particularly you, Doña Mariana, for confirming me in my, er, premonitions. And now I really must ask you all to excuse me …'

King Charles of France said 'Thomas!' and Thomas said 'Mariana!' and the next thing I knew we were both backing out through the double door and it was closing before our eyes. We

raised our heads and looked at each other. He smiled. I smiled
back at him.

'Where shall we go?' he said.

'Take me to a tavern. I am hungry and thirsty.'

'Yes, palace hospitality leaves much to be desired: either far
too much or nothing.'

'Do you know a good one?'

'I know all the good ones.'

10

Soon we were sitting in a private corner of a large room filled
with people and music, loud voices and soft intimate voices,
smells of cooking food and wet clothes, of steam and smoke. My
mouth watered. My eyes watered.

'Congratulations!'

'Uh?'

'You hit the month, and without using astrology.'

'What makes you think I didn't use astrology?'

He laughed. 'I should have known.'

'I was lucky. In a way. In another way, I was unlucky. I
wanted to consult the Emperor – and you, of course, maestro –
on the subject of alchemy, but I didn't get the chance.'

'He would have been most reluctant to answer, unless you
were alone with him. And that you will not be, not during these
days in Paris. Though there was a moment when I thought you
might soon be spending a lot of time alone with him!'

'Oh, that. That was a joke.' I blushed.

'Not entirely. If his young Romanness had not been there and
impatient for the good news, anything might have happened.
Charles IV of Bohemia is very susceptible to feminine wiles.'

'Wiles?'

'Beauty, then. Charms.'

A skinny boy cleared the cups and empty carafe from our table, came running back and began wiping it while a serving-woman stood waiting impatiently, toe tapping, to put down the tray of bread and meat and wine and olives she had brought for us.

'And you made two friends,' he said, while we all waited for the poor boy.

'That's true. I liked them. Shall I do her horoscope then let you have it?'

His mouth was full.

I followed suit. The olives were small, hard, green ones, not at all what I had been used to before I came north to Paris, but the wine was wonderful, the bread freshly baked and the meat at least edible. I noticed the people at the next table had a dish of some kind of meat in a sauce. I called the woman back. 'What is that they're eating? In the sauce?'

'Tripe lyonnaise, dem'selle.'

'Oui? J'adore la tripe comme ça!'

She went to fetch us a portion of tripe, and Thomas said, 'Let me have a copy. Send your original to the Emperor, as soon as may be.' He looked at me over his wine, and said, 'That won't be entirely good news either, will it?'

'We'll see.'

'Number of children?'

I swallowed a piece of bread, but had rejected the meat and was waiting for the tripe.

Was he testing me, or unsure of himself?

'None.'

He nodded. 'Right. So … Can I help you with the alchemy? No one can hear us.'

'Oh, yes, please. It was you I wanted to ask. I had no idea of meeting the Emperor.'

'So ask.'

'First I should say that I do not believe in alchemy, that my teacher in Spain, my spiritual master, considers alchemy a bastard science, neither truly of this world nor truly of the other, a spiritual means to a material end: the motive greed, the end unlimited wealth and the power such wealth bestows, and the means – any means that can be wrested out of true knowledge perverted by unworthy men.'

'Those are I assume mostly your master's words.'

I nodded.

My tripe came. It was delicious.

'Have some.'

'No, no, I do not care for tripe. In principle you agree with your master?'

'Of course. My master is a Kabbalist, and like all true Kabbalists he studies the Kabbalah for spiritual, not material, gain. Not for gold. The idea is somehow shocking to me.'

'Yes, I see that. So what is your sudden interest?'

'It relates to a quite different matter which I have been asked to investigate, and before I can proceed I must clarify certain points in my mind, points that at present I find very confusing. So confusing that I wonder if they were not meant to be confusing.'

'Such as?'

'I am confused about the ways in which words like "mercury" and "quicksilver" are used.'

'Quicksilver is mercury: argent vive.'

'Yes, I know, but they, and "sulphur", and even "silver" and "gold" are used in different senses – '

'That is true, yes, on occasion.'

'When Jabir ibn Hayyan, for instance – '

'You have read Jabir?'

I nodded.

'In what translation?'

'In the original Arabic, dottore. And I translated it.'

'Into Spanish?'

'Castellano, yes.'

'I see. Mm. Well, go on.'

'When Jabir, for instance, or ibn Sina – '

'Whom we call Avicenna, yes.'

'When they teach that we must produce the essence of fire, a tincture they call mercury or quicksilver, this is not the mercury or quicksilver we know.'

'That is correct. And the usage of Master Bacon of Oxford and the great Albertus, though somewhat different, is similarly confusing – to the novice, of course, not to the adept … There is this mercury and there is that mercury: call them vulgar mercury, and philosophic mercury or mercury of the wise or divine mercury – what you will.'

'I do. So that is not really a problem.'

'In discussing alchemy, there are many pitfalls, many difficulties: the distinction you mentioned is among the least of them.'

'But how and where might blood enter into it?'

'However, once you have the tincture which is the divine mercury, you can combine the sun and the moon, the moon being quicksilver …' He had been drinking and thinking, not listening. Now he said, 'Blood? What blood?'

'The blood of a virgin?'

'Oh no, not in alchemy. Urine, yes, and I have heard of the use of semen in preparing the primal tincture, but not blood or milk.'

We ate and drank, I finishing the food, he finishing the wine, and each thinking our separate thoughts.

Then: 'And the use of a simpleton?' I said.

'Ah, that, yes. It may be the corruption of the alchemist himself which prevents the union. It takes so many years and so much suffering to purify oneself, to separate the gross from the divine. But the fool may be by nature uncorrupted … The Holy

Fool.'

I had heard of that. Was that what Charlot had been? The Holy Fool?

I needed to get back to Raoul - but he would not have spoken to Mère Henriette yet. And it was the middle of the night.

'Is there any connection between that and the Fool in Tarocchi?' He had no idea, of course, of my personal interest in The Fool - the card I had chosen from among the fan of little cards held out to me by the old Gypsy woman at home by the sea in Spain.

He laughed. 'Probably. I haven't thought about it. But the Fool is depicted as ragged, isn't he? With holes in his rags - or is he wearing motley? And he is being whipped out of town as a vagabond?'

Whipped out of town? A familiar cold shiver ran up and down my spine.

But, 'In the one I saw,' I said, 'the vagabond was being harried by a dog, and the holes in his attire seemed to have been made by the dog biting him.'

'Hmm. Yes, that could be the Holy Fool. What does it signify in the Tarocchi, do you know?'

For me, taken literally? Mariana the outsider, la loca; at least, that's how the Gypsy woman had interpreted it. I improvised a more esoteric interpretation: 'I think maybe it signifies incarnation, but incarnation that is, in a sense, unadjusted. The soul out of place in this world. I may be reading too much Kabbalah into it, though.'

He laughed again. 'You may indeed. What are you doing in Paris, Mariana? You look and you walk and you talk like some great nobleman's courtesan; but the things you say, the things you know ... Don't tell me you are one of these famous girl-boys who frequent our lecture halls?'

'Are there others?'

'Oh yes. But I've only met one before. She liked it so much in red hose, a cod-piece and a short tight cote-hardie, that she decided to stay a boy for ever. The last I heard, she (now, to all intents and purposes, he) was a poet and singer at the court of the Duc de Berry.' He ordered more wine. 'Don't let that happen to you.'

'No, that won't happen, though I do enjoy wearing long hose for a change sometimes, instead of these skirts. '

We talked for another hour, then he walked me home.

Where a weeping Yahia informed me that Natalie had disappeared, a contemptuous Khadija (contempt hiding her distress) snorted that eunuchs were good for nothing, and a bewildered Ferchard, who had just returned from two days of drinking and mourning and had never met Natalie, threatened to move out of this mad house, this mad city, this mad country, and return to his native Scotland forthwith.

I went to my room and closed the door.

But that didn't solve anything.

I would see them one at a time.

Ladies first. Khadija, to get the facts.

Then Yahia.

Men last. Ferchard, to put him in the picture and discuss the whole situation.

'Khadija!'

But Yahia came running in, and fell on his knees.

'I thought I called Khadija.'

'Yes, Lalla Maryam – '

'But you wish me to hear your story before I hear hers.'

'No, lalla – not that, no – it is just that – I cannot wait!' He was trembling. 'I have waited!'

'All right, Yahia. Tell me what happened. From the beginning. When I left with Raoul, Natalie was upstairs with you … No, she had come downstairs, hadn't she. You followed me. What happened next?'

'Nothing happened, lalla. We went into the kitchen. We ate

some sweets. They were strange to her, but she liked them. We
drank some water. Then she said, "I'll be back in a moment."
"Where are you going?" I called after her, but she had gone.
Khadija said, "She needs a moment. Ladies do. You should know
that." We waited a moment. Two moments. Several moments.
Then I went in search of her. There was no sign.'
    'The doors? The windows? All closed?'
    'Yes, lalla.'
    'Did you ask outside?'
    'No, there was only Khadija and me, and we don't speak the
Nazrani tongue, and ... '
    He was right. And it was too late now: the middle of the night
and freezing cold.
    'So what exactly do you have to tell me?'
    'Nothing, lalla.'
    I was surprised. I'd been expecting him to claim that he
deserved a whipping.
    'Send Khadija in.'
    'Yes, lalla. But … I have to tell you that it is the will of Allah,
as laid down in the Law, that I should die.'
    'At least.'
    'Sidi Farquhar can – '
    'It is the will of your mistress as laid down in her diwan this
night, the 27th of December 1377 in the Christian calendar, that
Yahia the eunuch should refrain from airing his opinions when
they have not been called for and should bear in mind that he
belongs to said mistress, that she will decide whether he needs
punishing and if so what form the punishment should take.' I
paused for breath. 'His death, he should note, is not an option that
is open to her. Do you understand?'
    'Yes, lalla, but – '
    'No buts. I shall check the streets in the morning, speak to
those who are at their post every day all day. Now call Khadija,
then keep guard outside this door. Keep guard all night. If I

disappear, I shall be really upset!'

'Yes, lalla.' No hint of a smile. He was in disgrace: he had so decided.

And my nose? We had had none of these histrionics when he was supposed to be my bodyguard and I got jumped on.

'Khadija. Tell me.'

'If Sidi Farquhar had been here, this would not have happened.'

'I asked you what did happen, Khadija. Now, tell me, for the love of Allah.'

'Nothing happened, Maryam. One moment she was here, the next she was not: she had gone.'

'Willingly, do you think?'

'There was no scream, no struggle.'

'There may be other possible explanations for that … What do you think happened, Khadija?'

'I think she let herself out, and fled.'

'By herself.'

'Yes, Maryam.'

'And how was she, how did she seem, immediately prior to her departure?

'She was happy. She was smiling.'

'How do you explain that? Surely she would have been tense, nervous?'

She shrugged. The Khadija shrug that has infuriated me since my childhood.

'What was she wearing? It was very cold.'

'The same clothes she had on when she arrived with you.'

'And her cloak?'

'I do not know.'

'Yahia!' I called. He looked in. 'Go and see if Natalie's cloak is still here.'

We waited.

He returned. 'It is here, Lalla Maryam.'

'Thank you. Wait outside.' I turned back to Khadija. 'So she didn't go willingly. Or if she did, she hadn't planned to: it was a shock to her, and done in a hurry … Khadija, tell Ferchard I wish to talk to him, will you?'

'And me? Is there anything you need?'

'Nothing. I'll talk to you in the morning.'

Ferchard came, we kissed, he sat down. I looked at him. My father's friend. He was nearly seventy now, big still, white hair and short white beard setting off the northern sky-blue eyes. They had fled Scotland together in 1338 when the Balliols, whom they and their families had supported for so long against the Bruces, finally conceded defeat and the King, Edward Balliol, went into exile.

I told him all I knew, all I had done.

'You could have been killed. I shouldn't let you go out. What was Yahia doing letting you go out through the door first? And then this evening, letting this poor lass - what's her name? Natalie?'

'Ferchard, tell me about this funeral. Tell me everything you know about the late Sire de Montrouge and his family.'

'Right. Well. Apart from the house in Paris where his body was found, they have a large estate to the south west, in Anjou, on the Loire. It was there that Pierre was to have been buried, among his ancestors.'

'But how did you know him?'

'I met him in Thessaloniki, I don't know, seventeen, eighteen, years ago. In the spring of '60. It fits in with what you were saying. I was there with the Old Duke, fighting the Ottoman Turks. I had been in the south and seen Athens for the first time, and was on my way round by land to Constantinople, where heavy fighting had broken out. '

'You were fighting alongside the forces of the Eastern Empire. I remember you telling me.'

'What was left of them, aye. We had allied ourselves with the Bulgarians. Anyway, Thessaloniki was, as you say, a centre of the slave-trade at that time; still is, no doubt. Our friend was there in search of fresh young flesh for the stews of southern France. I wasn't interested, but we had a drink together with some of the others in a taverna on the waterfront. He was very distinctive with that red hair and those green eyes. He looked a lot like a Scot. He told me many people in the Poitou area look like that. I remember thinking that there must be some connection between the Gaels and the Gauls. Of course, the Gaulish language no longer exists, but it could well have been like the Gaelic we're using now. When I saw him again here, in Paris, some months back, I recognised him immediately. And he recognised me. I haven't changed much.'

'So you had a drink together.'

'How did you guess? But he was not the same man at all. Much more subdued. He told me that when he was young he dreamed of becoming Sire de Montrouge, thought being Sire de Montrouge would solve all his problems. It had not.'

'He must have been a rich man.'

'When a poor fool becomes a rich fool …'

We thought about that for a moment.

'So his problems were financial, mainly?'

'Aye. And I met his brother – that's Jean – P'tit-Jean, the new Sire. Pierre was to have been taken back home to the Castle in Anjou, as I say, nearly two hundred miles to the south west. But the weather is getting worse, they would never get through with a funeral cortège, so he was interred here.'

'Tell me more about this P'tit-Jean. Also about the steward or whatever who runs the estate down in Poitou – '

'Anjou. But it's near Poitou. There's a bailiff. Henri le Boeuf they call him. He's the one who found Pierre.'

'What kind of man is he?'

'Un boeuf.' He laughed. 'But I had the impression of a fair

man, a straight man, when I spoke to him: the man who carried
the estates through one disastrous Sire after another. P'tit-Jean is
the fifth in ten years. And all gamblers and drunkards.'

'Which is how they met you.'

'Now, come, young woman. That is hardly fair.'

'I heard that he was hanged in the posture of the Hanged Man
in the Tarocchi card. What did the bailiff tell you?'

'I imagine he knows no more of Tarocchi cards than I do, but
he did say that Pierre was found hanging by one leg. His hands
had been tied to the belt at his waist. He seemed to have been
drowned, by having his head immersed in a bucket of water. The
bucket was on the floor and there was water everywhere, as if
they had taken a long time and many buckets of water to finish
him off. Doing it slowly, and talking to him the while, no doubt,
whenever they took his head out of the water.'

'Ugh.'

'Le Boeuf told me of three other Sires de Montrouge, all as
bad as each other. Pierre may have been a triple murderer – I
mean if he killed to get the title – killed his spendthrift uncle and
his two drunken cousins whose only interest in life had been
bear- and bull-baiting, and gambling on cock-fights.'

'Not much different from Pierre himself.'

'Aye, the same, but less adventurous. Or, of course, it could
have been Pierre's half-brother, Jean, the new Sire de Montrouge,
who did all the killing.'

'Killed four times, you mean. So far.'

He grinned. 'Next time, he will be the victim. That is the only
justice there is in such families. How could there be any other?
Who would be willing and able to take them on? Who would be
interested?'

I smiled. 'So let them kill each other off one at a time. And
who is more likely to have murdered his way to the title, if that is
in fact what happened? Pierre or P'tit-Jean?'

'Oh, P'tit-Jean. Pierre could kill – and no doubt had – but in a drunken rage, not in cold blood like that, methodically working his way towards a title.'

'And is there another? I mean could P'tit-Jean be next on the list? Might this bailiff, this Henri le Boeuf, be the next in line to the title and estate?'

'From what I hear, there is no estate to inherit. Everything is mortgaged and belongs to some money-lender. There was a cousin present, a lady, the sister of the two Sires who preceded Pierre.'

'She has no son?'

'I see what you mean. If she once had a son who came to an unfortunate end … There was nothing about a son. Something about a daughter, but I wasn't paying attention.'

'I'd like to make the acquaintance of this Henri le Boeuf, and very soon. Where does the lady, the cousin, live? Do you know?'

'I only know that she is a widow.'

'And beautiful?'

'Yes. Beautiful. And sad. Sadder than she should be for the death of Pierre. Unless they had been close once …?'

'Ferchard, I must sleep now. I'm going straight to bed.'

I didn't go straight to bed, though. I lit another lamp and opened my almageste. Princess Anna … As I worked, I made notes. Everything was all right for the moment for most Librans, as I had thought, but next November tragedy would come into her life. Well, we knew that. And from then on her life would be much harder. Wenceslas was not the man her father had been, and she would have no man, no "father", she could trust until, yes, she married while still young and became a queen. The Queen.

And Maître Pietri, the money-changer … what was this? There was danger here, great danger, on the 29th and 30th of this month. And it was the 28th tomorrow! If I did not warn him, if he did not disappear for three days, he would turn out to have

been Tiphareth, the dying god whose symbol was the sun: Maître
Pietri was a Leo.

I undressed, extinguished the lamps, and fell fast asleep as
soon as I sank into the great goose-down pillow.

11

Next morning, everything was white!

Snow anywhere but high on the distant mountains was still a
novelty to me. I loved it! I put on my thickest boots, my warmest
cloak, and sailed out, with Khadija prophesying my early death
and what would she and poor Yahia do then?

I returned a few snowballs, laughing, and getting not just
warm but hot, then remembered I had jobs to do.

I asked the stall-holders in the Place Maubert, and all the
pedlars and beggars, but few had been on the street after dark.
All I discovered was that Natalie had been with two men and had
seemed to be walking freely. One pedlar knew, I thought, who
the two men were, but he wouldn't say.

Had they been the abbé's men?

I hurried over the Petit-Pont and across to the Pont-au-
Change, wanting to warn Maître Pietri. When I arrived, he was
busy, so I walked on by. Was le Cafard still keeping watch
outside the house in the rue Saint-Pol? I walked up Saint-
Antoine.

Yes, he was there.

I remembered our signal, stood at the door, looked up and
down the alley then walked to the corner.

He followed me.

'Don't tell me you've been here all this time, le Cafard, for I shan't believe you.'

'Non, dem'selle. But when I had nothing else to do. In case.'

'What happened to the abbé's men? The ones my eunuch brought out and left in the road.'

'Ah oui, those two. And there was the one who jumped on you. I tried to warn you. The one Dem'selle Natalie killed. She's fast with that knife, isn't she!'

'Yes.'

'They came with a cart an hour or so later and took all three away.'

'But they weren't all dead!'

He shrugged. 'Chucked them in the cart and drove off. But that Dem'selle Natalie ...' His blue eyes sparkled.

I turned away, and nearly left him. By the grace of God, I didn't. I said, 'Have you seen her again since then?'

'Yes, she was here last night, with l'Albanien and le Grec.'

'Le Grec?' I was thinking of Maître Guillaume.

'The Albanian's son – j'sais pas, moi – maybe he's not his son, but he's young and he's, like, his deputy.'

'And is he dangerous?'

'Oh yes. Not as dangerous as the Albanian, but he has two arms, and he kills with both. I saw him fight once. He cut the other man up in slices before he finished him off. But it was a fair fight.'

L'Albanien, and now Le Grec.

'This le Grec. Is he Greek? Or is he French, and le Grec simply a name?'

'J'sais pas, moi. He speaks real Parisian – not like the Albanian.'

'Or me.'

'Your French is good, dem'selle.'

I laughed.

I was impatient to go in search of Raoul and find out about Charlot. But first I had to warn Maître Pietri.

I gave the boy a couple of sous, and told him to keep watch here as often as he could.

In his little shop, or rather office, on the Pont-au-Change, Maître Pietri was still busy.

A small man, an aristocrat, to judge by his accent and by the red and grey velvet cote-hardie, the grey fur-lined cloak pushed back off his left shoulder, the red hose with dark red velvet cod-piece, and the galoches to protect him from the thawing snow.

As soon as he realised I was there, he fell silent.

Maître Pietri hesitated, then said, 'Dem'selle Miriam, what can I do for you? You should be at home before the fire on such a morning.'

At the name Miriam, the man – the gentle man – had looked up. Now he spat very deliberately on the floor, went to the door and opened it, and stood there breathing fresh air rather than breathe the same air as a Jew.

'Demoiselle, you must leave now, at once.'

'I came to warn you. I cast your horoscope, you will be in great danger – danger of death! – during the next two days, unless you flee the city, go into hiding.'

'Dem'selle Miriam. I thank you for your concern, but please, please, just go now.'

'Very well. But you, please, please, take this warning very seriously.'

What else could I do?

I went to the Lutetia. Raoul and Evrard were not there, but Kateline and Marc were. They wanted to know what was happening, what I had found out, whether Jaquet was still in the Châtelet …

I told them some (not all) of what I had discovered. I didn't want to say much about the Montrouge brothers, and I didn't mention the Abbé Soxxal – for such was his name. So I decided to tell them about the previous evening.

'The point, of course, is,' I said, 'that Maître Guillaume - the miser - was an alchemist. A successful one, by all accounts. And whoever killed him, whoever tortured him to death, was after his gold and his secret. Now I know a little about alchemy from my studies in Spain but I need to know more, so I turned to Maitre Thomas of Pizan.'

'You didn't!' gasped Kateline.

'The King's astrologer?' Marc, too, could hardly believe it.

'Yes, but listen. He had been invited to meet the Emperor - he and his "charming lady".'

'Oh, I've seen her! Yes!'

'But his charming lady has dropped him, so …'

'Oh no! He took you!'

'Yes! I was presented to King Charles V of France and the Emperor himself, Charles IV of Bohemia, and three of his children, Wenceslas, his heir, and Prince Sigismund and Princess Anna.'

'It's like a dream!'

'What were they like, Mariana?'

I told him, without mentioning the horoscopes, though I did say (I knew Kateline would love it) that I had read Princess Anna's hand. They were both open-mouthed.

I laughed, then grew serious again, and said: 'Unfortunately, that doesn't help Jaquet much.'

'You didn't find out what you needed to know?'

I shook my head. 'I don't believe Thomas knows much more about it than I do. And the Emperor - who does know, if the rumours are to be believed - could not discuss alchemy in front of the King.'

'That's so strange, isn't it,' sighed Kateline.

'What, that even the Emperor isn't free to speak - '

'Bah,' said Marc, 'being Emperor doesn't mean much these days. The King has far more power than him.'

'In France,' I agreed. 'But remember the Emperor is also hereditary King of Bohemia and elected King of Germany and in a sense too of the Papal States.'

'That's true, cherie.' Marc was always charming. 'Well, I have to go now. Kateline?'

'No, I'll stay with Mariana for a while.'

On his way out, he was stopped and questioned by two sergeants who had just come in. There seemed to be no problem. He was allowed to go.

'I'm hungry,' I said.

'And me. Shall we order some bread and cheese?'

'Mm. And some wine. It'll warm us up.'

When we had ordered, Kateline, who was Paris born and bred and knew everyone, said, 'I have an aunt - she's not really my aunt but she's a friend of Maman - I call her Tante Perenelle. She's married to an alchemist.'

'She is?'

'I don't know much about it - it's a secret, really, and you mustn't mention this to anyone, but if it will help poor Jaquet, then I might be able to arrange for you to come and talk to him about the work of Maître Guillaume.'

'What's his name?'

'Nicolas Flamel.'

'And he's a practising alchemist.'

She nodded.

The bread and cheese arrived, and the wine. And with it the two sergeants.

'We seek a student by the name of Jacques Couting. He speaks French, but with a marked English accent.'

'I regret, I cannot help you, sergeant.' Kateline fluttered her eyelashes at them, while I started in on the bread and cheese. The bread was hot, the cheese was delicious.

'Nor I,' I mumbled.

They stared at me. At my nose.

'Nor you what?' demanded the larger of the two.

'Nor can I help you, sergeant. What did you imagine I meant?'

They continued to stare.

The smaller said, 'You have an English accent, dem'selle.'

'Mi acento no es inglés, es español! Soy española! Do I look like an English boy?'

The drinkers at the nearby tables laughed.

'English boys come in all shapes and sizes!' quipped one.

'If that's a boy, my wife is too!' laughed another.

'Silence!' roared the larger sergeant. And in the sudden silence, the smaller one said, 'De dónde eres, señorita?' He spoke Spanish.

'De Cartagena. Me llama Doña Mariana de la Mar, y mi padre, Don Joaquín de la Mar, es alcalde de Los Alcazares.'

'She is Spanish,' he told his comrade. 'A thousand pardons, señorita.'

They went.

A man at a nearby table called, 'We want a boy to work in our glove shop.'

But Kateline snapped something at him that I did not catch and he closed his mouth and turned away embarrassed.

'What did you say to him?'

'I said I knew his wife and from what I'd heard a boy was the only thing he did want.'

'Kateline!' I stared at the man, who was still embarrassed in front of his friends. 'But is it true?'

She shrugged the Paris shrug.

I laughed.

She gazed at me. 'I've never seen you speaking Spanish, being Spanish, before. Everything changes. Your eyes flash, your foot stamps: suddenly you are a Spanish lady, Doña Mariana, not the Dem'selle Mariana we know.'

'You'd be the same if you lived in, say, London, and spoke English, then suddenly went into French. Your whole manner would change and surprise everyone: their Katherine, whom they thought they knew, would become Dem'selle Kateline, a stranger, a foreigner …'

'Mm.' She liked the idea. Then: 'I didn't know your father was Spanish, too? I thought you said once that – '

'Like you, mon ange, I don't always tell the truth. I'm really only half-Spanish.'

'And half-English, but that was not the time to say so.' She laughed.

I was going to protest at the "English" – after all, Scotland is not England whatever the Kings of England may believe – but she was still talking so I let it go. What did it matter?

'And you used to spend all your time in the sea, didn't you say? Like a little mermaid? Oh, Mariana, that's so fantastic.'

'Not all my time,' I laughed, 'but yes, a lot of it, at least half of each day, until I was kidnapped and sold into slavery and became a prostitute.'

'Oh yes, you told me about that. It must have been so awful!'

The last of the wine accompanied the last crumbs of cheese and bread.

A man at the next table had been listening closely to what I was saying.

'Are you waiting for Evrard?' she asked.

'No, for Raoul. He's been talking to Mère Henriette again. I think I'll walk round to his place, see if he's there.'

'D'accord. And I'll go and see my Tante Perenelle.'

'Where do you work?' the man at the next table asked me as I stood up. He was the one who'd been taking all the interest in us. In me.

Before I could respond, Katelina said, 'She doesn't, Not any more. And if you'd been listening to the earlier part of our conversation as closely as you were listening to the last part, you'd know she's not a she at all, she's an English boy in disguise.'

More roars of laughter as everyone looked me up and down.

'But perhaps that's what you like – English boys. Hey, does anyone know if there's a house anywhere in Paris specialising in English boys? This gentleman ... '

The man, whose name I was later to learn was Martin, stood up and confronted Katelina. 'Shut your mouth, bitch.'

'Touch her and you die,' I said.

I meant it, but of course no one took me seriously – except perhaps Martin.

'Ah, the Engleesh boy has teeth!'

'The Engleesh boy has breasts, too! Look at them!'

Everyone was ordering more drinks and having a great time.

'There's a house in the Rue Tire-Putain where they've got a couple of English boys.'

'How d'you know?'

Laughter and mockery.

'Show us a bit more of your breasts, love!'

Martin had had enough. 'Don't tell me you're not a whore still, Marian. You always have been and you always will be.'

With that, he strode out. And we followed, to everyone's disappointment.

'It's true, everyone knows you're a whore, don't they. Or at least that you used to be,' she added quickly.

'He called me Marian! He seemed to know me.'

'He'd heard me use your name.'

We were standing in the alley now, ready to go our separate ways. Suddenly she didn't seem so sweet, so friendly. 'Yes, he seemed to know you very well. Are you sure you – ?'

'No! I've never seen him before!'

She gave me a look that meant she didn't believe me. An all-whores-are-liars-look.

Then turned away and left me standing there. Not even the kiss on both cheeks we always gave each other.

Ah, well ...

First, talk to Raoul. Then go and see Jaquet, dressed as I was.

After that, go home and change: I wanted to visit La Adriatica, and try to get to the Albanian, dressed as a man.

I met Raoul on the bridge as I was crossing from the university side of the river, the Rive Gauche, to the Île de la Cité, the island that had once been all there was of Paris, or so they said. Paris had been known then as "Lutetia". (Frequenting taverns can be educational.) The island was still "the City", and it housed the great cathedral of Notre Dame, its buttressed roof and twin towers now coated with snow. We stood there for a while in silence, gazing at the river. It hadn't frozen yet, but it would, it looked sluggish already, as though it was slowing down, preparing itself.

I sighed, and spoke without looking up from the river. 'Did you see Mère Henriette?'

He nodded. 'She says she knows nothing of any other girl – or any baby with dark hair who was with the miser and Lule when they arrived in Paris. Natalie was born later, here, after they arrived. And her hair and eyes were always the colour they are now,' he laughed. 'But there was a third brother, Charlot. She hardly knew him because Hugues, her husband, the eldest brother, wanted nothing to do with Charlot, who was a simpleton and an embarrassment. Guillaume looked after him. They all still lived on one of the Îles Normandes then, they hadn't set out yet on their travels. When they did, Charlot accompanied Guillaume. They spent some time wandering around Brittany, where they fitted in, both of them being pure Breton in appearance, dark hair, blue eyes, almost like twins except that Charlot was very tall and thin while Guillaume was small, and Charlot's vacant smile was quite unlike Guillaume's expression, which was – "foxy" was Mère Henriette's word.'

I laughed. 'She didn't like him. Alert, she means, I suppose. And curious. Did she say whether Charlot helped Guillaume at all, whether Guillaume used him in his work in any way?'

'Yes. Guillaume used to scry (is that the word?) in some sort of magic mirror. Not a mirror like a mirror of glass or metal, but water in a flat shallow dish, and he peered into the water. Only he wasn't very good at it. Charlot could see much more clearly what was happening in the mirror. He didn't understand what he saw, but he described the images to Guillaume, who did understand. At least, that's what Hugues told her. Hugues didn't approve of it, but he believed it. Mère Henriette, on the other hand, thinks it's a lot of nonsense.'

'I see. Did you discover any more about their travels? Where else they went?'

'They were in Toulouse for some time. Then Spain, she doesn't know where, but a long time in Spain, then Ibiza – '

'Then Thessalonika, then back to Spain again.'

'Yes, and that last time they were in Spain they definitely went to Toledo, she says, and to Compostela.'

It sounded to me as though Maître Guillaume had been in search of something: some arcane knowledge. Toulouse? Spain? That meant the Zohar, Kabbalah. It could also mean alchemy.

Had he found the knowledge he sought? And if so, where? Presumably he had, at the end of his long quest – which was why it was the end. 'Ask her if she knows what the last place was before Guillaume decided to settle in Paris.'

'She doesn't. She's very vague. She knows a few names, that is all, because sometimes, when he was talking to Hugues, Guillaume would mention a place he had visited – or in later years, when he was talking to Jaquet. He tried to be a father to Jaquet after Hugues died, but that petered out as he grew older and Jaquet grew up.'

'And both Jaquet and his father used to hurry home and tell Maman what the black sheep of the family had been saying.'

'Something like that, yes.'

'Did she know brother Charlot's date of birth?'

'The twenty-ninth of January: which makes him an Aquarian, doesn't it?'

'Mm. The time?'

'She had no idea.'

'Well, it's something. Listen. I must get to Jaquet. When shall I see you?'

'Alexandre l'anglois, this evening?'

'If you like. After Compline, say. I'll try to be there, but if I'm not I'll see you in the morning at the Lutetia.'

'D'accord.'

Jaquet was the same, not yet growing weak, praise God, from the lack of air and light, and from the filth all around him.

I told him what we had discovered about his long-lost Uncle Charlot.

'But yes, I remember now. It comes back to me. When he talked about Spain, that's right, he was never alone, it was always "we" did this, "we" did that. It was so long ago. I remember him describing the Pyrenees; it must have been him, no one else has ever described the Pyrenees to me. They were in a village high up – high, high up – it was early summer and the snow was melting and all they could hear was water rushing, rushing, rushing, all day, all night … They were staying at an auberge, and everything was good, and they were coming home to France across the mountains, and from where they were it would be all down now, down the paths beside the glaciers (It sounds so clean, doesn't it! I wish I was there!) but then – no, that was the first time. The second time something had gone wrong. I don't think he ever told me what, I think I felt it. But, oh yes, he told me about the mountains, the snow, the peaks at sunrise, the water – "Ah, les sources!" he used to cry, remembering – and about that village, many times. He wanted to return, live there. He was not, not at all, not in any way, a Parisian. Then he would stop talking … I don't know, I was only young.'

So it was there. Or was it? Was he already on his way back?

'But what has all this to do with me, Mariana? How long will it be, now?'

'I'm sorry, Jaquet. I don't know. I'm still feeling my way. You must be patient.'

'I have been!'

'You must go on being.'

He stroked my fingers. Every time he stroked my fingers, he thought of Natalie. 'Why will Natalie not say that I ...?'

'I don't know. And now I've lost her.'

'Lost her?'

I told him what happened, that I suspected she was back with the Albanian.

'Is she safe with him?'

'If it was him, he must believe he can protect her better than I can, better than Yahia can.'

'The eunuch?'

I nodded. 'Mm. And judging by the ease with which he abducted her, I'm sure he's right.'

He thought about that, then said, 'Natalie would never refuse to make the statement that could get me released just because she was scared of this Sire de Montrouge or the priest or whatever.'

'I think she would.'

'No, there is something else. Someone else. Someone she hasn't told you about yet.'

I stared at him.

Yes. I had to find Natalie.

12

Dressed in my soutane as Magnus of Orkney, my student alter-ego, I set out once more. My only problem was that with my grazed and swollen nose it would be hard to tell the difference between me – Magnus – and the now-notorious Jack Cutting. I knew I was Magnus today, but would anyone else?

It was getting colder again and more snow was falling as I approached La Adriatica. It was a large building for a bordel. I rang the bell at the main door, tucked my thumbs into the narrow belt in the approved fashion, and waited.

The door was opened by a female midget, a tiny human such as I had come across once or twice in Spain but had never seen in Paris. Behind her stood a blond-haired giant who would have been able to put his arms round my huge Yahia and pick him up, to rest his chin on Yahia's head.

It was time for me to buy a new body-guard.

I loved Yahia, though. Maybe I'd keep him just for harem duties.

I'd tell him. See what he said.

'Who do I speak to?' I asked them both, my head going up and down like a chicken's.

The black-haired midget was probably the more dangerous of the two.

I spoke down. 'My father sent me.' I pulled out a silver sou. 'He says I lack experience.'

It was the midget who spoke. 'That is easy.' She held out, and up, her hand.

I ignored it. 'I have experience of which he knows nothing.'

Do the dead witness our lives, our deeds?

'That too we can accommodate.' Her hand was withdrawn, still empty.

'I should like to discuss my, ah, special needs with Mère Veronique …'

'I regret Mère Veronique is unavailable at present.'

'She will be available soon, I have no doubt.' I tossed the sou into her outstretched hand, she caught it, tested it with her teeth.

'Meanwhile,' I went on, 'I should like to pass the time with someone young and sweet and slender and fair ... '

'How young, messire?'

'Oh, sixteen, eighteen.'

'That too is easy. Hans! Escort the young gentleman to Gwyneth.'

'And the English student?'

'Tell him his time is up. Remain outside the door while this one - ah, here he is.'

The English student turned out to be Peter Crofton. Not one of our crowd, but I knew him because we attended some of the same classes. And more to the point, he knew me: he was one on the very few who had seen through my disguise without needing to be told.

He grinned. 'Mariana?'

'I'm here to see Mère Veronique. On business.'

'How very intriguing. And dressed as a boy. But listen. Be careful. They're searching everywhere for an English boy with an injured nose. They questioned me. I am English, d'accord, but I don't have an injured nose. When I pointed this out, one of them raised his fist and said "We can soon fix that!" All right, you can laugh, but really, you must be careful: you do have an injured nose. You haven't been masquerading as an English boy? A certain "Jack Cutting", by all accounts?'

'Moi?' The picture of innocence.

He studied me. 'No, you're from Spain, aren't you ... I hear you met my friend Philippe - as Doña Mariana. I don't think he realises Mariana and Magnus are one.'

The midget cleared her throat.

'I'll leave you to it, then. He was very taken with you, was Philippe.'

'Au'voir, Peter.'

Gwyneth was seventeen, and from Wales. She knew hardly any

French, only Welsh and English, so we spoke English. We sat on
the bed and whispered of her homeland and how she had come to
be in Paris, and I made her laugh. I don't think she laughed often
in La Adriatica. Then she whispered, 'But don't you want to do
anything?'

   'Not really. I'm a girl.'

   Her eyes opened wide.

   She was shocked.

   And then, believe it or not, she was embarrassed!

   She pulled her shift down over her thighs, back up over her
breasts.

   I laughed, opened my cote-hardie and my shirt, and revealed
my own bandaged-flat bosom.

   She relaxed. 'It's just that I've never – it's never – there's never
been a woman in here before while I've been doing this.'

   'I understand. There are things we do with men – in front of
men – we'd be ashamed to do in front of a woman. Perhaps not
ashamed, but shy.'

   'Yes.'

   'Had you lived all your life in Cardiff?' That was the port
where she had been traded to a ship's captain.

   'No, I grew up in the mountains. But we were too many, my
da had to sell one of us. I went to Cardiff to be a maid. I learnt
English there. I had to.'

   'And your master sold you?'

   'No, my mistress.'

   'Why? No, don't tell me. I can guess.'

   She was very sweet. Far too sweet for her own good. But
what could I do?

   Loud footsteps coming.

   Too loud.

   Jack Cutting.

   Be a girl again, quick?

   Too late.

I did up my tunic, adjusted my hair.

'He's in here!'

The curtain (there was no door) was swept aside. Two sergeants burst in. Fortunately, not the same ones.

'Jacques Coating?'

I looked at Gwyneth.

She looked at me.

'You!' he roared, pointing at me. 'Stand up!'

I stood up.

'You are Jacques Coating!'

'I am not Jacques - what was it? Couton?'

'Coating.'

'Cooting. I am Magnus MacElpin, and - '

'Where are you from?'

I couldn't say Spain again.

'Scotland.'

'L'Écosse. C'est en Angleterre.'

'C'n'est pas en Angleterre! C'est un pays, un royaume, un peuple!'

'And your father?' one asked, in English. Good linguists, these sergeants.

'Comment? Je ne comprends pas.'

'Tu ne parles pas la langue anglaise?'

'Dans mon pays on parle gaelic. A bheil sibh a' bruidhinn a' Ghàidhlig?'

He looked baffled. Disbelieving, but at a loss how to proceed.

Then an old lady's voice cut through from outside. 'Le jeune homme qui m'attend est là?'

'Oui, madame,' said the midget who had led the sergeants to me.

'Et les sergeants? Qu'est-ce qu'ils veulent?'

'Rien, madame. Rien.'

They went, with their tails between their legs, and the midget gave me an evil look.

I gave her the sign for warding off the evil eye, index finger and pinky extended like two horns straight at her.

She squeaked.

'What was that?' Madame demanded, turning.

'Rien, madame.'

'All I ever hear is "Rien madame". The next time I hear "Rien madame" I shall not believe it. Someone will taste the whip.'

She held out her elbow for me to take her arm. After we had gone six or eight paces, she gave me a strange look.

In her private room, with the door closed, she said, 'You are a woman. Hardly more than a girl. What is this nonsense?'

She nodded to a stool by the fire. Herself, she sat in a big upright chair with cushions on the seat and at her back. She sat very straight.

I remembered what La Mireille had said: this woman was old but she wasn't stupid.

I explained. In full.

'I see. And why could you not have come straight to me? Why this performance with the Welsh girl?'

'I did ask to come straight to you. I even gave your diminutive door-keeper a silver sou. But to no avail.'

'Did you indeed. Well now, let me see … You prefer to meet the Albanian man to, ah, man.'

I looked at her. Old, yes, and small. But still strong-willed, still fiery. I remembered the threat of the whip, knew she had meant it. Knew I wanted her on my side.

I said, 'What would you recommend, Mère Veronique?'

'I would definitely not recommend any strange man – or boy – to approach the Albanian. Unless he is tired of life.'

'Then …?'

'A beautiful woman, or girl, at least gets a moment or two while he looks her up and down, judges her as he might judge a freshly-plucked capon strutting around thinking itself something special.'

'This Natalie is important to him.'

'D'accord, but will he believe you are important to Natalie? At any rate, if you go as a beautiful woman (and I can see that you are) you will get a hearing. As a boy, you will simply get your throat slit.'

I remembered le Cafard's words.

'Go home and change. Do something about that nose … But on second thoughts, that may amuse him, with women he is unpredictable. It may even gain his sympathy. Then come back here.'

'Should I bring a bodyguard?'

'Non! I shall arrange for one of my girls to accompany you, one he knows and likes.'

13

And so it was that as evening fell in what should have been by Andalucían standards the middle of the afternoon – I didn't mind, it was different, this darkness during the day, my father was wrong when he said I would hate the north of Scotland in winter – I found myself in a boat going up-river with Notre Dame on our right, and the gibbets and wheels, all full today, on the quay to our left. My companion was Marie-Élise, a cheeky but very sweet little blonde of about my age who assured me that the Albanian was gentil as long as you didn't bore him. 'Men mustn't upset him, women mustn't bore him.' Perhaps I'd read his – one – hand: that should be anything but boring!

There was an icy wind on the river and it was bitterly cold. We were passing the palace now on our left, and on our right, the Île-aux-Vaches, a flat green island where cows were kept for their milk; but my heart was still with the men on the wheels, alive, though broken and in agony, unlike the lucky ones whose

heads alone were on display. Uncle Yacoub was quite right: 'The
Christian God shows little compassion, despite the teachings of
their Jesus Christ. Find a great church and look around,' he
would say; 'not far off you will see the instruments of torture.'

We were put ashore at the Porte Saint-Antoine, and there
Marie-Élise spoke to an urchin who guided us through a series of
almost pitch black alleys where we kept slipping and sliding on
lumps of slime – I know, but that's what it felt like – till we came
out into a place which, Marie-Élise whispered, was the Cour des
Miracles. 'All the houses around here belong to them,' she said.
'Everything here.'

I looked round. I could see little in the dark, but the lights of
lamps and fires showed through flapping doors and shutters.
Everything was in a state of disrepair.

'Why is it called a Cour des Miracles?'

She laughed. 'Here the crippled walk, the blind see again, the
—'

'No …'

'Yes. There! Watch!'

Even as I looked, a one-legged man caught in the light from a
window undid something beneath his cloak and a second leg
dropped down beside the first. He put his crutch on his shoulder
and walked into one of the houses.

'I see,' I breathed. 'They are pretending. And the Albanian?
Does he have two arms really?'

'Oh no. He never pretends.'

He never pretends. This was a man to take very seriously.

The urchin, who had gone off by himself somewhere into the
darkness, now returned. 'He will send someone for you.'

'Who?'

'L'Albanien, dem'selle.' He looked at me as if I was stupid.

'Ah. When?'

He sighed. 'When he is ready, dem'selle. You wait here.'

It began to snow again.
      Two sheep, "liberated from Les Halles", were also waiting.

I began to wonder whether coming here had been entirely wise.
      "If you are unhappy where you find yourself, and uncertain
whether to step forward or step backward, step forward." Uncle
Yacoub. He was right.
      Give it a few more moments ...

'That's it. I'm going in,' I said.
      She grinned.
      I liked her.
      'In where?'
      'Don't you know?'
      'No. Usually he is out here in the place. There is a big fire,
meat roasting.'
      I looked round, nodded towards the house that was brightest
lit. 'Let's try that one.'
      We walked across to the doorway and looked in.
      I had thought he would be tall and dark. He was not. He was
small – quite short, very thin and wiry – and his hair and beard
were straw-coloured.
      No one else had noticed us, but he was staring straight at us.
At me.
      'That's him,' whispered Marie-Élise.
      Capons were stupid things. Me, I just wanted to run, to hide.
At least get back out and wait my turn with the sheep.
      He beckoned, and suddenly everyone had noticed us,
everyone was staring.
      We stepped forward. We were in. There was no turning back
now.
      There had been no turning back before.
      He gestured to Marie-Élise to stop. It was me he wanted.
      It was like a tavern. A particularly sleazy one, even by

Parisian standards. But if everything was free?

I walked between two tables, benches packed with ragged men and women who looked me up and down as I passed. Did they then turn back to their food and drink? I don't think so. I could feel their heads follow me as I passed the next table – where a man put out his hand and grabbed my skirt, pulled me towards him. I twisted, raised my skirt, kicked out at him as Ferchard had taught me, catching him on the side of his head as he turned to his neighbour, laughing – and at the same instant a knife flashed by, piercing the hand that pulled my skirt. The man flew sideways, the hand with the knife stuck through it held out in amazement.

I looked at the Albanian. His arm was still extended. He pulled it back. Nodded to me to come closer.

I went right up to his table.

Behind me, the man's howls of pain and rage subsided to a whimper as he realised the peril he was still in.

The Albanian gestured to the man's companions to throw him out. Then he picked up a grilled rib of some kind, chewed the meat off it, his eyes fixed on me.

They were pale blue. Like Lule's. Was he her brother? Or had he been her husband, once, before Thessalonika? Before the fighting and the raid on their village? No, her husband had probably had brown hair, brown eyes, like the baby daughter that went missing somewhere in Spain.

'You are fast,' he said. 'You saved the fool's life.'

Yes, the knife would have pinioned the man's hand – and my skirt! - to his chest if I had not –

'Your leg moved so fast my knife almost hit that, hit you, instead of him. And I never miss when I throw a knife … Where did you learn that?'

'A friend of my father's, an old soldier, a Scot. He teaches me what he learnt on his travels. He learnt to fight with his feet in Alexandria.'

'Alexandria … And you caught him off-balance as he pulled at your skirt.'

I nodded.

'Marie-Élise!' he called. 'What will you do for us tonight? Will you dance for us?'

'No, I will sing for you.'

From where she stood, beside the place vacated by the man who had grabbed my skirt, she sang a sad little song about the apple trees in her village – one apple tree, under the branches of which she lay as a baby, played as a child and where she first knew love …

We listened, his eyes still on me. And when she had finished, he shouted: 'Marie-Élise! When you go back to your village you'll find that your apple tree has been chopped down!'

'No!'

'Yes! I will send someone to chop it down if you don't sing us something more cheerful than that!'

Everyone laughed and agreed.

Then someone started playing the lute and a girl joined in with a tambourine.

'And I want to see you dance!' he shouted over the music.

She smiled, and shook off her cloak, which was caught by the man behind her as it fell, an old man who sat holding it reverently while she raised her arms above her head and began to dance, and then to sing again, a fast happy song in a language I did not understand – save that I caught the names Lancelot and Guinevere. A happy song about those two? I would ask her afterwards.

Suddenly, he kicked out at the bench opposite him and three men went flying over backwards. 'Did no one ever teach you to offer a seat to a lady, pigs?'

All three were killers. Now all three picked themselves up smiling, humble, apologetic. They sat me down in the middle of the bench, then sat back down with me, careful not to crowd me, and carried on eating and drinking.

He picked up a sausage and held it out to me.

I eyed it suspiciously.

'No, go on, eat it! It's good!'

I was about to take it, then changed my mind. I leant forward and bit off a piece, leaving him holding the rest.

He was right. It was delicious.

I was right, too. He had hand-fed me. I was under his protection now.

He smiled.

Bit by bit, he fed me the rest of the sausage. He fed me in silence. And though Marie-Élise was singing and dancing behind me, his eyes never left mine. And my eyes, like a feeding baby's, never left his.

I was sending silent blessings, too, to Mère Veronique: if I had come dressed as a boy, I would still be outside in the snow. With the sheep.

When the sausage was finished, he passed me a chunk of bread and a cup of wine.

'I think you must be Lalla Maryam,' he said suddenly, in Arabic.

I nodded.

'I learnt Arabic when I was a slave. One of my men here is from Algiers, another from Granada. I speak Arabic to them. For privacy. It will give us privacy, too. What we have to say here is not for other ears … Are you looking for Natalie? Or did you come in search of information from me?'

'There are one or two questions I should like to ask Natalie while I am here, but – she is safer here than she was at my house, where it seems anybody could just walk in and help themselves to her.'

'Not anybody!'

'No, all right – '

'But it is true, you do need a bodyguard with balls.'

I laughed.

'Like these three?' I said, glancing to my left and right.

'I don't have a bodyguard. I don't need a bodyguard.'

Go on, say it.

'I have balls.'

Right.

These men from the mountains. The men from the Sierras in Spain were the same.

'I can see that,' I said - he glanced down at himself! - 'and I assume she is safe with you.'

'She is. I am her uncle. Tell me how you come to be concerned with her welfare.'

I told him, briefly, and when I had finished, he said, 'So let me guess what you want to ask me. You want me to tell you about Lule, my sister, before she - we - were captured by the Serbians, may God's curse rest upon them! You want me to tell you about a little girl with dark curly hair and shining black eyes whose name, by the way, was Tara. And you want me to tell you all I know of Lule and Natalie, and of Guillaume Le Grec ... Natalie told me that sometimes you dress as a man, a boy, one Jacques Cotine. That as Jacques Cotine you were jumped the other night and she saved your life.'

'That is so.'

'Natalie, too, knows something of fighting ... Because you are on her side, and because I share your desire for justice in this case, I will tell you. But much of what I say is not for Natalie's ears. She does not know who her father was, nor must she ever know.'

'Of course.'

'Good. Then come with me.'

14

The Albanian led me up to the first floor, then along the landing to a closed door. A blind beggar was standing guard. When he saw the Albanian coming, he sprang to attention.

'Take those things out of your eyes when you're up here,' the Albanian snapped.

More pretending.

The beggar put his fingers to one of his eyes and took out a piece of puss-soaked muslin. Then did the same with the other eye.

We went in and he closed the door behind us. A fire was burning in an open brazier. There was furniture – expensive furniture, a table, chairs such as you never see outside the palaces of kings and bishops – but he threw himself down on a bearskin spread over a palliasse on the floor and motioned to me to do the same. I declined, sat on a cushion-covered bench at his feet and looked down at him.

'Natalie is in the next room. Asleep, I hope. Now where shall we start?'

'At the beginning? You and Lule in Albania?'

'Our village was not in Albania, it was in Serbia. Up in the mountains, the peoples are divided by villages, not by borders. It can be peaceful for a while, so peaceful people begin to make friends, the young may even want to intermarry, but something always happens, then vengeance is taken and the fighting starts again.'

'So do you speak Serbian, as well?'

'Oh yes, up in the mountains we speak all the languages.'

'Then before you go on (I am sorry to interrupt and it won't happen again) but does the word "chuvar" mean anything in Albanian or Serbian?'

'"Chuvar"? Yes, it is Serbian. It means guardian, watch-dog, keeper … And please do interrupt if you have a question. Better that than forget the question.

'At that time, fighting was going on, not so much between the villages as between our villages and Serbian brigands, who were raiding the villages, looting and killing and taking prisoners to be sold as slaves. And that is what happened to us. We had no warning – our chuvar must have been sleeping – and suddenly we were fighting for our lives. I saw Reda, Lule's man, killed. I saw Lule seized. I tried to get to her, to save her, save the baby, but … I woke up in the back of a cart. When they saw that I was conscious, they kicked me out and I had to walk, tied neck to neck with the other men. We were on our way down to the Aegean, to the slave-markets of Thessalonika. I saw Lule from time to time, but we couldn't talk. The women and small children were in carts. When we arrived, we were herded into separate buildings and I saw no more of her or Tara. Eventually, though, I heard that she'd been sold to a French astrologer. "Tell me more!" I begged. "Find out all you can!" They discovered that he had come there from Ibiza. That his name was Guillaume Le Breton. That he had an idiot brother called Charlot. That he was not a bad man, would be kind to her and Tara …

'A few days later, I was taken to Candia, on the island of Creta. There, I was one of eighty Albanian and Serbian men who were sold as a job-lot to an Arab trader. He took us to Barka, in north Africa, where we worked on building projects for ten years.'

I watched him as he spoke. He, like me, had been a slave, but he had had a far worse time of it. To be a slave on a major building site is almost as bad as being a slave in a mine, or so they say. Not many survive ten years. He had. Then he and the other remaining Albanians and Serbs had been loaded on board a ship again: to be transported to Al Khums, from where they would be taken to work in the mines out in the desert, or so it was rumoured. They never found out, for their second night at sea one of the Serbs, Mikhail, worked himself free of his bonds and untied the rest of them.

'Oh yes, by then we were all friends! Life is always a matter of "us" and "them", have you noticed? And now we were us and the Arabs were them.' He laughed.

Oh, I had noticed, yes. I had also noticed that very few people saw beyond it.

They seized the ship, threw their "masters" overboard (ex-slave-traders do not make good slaves, are best despatched quickly) and headed west for Malta. They stopped at Valetta to pick up supplies and satisfy one or two urgent needs (such as visiting the portside brothels, bien sûr) then sailed south in the hope of some rich pickings to augment the small amount of gold they had found on their ship. Before the day passed, they were hailed by an Arab ship, a corsair. They closed with it; then, when the two ships touched, boarded it suddenly, unexpectedly, and within minutes had slaughtered the whole crew. In the hold they found slaves, and in the Captain's cabin a treasure in gold and precious stones. They were rich.

But what to do with the slaves, most of whom seemed to be young people, children. They couldn't throw them overboard. Finally, they decided to take them to Ibiza, which was not far away, and sell them. He had gone along with this because it suited him very well to be dropped off on Ibiza with a bag of gold.

'But you remember "us" and "them"?'

I laughed. 'There was no longer any "them". So – '

'Oh yes, there was. The Serbs. And for the Serbs, "them" was once again us. Why should "we" share the gold with "them"?'

'They set on you one night.'

His mouth and eyes twitched in what I took for a grin. 'Right. We'd been expecting something, of course, but even so, many of us were killed. And many of them. In the end, there were nine of us still standing, three of them. They knew they could expect no mercy. They jumped overboard. There was land in the distance – Sardinia, to the north – but they couldn't swim, they were men of the mountains.

'I should have said that I was not one of the ones still standing. I'd had my left arm hacked off at the elbow, as you see it now, and was flat on my back, losing blood fast. They saved me. I was fortunate.'

They'd dropped him off on Ibiza with one other who wished to accompany him. Each of them, under their rags, carried a bag of gold and three precious stones: his were sapphires because they reminded him of his sister, his companion's were mixed, one large diamond, one ruby, one perfect emerald.

I asked him what had happened to his companion.

'Besnik? He died when we were set upon by thieves soon after we arrived here in Paris. He was injured, but the thieves – the two who still could – fled into the night, leaving the rest of their number dead or dying at my feet. My reputation as a one-armed killer stems from that first encounter with the Paris underworld, and it was then that I decided not to fight and fear the underworld (Was I not a rich man? Doubly rich now that Besnik had died) but to join it, to become their leader. These houses here all round the square – my army of beggars and whores and thieves all think we squat in them. They laugh at the rich owners too fearful to come here with the sergeants and evict us. We do not squat in them. They are mine. All the property in this whole quartier now belongs to me.'

When he and Besnik arrived on Ibiza, it had been ten years since Maître Guillaume and his little family had left there. Few people remembered them. He learnt however that Lule and Tara had gone from there to Barcelona, not to France.

Enough. They followed.

In Barcelona, they could learn nothing, until, talking to some old men in a tavern by the harbour – men who knew Arabic, for no one of course spoke a word of Albanian – they found a man who did remember: about ten years ago, yes, a French astrologer and his wife had been attacked on the road as they came up from

Valencia; the man's brother had been killed, the baby injured, its
head, it no longer responded properly. They had gone on to
France, across the mountains. Yes, one of the others remembered
now: he had asked the man, whose name was le Grec, yes, why
he was taking the injured baby up the mountains, and le Grec had
replied that he knew a witch there, in Andorra, one who would
cure the child if anyone could.

He and Besnik had bought horses and mules and hired guides
and made their way up into the mountains. There, high up near
the pass that takes travellers over and down into France, they
found the witch, and heard that the baby had died before
reaching Andorra.

Now he blamed Guillaume, le Breton, le Grec, whatever his
name was, swore he would kill him!

But the old woman calmed him, assuring him that, from what
the parents had told her at the time, the child could not have
lived.

She would say nothing else.

'Then we travelled on as fast as may be till we reached Paris.
We heard of the return of the Pestilence – it was the summer of
1371 – and though everywhere they assured us that it rarely
struck adults this time around, and had become known as the
Children's Plague, I had a premonition. In our family we do, we
are sensitive, which is why Lule was so good with Tarocchi
cards. And I was right.

'I found Guillaume le Grec. I found Lule. And days later, I
lost her again. I see now that I was lucky to have got to her in
time, but then I thought myself accursed, and being Albanian –
being me – I cursed right back, cursed gods and men, and have
been cursing ever since …'

A long pause. I gaze down at him. Beginning to understand him.
Or so I imagine ... 'But now, with Natalie here,' I say, gently, 'the
rage has become less?'

He turns his cold blue eyes upon me and for a moment I fear I am about to feel that rage, to learn at first hand that his rage for his lost sister can never become less.

'Not just Natalie.' He goes to the door, opens it. 'Fetch me le Grec.'

We wait in silence.

A boy enters. A beautiful boy. Lule in boy's clothes.

'This is Dem'selle Mariana. Mariana, my nephew, le Grec.'

The boy comes forward, bows, kisses my hand. 'Enchanté, Dem'selle Mariana.'

'Mariana is a friend.' The Albanian gives me no chance to speak. 'All right, you can go. The lady and I still have things to discuss.'

The boy grins at me as he turns and leaves.

'Now let me tell you the story as I had it from Lule, shortly before she died.

'It was generally known on Ibiza that Guillaume Le Breton was an astrologer. He let it be known. It was how he made his living. It was not generally known, though, that he foresaw and farsaw by means of a magic mirror. Nor would anyone have guessed that his brother Charlot, a simpleton, could see things in the mirror much better than Guillaume himself could. And it was not known at all that Guillaume was an alchemist who had come very close indeed to realising his dreams. There was just one small detail – maybe two. And he had heard from a Jew in Thessalonika that in León, in Spain, there were masters, Kabbalists, who would be able to help him. León! So close! He had been to Spain before, but to Toledo and to Córdoba, and had learnt much there. But no one had told him of the masters in León. They were so secretive! Well, they were right to be. He decided to sail for Spain.

'However, before Guillaume could leave Ibiza, Pierre de Montrouge came into his life – and into that of my sister, and my niece. Pierre wasn't interested in astrology, but he was interested

in beautiful women, especially beautiful slaves. He came to
Guillaume seeking information about where Guillaume had
bought the beautiful Lule. Were there more like her? At what
kind of prices? Could one deal directly with the Serbs, cut out
the middle man? He was also interested in having his fortune
told (like all gamblers he was superstitious) and he had learnt
somewhere, no doubt from some other Albanian slave, that
Tarocchi originated in, or at least came into Europe via, Albania
and Hungary, and that the only authentic readings were those
done by Albanians and Hungarians. So he persuaded Lule to do a
tarocchi card reading for him. Do you know anything of
Tarocchi?'

'Not really. My teacher did not take Tarocchi seriously,
though there are Kabbalists in Spain who do.'

'Lule started that day with a simple eight-card reading. Card
number eight, the important card, the final card, turned out to be
the Hanged Man. He would not listen to her explanations of the
other seven cards, the order, the interpretation of the Hanged
Man, oh no. He was drunk, of course. He accused her of
predicting an evil fate for him, made her start all over again. The
first seven cards were mostly different, but the eighth was once
more the Hanged Man. Now he was frantic. He was a fool as I
have told you – though not a Fool, in the Tarocchi sense, the
sense that Charlot was – and he was quite sure that here his fate
was being decided. He insisted on another reading. This time,
when they came to the final card, the answer to the question, it
was the Moon, indicating simply that his worries were unreal, he
was imagining things. He laughed. He relaxed. Then suddenly
demanded to see the Hanged Man. It was at the bottom. She had
palmed it, added it after he had shuffled. Furious, he demanded
one last reading, with more cards, and the Hanged Man included
in the shuffle. So this time she dealt the Thirteen-Card Spread:
and the Hanged Man turned up at the end, card number thirteen,
of course.'

'Of course?'

'Well, it would now. Tarocchi works like that. Fate gets stuck.'

'I see. No, I don't see. That is a very strange thought … Do you think there might be any chance of me taking lessons with Mère Bòrbala?'

'You know Bòrbala?'

'Natalie mentioned her.'

'Ah. You'd have to speak to her – Bòrbala. When all this is over. Anyway, Lule tried again to interpret the cards for him, but he wouldn't listen. He flounced off with a threat to her life – as though killing the seer will make any difference. And that was that.

'They went to Spain, to León, and Guillaume found the answer to his questions. One was that the "water of life" he needed in the first part of the process was "golden water" and not "white seed" as he had believed. Do you understand these terms?'

'Oh, yes.' "White seed" was semen, in Kabbalistic terminology; "golden water", presumably urine.

'So … it was just that?'

'No, it was not just that. He had to use Charlot, as he did with the magic mirror. He himself was too corrupt, too worldly. Everything possible had to be done by Charlot. Guillaume had to avoid handling anything. Even the urine had to be Charlot's. And that worked. Gold. At first, a little. Then a lot … A lot, Lule told me, and why should she have lied? To me, her brother? And on her death-bed … A lot … But "Only make what you need," they had told him. "Use it only for yourself. Do not make all your family and friends rich." "Keep it secret." "Do not mention Spain. It is already rumoured that there is more gold here in the north of Spain than there ought to be." "The Inquisition want the Pope to authorise them to treat Jews as heretics and put them to the Question: what question do you think they will ask?" And so on.

'The same masters in León who had taken Guillaume into

their confidence, took Lule also to their hearts. They showed her
the Spanish, the Kabbalist, way with tarocchi cards, something
none of us had known existed. The cards are laid out with the
sefirot in the pattern of the Tree of Life, a card to each sefirah, or
more comprehensively, and allowing for more cards, according
to the figure of the Divine Man, Adam Kadmon.'
    'You know a lot about this.' I was impressed.
    'I followed it up, have found out all I can …'
    Fearing discovery, the masters in León had sent them down to
Valladolid and Toledo with the names and addresses of
astrologers in those cities. They told Guillaume to pursue that
interest now, exclusively, lest anyone should follow and start
asking questions. And that is what they did, crossing Castilla this
way and that, a long, long journey. But after they left Toledo,
intending to travel north to Saragossa and so over the mountains,
where Guillaume knew an old woman he dearly wished to speak
to once more, Lule's cards began to read ill: she foresaw the
death of baby Tara and of Charlot, disaster for Guillaume and
herself. Guillaume, panicking, set up his magic mirror: and
Charlot, too, could see nothing beyond his own death, lying
somewhere on the floor, in a pool of blood.
    They changed their plans, headed east, instead, for Valencia,
to take ship from there for France.
    Lule's cards still fell ill.
    Charlot remained unable to see anything but his own death.
    And in Valencia, a man came to their room at the portside inn,
knocked on the door.
    It was not bolted, there was no bolt. If there had been, a strong
man or woman could easily have burst it open.
    What could they do? Pretend they weren't there? As they had
been pretending ever since the signs started appearing and they
changed their route?
    But Guillaume had read Charlot's horoscope for the next few
days when they breasted the hills to the west, and the sea and the

city of Valencia first came in view: Valencia the beautiful, his favourite city from his travels in his youth, spread round the great blue bay. Today was going to be the day for Charlot. If he survived today, he would live for ever.

He opened the door.

It was Pierre de Montrouge. Alone. Smiling. Drunk.

He seized Guillaume's arms, kissed him on both cheeks.

'I got in only yesterday. Asked around for any old friends of mine. And who should I find here? You and the superb Lule! Let us have a drink!'

He shouted down the stairs for coñac, then came right into the room.

'But where have you been all this time?'

'Oh, wandering through Spain, learning more of astrology. There is always more – '

'Et toi, ma jolie?'

'I accompany my master.'

'Learning more of your art – of your magic … of Tarocchi?'

What was this emphasis on the word "magic", Guillaume wondered. Was it simply that she had some other magic – a simple tribute to her beauty? Or was it threatening? He could so easily denounce her as a witch, accuse her of putting a curse on him, and she would be burnt: in Spain and the south of France witch-burnings were everyday events now. He would have to be very careful. He could not afford to have someone like Montrouge for an enemy.

'A little,' Lule replied into the silence.

The silence continued.

Pierre said, 'You seem unhappy. Frightened, almost. Both of you.'

'No. Oh, no,' Guillaume murmured.

'Yes, I say!' He gazed at Lule, glanced at Guillaume, then looked back at Lule. 'Could it be those readings you did for me, Lule? Those false readings? As soon as I heard you were here I knew we had been brought together once more for you to do a proper reading … You don't say anything?'

'What is there to say, messire? Those other readings were false only in that you read the cards for yourself, you would not let me read them, interpret them, for you. And what do you know of interpreting tarocchi cards?'

'For one reading, you had actually palmed one of the cards, if I remember rightly. If I were to mention that in certain quarters … Still, this time you shall interpret, my sweet, and I shall – '

There was a knock at the door. The coñac had arrived.

He gave them each a drink, even Charlot, whom till then he had ignored.

'Salud!'

They all drank.

The baby, in the middle of the bed, stirred, gave a small cry, settled down to sleep again.

'But first, you shall tell my fortune, Maître le Breton. I have heard good reports of you.'

'No, no. I cannot. Not now.'

Lule gave Guillaume a pleading look. Do it! Get rid of him!

Guillaume shrugged. 'Oh, very well. Charlot, prepare the mirror.'

They all watched as Charlot rummaged among the bags and found the silver dish, placed it on the floor, filled it with water from one flask and added a few drops of some kind of oil from another.

'Pick it up,' Guillaume instructed Pierre.

'Hein?'

'Just pick it up. In both your hands. Hold it still. No, that is no good. Give it back to Charlot. Right. Now kneel down,'

'What?!'

'Kneel.'

The big man knelt.

'Sit back on your heels. All right. Now hold the dish in front

of you. Give it to him, Charlot. Let it down, let it rest on your
thighs then, if you can't hold it steady ... Yes, that will do.
Charlot?'

He and Charlot knelt in front of Pierre, facing him, close
enough to be able to peer into the dish. Then Charlot held out the
middle finger of his left hand and Guillaume produced a needle
from somewhere, took hold of Charlot's finger, and pricked it. A
drop of blood welled out, was shaken into the dish, then a second
drop.

'Stir it, Charlot.'

Charlot dipped the finger in, gently stirred the water and
blood and floating oil, then removed his finger: and sucked it
clean, which was not part of the ceremony but certainly
confirmed that he was an innocent. A Fool.

They waited.

An image formed.

They saw Charlot lying in his pool of blood again; even
Guillaume saw it this time. He gasped.

'What is it?' demanded Pierre. 'What can you see?'

'You must leave,' said Guillaume. 'Now! Before - '

'Wait.' It was Charlot. 'I see a man - this man - standing
before a great house with grass and trees all around. He is
wearing fine clothes and is surrounded by people who admire
him, look up to him, depend on him …'

'That - that - ' stammered Pierre.

'You will one day be rich, be courted, be, I imagine, the Sire
de Montrouge,' Guillaume told him. 'Now leave us, at once, I beg
of you.'

'Wait,' said Charlot.

Guillaume glanced back down into the mirror, not expecting
to see anything much. Saw the Hanged Man of the tarocchi pack,
but not a card, this time: reality. And Pierre de Montrouge was
the Hanged Man.

'That is nothing,' he said quickly, and tried to take the dish from Pierre.

Pierre resisted. 'What is it? It's –

'Nothing that concerns you. You have your answer. Now go!'

Guillaume gave the dish a tug and it contents flew back onto his grey hose and over the floor.

'What if it is not true? If – '

'Charlot saw it. He does not lie. He cannot. If he saw it, it was there. And if it was there, it will come to pass.'

Pierre got to his feet.

'Now go,' said Guillaume.

Charlot, looking up at the others, realised he too should stand up.

'Yes, yes. But first, Lule must read the cards for me one more time.' He offered the coñac around.

They declined.

He drank, sat down on the bed, waking the baby.

The baby started crying.

Lule went to pick it up.

'Leave it,' he told her.

'It will cry.'

'Let it cry. Come here. Bring your cards.'

The baby screamed.

Guillaume picked it up.

It quieted.

Lule fetched her cards from a bag, gave them to Pierre to shuffle.

He checked that the Hanged Man was in the pack, shuffled, and handed them back to her.

She began to lay them out.

The baby started crying again.

Charlot took the baby. It smiled. It liked him.

As Lule laid out the cards, she turned them up, one by one, commenting briefly on each. He showed no interest. It was just that last one, card number eight, that he was waiting for.

She took it off the top of the pack, turned it over. The Hanged
Man.

He swept the cards off the bed in a rage and as she bent with a
cry to pick them up he slapped her, grabbed her by the hair, hit
her again and, when she screamed out, punched her in the mouth
to silence her.

Guillaume was no fighter. The first thought that came to him
was that the penalty for assaulting a nobleman was death. The
second thought was that Lule could have had a master who beat
her all the time. The third, though, following hard on the second,
was that, as it happened, he was Lule's master, not Pierre de
Montrouge. And when Pierre gave her that final punch,
Guillaume ran at him.

Pierre threw her to the floor and drew his dagger.

Guillaume stopped dead.

'Sit down. There. On the floor.' Pierre indicated the foot of the
bed. He looked round, saw some cord used for tying luggage and
used it to bind Guillaume by the wrists and neck to the end of the
bed.

Next, he picked Lule up – she was still unconscious – and laid
her backwards over the side of the bed. He grinned, and lifted her
skirt, pulling it up over her body till she was naked all the way
up to her breasts.

Then Charlot, who had been watching with his mouth hanging
open, suddenly thrust the baby down onto the bed and leapt at
Pierre. With an oath, Pierre threw him off, or tried to, but Charlot
was big and hung on and they both fell onto the bed and rolled
over Lule; now Charlot was on top and Pierre kicked out and his
booted foot slammed into the screaming baby sending it flying
up into the wall which it hit with a thud and then fell back onto
the bed. Silent.

Charlot stared at the dead baby in horror. And as he stared,
Pierre pushed him off – and cut his throat. He fell to the floor
and lay gurgling and rasping, then silent, in the spreading pool of

blood that he himself had so often foreseen – and Guillaume was
now seeing in reality, though so shocked, so horrified was he that
he could only stare like a corpse at the shambles around him. He
would be like that for days. It would be months before he
recovered fully. If he ever did.

Lule stirred.

Untroubled by the blood, by the pain, by the deaths, Pierre
took off his tunic, pulled down his hose, and spread her legs.

She woke, opened her mouth to scream, and he slapped her
again. Then, while she wept and coughed and spat out blood and
bits of broken tooth, he took her … Afterwards, he spoke to
Guillaume, said she was too good for him, he not man enough
for her, did he not see how such a woman should be treated?
Then he took her again …

When he finally left, Lule picked up the baby and sat on the
floor beside Guillaume nursing it, for it was still alive; crooning
over it, hour after hour, while Guillaume, beside her, still tied up,
showed no reaction. He had lost his wits.

'Lule said it was the chamber-maid who found them like that
next morning and started screaming, and her screaming woke
Guillaume and brought Lule herself to her senses.

'The room was cleaned up, and though Guillaume could do
nothing, Lule managed to get a physician to come and look at
Tara and to arrange for Charlot to be taken away for burial. The
physician nodded and sighed over the child, said babies were
very delicate, said babies had great powers of recovery, said time
was the best medicine and only time would tell. Perhaps if they
knew the child's date and time of birth … Lule gave him a
Castillian silver peseta and sent him away.

'She also made official statements for the court, naming Pierre
de Montrouge. But Montrouge had gone.

'There was nothing to be done.

'They stayed two weeks, three, Lule wasn't sure, then set off
once again on their travels: this time north by land to the

Pyrenees, to Andorra. For Guillaume had talked so much of the old woman there, the witch, that now, with Guillaume not speaking at all, Lule felt that the witch was the one person who might be able to save little Tara.

'She also thought the witch might be able to help Guillaume to scry – and to manufacture gold – without Charlot. For all the gold they had was what they had made before they left León.

'Tara died in the foothills of the Pyrenees, as I said, before they ever got to the witch.'

He looked at me.

'And on the other question?'

'No one knows, for Lule was not present when Guillaume talked to the witch.'

'He had recovered then?'

'To some extent. But he became much quieter, much more secretive, especially about his work. When they settled here in Paris, using a new name, le Grec, Lule began to make money for herself and her children by inviting people in and doing tarocchi readings for them. But that was downstairs. Upstairs, Guillaume kept himself to himself – and at least when Lule was alive showed no sign of running out of money. Certainly, he never again felt the need to work as an astrologer or fortune-teller to earn a living.'

'Natalie said that while your sister was alive, Guillaume was always kind and generous. It was only after her death that he began to shut himself away, get a reputation for being a miser.'

'There is some truth in that. Certainly, he was never really happy again. But the secretiveness stemmed from the shock of that night in Valencia. It was evident when he was in the Pyrenees with the witch. She is secretive too, I told you. They probably all learn to be so in the end.'

I thought about Thomas of Pizan, how unhelpful he had been, doing little more than repeat my own words back to me. Did he in fact know no more than that? And this uncle Kateline had mentioned: would he be willing to talk, really talk, to me?

The Albanian was running out of time, and (I suspected) patience. I smiled. 'When you said "her children", you meant Natalie and le Grec, I assume. Can you tell me any more about them? Like who their fathers were. And how le Grec came to be in your care.'

'Natalie's father was Pierre de Montrouge.'

It explained everything. Why poor Guillaume couldn't look her in the eye. They were Pierre's eyes. And that was Pierre's hair. And why her poor uncle here didn't know what to do with her: the daughter of his beloved sister was also the daughter of his worst enemy. And she didn't know. Must never know.

'The boy's father,' he said softly, 'was Guillaume le Grec, of course.'

Of course. Well, not of course, but the Albanian was not the kind of man to whom one mentioned his sister's infidelities.

'I took him after Lule died because it was him Montrouge would use to force the secret out of Guillaume if he ever caught up with him again. And I was sure he would.'

'When you say took him, do you mean abducted him? Or do you mean with his father's consent, his father's agreement?'

He laughed. 'I would have abducted him if Guillaume had not agreed. But he knew the danger only too well.'

'And Natalie?'

'Natalie was not his daughter, and had not been brought up to think of herself as his daughter. Lule taught her to obey orders and get on with her jobs in the house. She didn't seem to be a daughter, that was the main thing. Of course, now things are different and she is in danger.'

'And though she was no daughter there, she is a niece here; she is likely to have a much pleasanter time.'

'You do not know the Cour des Miracles, ma fille. Life here is not pleasant for anyone. It is a means of surviving, for some, for a while. And she has not been brought up to it. By some standards she may have had a hard life: by our standards she has had a very easy one. I shall keep her hidden - and keep her pampered - for a while, till the danger is over. Then she will have to choose.'

'I see. But how did you know this would happen? How did you know that one day Montrouge would realise Guillaume was an alchemist?'

'Very astute. Because when he placed Lule on the bed to rape her, when he lifted her skirt, Guillaume shouted "Stop! I'll give you gold! All the gold you can possibly - !" But then Charlot attacked Pierre and the moment passed. And when later he set about raping Lule in earnest, Guillaume sobbed "You fool! I would have made you rich!" And Lule leant over even while Pierre was fucking her and hit Guillaume hard across the face and Pierre laughed and cried out, "Who's the master here then, eh?"

'For months, neither of them recalled Guillaume offering Montrouge gold or Lule hitting him. It was the least of what happened that night. But when it did come back to them, one evening while they were speaking of Charlot and his heroic attempt to defend her, they realised what had been implied by the words and by Lule hitting her master: that it must have been obvious even to Pierre once he began to think about it.'

There is a loud knock on the door. 'Signor Alban!'

He gets up and goes out, closing the door behind him.

A moment later, the blind chuvar opens the door and announces that he has been ordered to escort me home.

15

Next morning, as usual, Yahia brings water and helps me wash.

When he has gone, I do my belly-dance routines. Then I sit cross-legged and meditate as Uncle Yacoub taught me all those years ago, focusing today on Malkhut, the Queen, the feminine aspect of God, the point of contact and access between this lower world where we live out our lives in exile and the upper world to which our souls long to return.

But I am distracted.

What is all this about alchemy? Did Yacoub, my uncle and rabbi, not dismiss it as an unworthy pursuit? And yet now I am hearing of great masters who not only transform base metals into gold but apply their knowledge of Kabbalah to Tarocchi!

Perhaps I might learn something from the uncle whom Kateline is arranging for me to meet.

I stand up. Dress – cold now – and go downstairs.

Ferchard is sitting at the table in the kitchen where we usually eat informally.

'Has le Cafard been in?'

'Not yet.' It is Khadija who answers. She puts a cup of warm milk in front of me.

I push it away. 'Make me a tisane.'

'You need to eat. Have some bread – here, it's fresh, still warm.'

'I don't need to eat. I'm getting fat.'

Khadija sniffs and gives up on me. She has been trying all her life to get fat, without success: she is always too busy.

'Your nose looks better,' Ferchard says.

'Thank you. My nose is the least of my problems.'

He smiles. 'You think so? They're describing Jack Cutting as having a bruised and swollen nose. I was with a young lad last night, having a drink after the cock-fights – he's from Sterling, studying here – it was grand to speak the Gaelic again – '

'We always speak the Gaelic. What are we speaking now?'

'Aye, but this made a change. And the sergeants were extremely interested in him when they came round, especially as

someone had recently punched him on the nose. They said there
was a report that Jack Cutting was not from London at all, he
was from Scotland - he'd been caught in a bordel, but had got
away again somehow …'

Oh dear.

'So Doña Mariana,' he concludes, 'had better be very de la
Mar - very Spanish, and very, very feminine - for some time to
come. And that will be no bad thing.'

'If she is Demoiselle Miriam ben Amar occasionally? I have
to go and see someone who - '

'Just don't be English - or even Scottish, for the moment, not
even the you you were born to be, your father's daughter, God
rest his soul - and don't be a boy. So. Tell me. What did you find
out yesterday?'

He is a good listener. At the end he simply says, 'You took a
great risk going to see this Albanian. If I'd known you were
going to see him, I'd have forbidden it. Still, it sounds as though
from now on he will be an ally.'

'An ally?'

'Any friend of Natalie's is a friend of his. They have a simple
code of honour, these men from the hills in little countries like
Albania.'

'And Alba.' Alba is Scotland.

He laughs. 'Exactly so. In Albania they would say that you've
been granted besa - the status of an honoured guest, an honorary
member of the fis - the clan. Any insult to you is an insult to
them, any attack on you an attack on them: and it will be
avenged.'

'Ah ha. I see. The Moors have a similar concept of honour, at
least up in the mountains they do, in the Rif and the Atlas …
None of this helps us get Jaquet out of Le Châtelet, though.'

'The lass still won't speak up?'

'I wasn't even allowed to see her … There is something else
there, something strange that she hasn't told me yet.'

He was gazing at me. 'And there's a page-boy gone missing.'
Why did I make him think of page-boys? 'He was with Pierre the
night he died by all accounts. We must find him. Which
shouldn't be too difficult: he's black. And we must learn more
about Pierre's family – P'tit-Jean and the widow. P'tit-Jean, it
seems, is quite unlike the last three Sires de Montrouge.'

'In what way?'

'He does not frequent cock-fights. He does not gamble. He is
not in debt. And he does not like Paris.'

'Is that so?' I remember him in Maître Pietri's office, where he
looked to me just like a spendthrift aristocrat in need of a
substantial loan. If it was not to pay his own debts, perhaps it
was to pay off his late brother's.

But Ferchard is talking about the widow again. 'She's gone
back to Brittany, travelling with P'tit-Jean at least part of the
way.'

'Brittany?'

'She has a house in St Malo where she spends most of her
time. All of it, now.'

'Go after her, Ferchard, please. Go at once, now, urgently, and
bring her back here to Paris. Tell her it concerns her daughter.'

As I cross the Pont-au-Change on the way to meet Kateline, I see
people clustered outside the little shop Maître Pietri uses as his
office.

I run over to them, push through – 'Let me through! I know
him!' – and come to the door. He is lying on the floor in a pool of
blood. So. P'tit-Jean. Not in Paris, eh, Ferchard? And not in debt?

I back out through the growing crowd, suddenly aware of the
smell, a thing I have grown inured to since coming to France, but
now it is not just the smell but the smells all at once, for an
incident like this provides the only occasion when lice-ridden
beggars reeking of their own filth press up against the clean and
wholesome, and those who rarely wash (never in winter) against

the freshly-bathed and sweet-smelling. As I pull clear, a man tugs my sleeve. 'Dem'selle Miriam? Come with me, please.'

He takes me into the shop next door but one, a goldsmith's, and says, 'He left this for you.'

He holds out a small packet.

'Who?'

'Maître Pietri. He knew somehow that would happen – or at least feared …'

I take the packet, open it. A short letter. And a gold medallion representing Malkhut, Melkah, the Queen of Heaven and Earth, beautifully done …

It may turn out that you were right. I have for years been buying occasional pellets (and I mean pellets) of gold from our deceased friend; I know nothing of the provenance of this gold, but his enemies believe that I do, or at least that I may, and they are ruthless. I should like you to have this medallion. Keep it. Wear it. Do you know Kabbalah? The design was intended to represent Malkhut, but when it was done they said to me: 'You cannot make representations of the Sefirot! To do so is to carve an image of God!' 'This is not God,' I protested, 'it is a woman – look!' 'Malkhut is one of the aspects of God!' They paid me well for it and took it away and ordered me to make no more the same. This is not the same. In that one the Queen of Heaven was clothed. This, which portrays her naked, could, I see now, serve as the image of the World. Let us say then that that is what it is. Stay beautiful. Have beautiful children. But do not try to save men from their fate. It does not work. Farewell. Pietri.

I never did learn your first name.

I thank the goldsmith and walk away.

Was that what I was doing? Trying to save men from their fate? Vanity of vanities? Should I then simply leave Jaquet to his fate? Was I wasting my time and everyone else's? And risking my life and everyone else's into the bargain?

I stop at one of the gaps between the buildings, move out of the wind, look down at the swirling, icy water. I hold out the medallion. Let it go? A representation of one aspect of God as a naked woman? Blasphemy. And yet to say I should not, must not, fight against fate is a greater blasphemy. For that denies the freedom, the Godhood, in each one of us. I saved Abd-el-rahman ibn Khaldoun and the sailor from the slave-ship from their fate. I will save Jaquet le Breton from what promises to be his.

I open my hand, look at the image again. She is beautiful.

Was it fashioned during the last day or two, I wonder? And slip it into the pocket I carry at my belt.

I met Raoul first. He told me Kateline had things to do and would see us at the corner of the rue des Écrivains at midday.

'Écrivains?'

'Near St Jacques de la Boucherie. I'll show you.'

'Do we have time to go back to Guillaume's house? I want to have another look at something in the laboratory.'

Le Cafard was not there (probably at my house, having breakfast) but a sergeant was stationed outside the front door.

A good thing I knew the back way in.

We walked on past him, up a side alley, and so came to a little arched door in the high brick wall.

Raoul tried it. It was locked.

'Now what? Shall we go back to my place ...?'

I produced the key from my purse, and opened the door.

He gaped.

The courtyard was small, but clean, and had pots that had obviously once contained sweet-smelling herbs along the walls that faced south and east.

The back door of the house opened with the same key.

Inside was cold and dark and smelt the way empty houses do,

especially during the winter months.

There was a sound from upstairs. A thud. A bang.

'Let's go.'

'Oh, come on, Raoul! We've only just arrived.'

'If your poor nose – '

'It's not my nose you're thinking about.'

'Actually, it is.'

He gazed at me.

It was.

Such strange things, men.

'Come on – but quietly!'

We crept up the stairs – creak – creak – creak – each one making more noise than the last.

'They must think an army is coming!' he whispered.

I laughed. 'Better. Perhaps they'll jump from the window.'

We stood outside the laboratory for a second, then pushed open the door. A window was swinging, bumping the frame.

'They've gone.'

'There was no one. It was the window banging in the wind.'

But I was not looking at the window.

The snake was on the floor below its box. I pushed it with the toe of my boot. It was limp.

'Dead,' murmured Raoul.

'Someone got here first.'

'How do you know it didn't just die? Cold. Hunger.'

'It would surely have "just died" in its box.'

'Mm. But what makes you think ...?'

'It's name was Chuvar. Which means "the guardian". In Serbian. Lule spoke Serbian.'

'I thought she was Albanian.'

'She was. But their village was in Serbia.'

'But why would she choose a Serbian word for – ?'

'I don't know! Perhaps she considered Serbs to be snakes, and therefore snakes to be – '

'Snake may be a general epithet for Serbs among Albanians.'

'That would not surprise me. Now can we get on?'

'The Serbs probably refer to Albanians as dogs or pigs or … like the French and the English ... or the people in my village and those foxes in the next village, just fifteen minutes away.' He laughed. 'But then they are foxes.'

I had stopped listening. The cavity beneath the box where the snake had lived was empty now, though there were still a few scraps of paper. I fingered through what remained.

Raoul watched me. Watched where bits of paper fell as I discarded them. 'You're right. Someone has been here. They even threw out bits of paper in the exact same way you are … What's this?' He picked up one piece which was bigger than the rest and had been on the floor already. He passed it to me. 'There's something written on it. It's Hebrew, but …'

It was the occult form of Hebrew that Kabbalists sometimes prefer to use, making it incomprehensible to all but another Kabbalist, one who knows the terms and content already, knows what to expect.

'I'll take it home with me and think about it.'

'Two heads are better than one.'

Two bodies are better than one, he meant. I agreed, but I feared I might miss Kateline.

When we came out, le Cafard was back at his post, but down the road a bit where the sergeant wouldn't notice him and he was more out of the wind. I told him to leave the house now and go in search of the black page-boy. He grinned. This was work he preferred.

The wind blowing off the river had grown worse. As we made our way to rue des Écrivains I could hardly speak, but I wanted to give Raoul some jobs to do. 'Where are Evrard and Marc?' I shouted. 'There are so many things to be done and time is so short.'

'Evrard's gone to his village,' he shouted back. 'Marc's trying, in his own way, to get Jaquet released.'

'Listen. Do you think you could ask Mère Henriette about Maître Guillaume's son? Yes, son. The boy is about sixteen now, and known as le Grec. Get her to tell you everything she knows – especially about the boy's parentage and why he left his home after his mother died.'

'Right. But he would replace Jaquet as the miser's heir!'

'Exactly. Which is why Mère Henriette chose to forget his existence … The other thing is: as I seem to have missed brother P'tit-Jean here in Paris, I might leave suddenly for Anjou or wherever – I mean, should the opportunity arise – and I may not be able to let you know.'

And Jaquet?

'Mariana, don't take any more risks! This P'tit-Jean ... '

'I'll be careful. And I shan't go as Jack Cutting, I'll go as Lady Marian MacElpin. A visiting aristocrat. He'll kiss my hand, be very sweet.'

'Let's pray that is all he does.'

'It will be you taking all the risks. I need you to go to the Albanian.'

'The Albanian?'

'Go by boat to the Porte Saint-Antoine, and find a street urchin to take you on from there. Say you have a message from Doña Mariana. And when you get to him, tell him you have some questions from me for Natalie. She knows you, there will be no difficulty. If there is, say you are my – my man.'

'I wish I were.'

'You are. For now, at least.'

'Hmm. And the questions?'

'First, Natalie's memories of her brother when he was still living at home with them. Second, what happened that night, the night of the miser's death, after Pierre de Montrouge had left the house? Did she see Guillaume again? Did she hear him again? Who opened the door when someone else came? For I believe someone else did come. If it was her who opened the door, then who was that someone else? How long did he stay? Did she see him when he left? And if she did not open the door, what did she hear, what could she guess? Look, there's Kateline – and Marc.'

We told Marc that Jaquet was not Maître Guillaume's heir. Would that help? It should. And if Raoul would accompany him to the office of the avocat who was representing Jaquet – they needed another signature: one from Raoul, who was a theologian and of a good family, would do very well – then he, Marc, would accompany Raoul to the Porte Saint-Antoine, at least, and if possible right into the Cour des Miracles. Raoul was delighted, and off they went.

'Tante Perenelle is waiting for us,' said Kateline. The smile was strained.

Perenelle was sweet, much younger than I had expected, still in her twenties, and like a child with her ready laugh. She worshipped her husband, the professional scrivener and secret alchemist, a plump little man of forty or so with red hair and a red beard.

We talked a little of me, where I came from, what I was doing in Paris, and I could see that they were both fascinated by my Spanish background and my training in Kabbalah.

'I've been telling Nicolas for ages that he should journey to Spain.'

'Just wants to get rid of me,' he joked. But like all older men with sweet young wives, he was never quite sure. Better.

'Silly. Tell Dem'selle Mariana.'

'It is a secret, Dem'selle Mariana – '

'Mariana, please.'

'Mariana. I like that. So, as I say, it's a secret, but as Kateline has told you already that I – '

'Anything you say will go no further, Maître Nicolas. And I trust you will treat what I say, too, in the strictest confidence.'

'Naturally … A few years ago – '

'A few? Twenty!' laughed Perenelle.

'Yes, twenty. It was in thirteen fifty-seven. I bought a book which changed my life. Let me show you.' He went to a cupboard set in the wall, unlocked it with a key, and took out a large brass-bound book. 'You see? These letters and figures on the cover? I knew even then that they were neither Latin nor French.'

'They are Hebrew.'

'Yes, I know that now. And some of these figures are Egyptian. On the first page, look, it says: "Abraham the Jew, Priest, Prince, Levite, Astrologer and Philosopher, to the Nation of the Jews dispersed by the Wrath of God in France, wisheth Health". He means it for the Jews in France, to help them survive, enable them to lend gold by the bag-full that will never be repaid and to pay their taxes and protection money …'

'May I?' I wanted to hold the book, glance through it.

'Mariana, there is a curse on anyone who reads the book being neither priest nor scribe. Look.'

'You?'

He smiled. 'I am a scribe.'

I smiled back at him. 'Me too.'

It was nearly all pictures.

'That picture there,' he pointed, 'that is Saturn, who is time, age, death. And that is Mercurius with the caduceus in his hand: he can overcome time and age and death.'

There was a boyish smile on Mercurius' face, shock and fear on Saturn's ageing features.

I said, 'And the whole of alchemy hinges on what constitutes the Philosophic Mercury, the Divine Tincture – or the Philosopher's Stone, in other words.'

He looked at me. 'Exactly … But what do you make of this one? It has been called the Massacre of the Innocents by some I have consulted – I show individual pictures occasionally, almost never the whole book – but the dead there are not children.'

'No, you are right. And the King and his two followers seem to be in pursuit of the culprit – of Death, shall we say? Couldn't they represent stages in the production of the Philosophic Mercury? With the King on the white lion as the final stage?'

'That seems more likely … This here is the caduceus again. Mercurius represents immortality, life over death.'

'But what are these?' There were two pictures of snakes. One showed many snakes in the open country, seemingly free and happy. The other showed a single large snake, crucified, hanging by its neck and tail from two long nails driven into the arms of a wooden cross.

He shrugged. 'I don't know.'

'The snake is a symbol of immortality.'

'And all these snakes here? Does one snake die that the others may live and have life eternal …? But what else can a snake symbolise? Lust?'

Yes, of course. 'You mean this picture with all the snakes may depict natural innocence, while this other one shows lust crucified?' He hadn't, but it is always wise to give a man the credit for good ideas.

'Something like that.' He sighed. 'I call this book "the Book of Abraham the Jew". It is the one that started it all. But do you know any of these others?'

He went back to his cupboard and produced five more wonderful books, two of which I knew while the others I had only heard of, including that of Artephius, which I begged to be allowed to come back and read at my leisure one day.

He sighed again. 'Perhaps Perenelle is right: I should go to Spain.'

I told him of Maitre Guillaume's journeys to Spain, that it was in Spain that he had first achieved a transmutation. And as I spoke I thought about him and Charlot – and the snake. I would have to ask Nicolas about that picture. I wanted to know who had seen it. But first, I had another question: in a picture in one of the books, a man was pissing into a shallow dish; or was he masturbating? I asked Nicolas.

Perenelle and Kateline both laughed, and Perenelle blushed. It would take more than that to make Kateline blush.

'Pissing, I suppose,' Nicolas said. 'But look at this one.' It was a boy - or possibly a hermaphrodite, a common symbol in alchemy - standing inside a glass retort, also pissing: there seemed to be a pool of urine in the bottom of the retort. 'But with Kabbalists and alchemists, I have discovered, what something seems to be is rarely what it is.'

I smiled. My mind was on Natalie now. I had not asked her about urine.

'The urine would have to be that of a virgin?'

He nodded. 'Of course. And pure in mind, as well as in body. Innocent.'

'Could she be a - '

'Not "she". It has to be a boy - or a man, if such a man can be found. The urine produced by a girl or woman is too strong; the authorities all agree on that.'

Interesting. I'd always supposed that men's piss was the stronger: the stench emanating from the walls and alleys they favoured as pissoirs certainly gave that impression.

'I used to get urine from street urchins - blood, too - but I've stopped those experiments for the moment. Now I'm reading and thinking deeply about the use of the Philosopher's Stone as an elixir of life, trying to ascertain whether the Stone that gives life is the same as the Stone, the Philosophic Tincture, which transmutes all metals into silver and gold. When I'm ready, I'll recommence my experiments. But shall I ever be ready?'

'I think you are right, you do need to go to León, Maître Nicolas. I agree with Perenelle.'

He nodded glumly. Obviously not one for the open road. I had a strange thought: I said 'If you found the Elixir of Life, you wouldn't want to spend all eternity in Paris, would you?'

He gazed at me. 'No. No, I shan't want to do that ... Most of it, though.' He was in earnest.

'May I see your hands?'

'My hands?'

'Chiromancy is one of my main interests, along with astrology. And the Kabbalah, of course.'

He held out his hands. 'As above, so below. The microcosm. The large in the small. One's whole life written in each hair, if one could but read it. The ocean in each drop of water: not just the ocean, the world, the whole universe. Does it not say something like that in the Book of Splendour?'

The Book of Splendour. The Zohar. 'Oh, yes.'

On his left hand the Line of Life curved right round the Mount of Venus and, without touching the First Bracelet, reached the back of the hand before it disappeared. On the right hand, it was the same. I had never seen such long Life Lines before. But what was stranger was that on the right hand only, meaning it was perhaps not something he had been born with but something that had developed during his life, there was a second Line of Life running parallel to the first, traversing the "foothills" of the Mount of Venus: all right, it was just a Mars Line, if you like, but I had never seen, never heard of a Mars Line like this, as long and as deep as the Life Line itself and running exactly parallel to it. What did it mean?

I gave him his hands back.

Perenelle was looking from him to me, from me to him. Where had Kateline gone? I hadn't noticed her leave the room.

'I'd like very much to come back and read your hands properly sometime, Maître Nicolas, and cast your horoscope. Unfortunately, I have to go now. I promised to visit Jaquet le Breton in the Châtelet.'

'Ah yes, poor boy. It is so kind of you to try to help him. If I can do anything ... '

'There is one very important question I should like to ask you, Maître Nicolas.'

He nodded. 'Of course.'

'Who else have you shown these pictures to? Especially the picture of the Crucified Snake.'

'Recently, you mean?' He mentioned a few names, none of which meant anything to me, and none of whom had shown any particular interest in that picture.

Then Perenelle said, hesitantly, 'There was the Abbé Soxxal – oh, about six months ago.'

'Ah yes, I forgot about him. He was against alchemy, of course. Concerned that I might be practising it, not merely studying it. I think I managed to put him off the scent.'

I doubted it.

'And the Queen in Normandy,' said Perenelle.

'Ah, yes, but we mustn't … ' he interrupted, then looked at me, appealing to me not to pursue the matter.

I smiled. 'If you mean the Countess Blanche d'Evreux in her castle at Gisors, then her secrets are safe with me.'

'You know her?'

'I had long talks with her when we were both in Avignon. But not on the subject of alchemy. Our common interest was something quite different.'

But I had to go. We arranged that I should send a message through Kateline when I was free to visit them again, and I took my leave.

Pietri's little shop was all closed up now. The world changed. Moved on. Nothing was for ever. The whole world changed each moment, did we but know it.

As I crossed the street to the Châtelet, a beggar approached me.

Suddenly the beggar was thrust away and I felt my arm grabbed. I was being attacked by two men, both trying to get

hold of me, my arms, my body. One grabbed one of my breasts,
a hand squeezed, hard.

I whirled round.

The man shouted: 'She is a woman!'

'No matter! Bring her anyway!'

I whirled again, desperate to free my arms, my legs, but it was
hopeless, the long, thick skirt and petticoat were like deep water,
like a nightmare of being unable to kick –

Beside me, a cultured voice said, 'May I be of assistance,
dem'selle?'

A horse, the rider leaning down, offering his hand.

'You may indeed, messire!' I jumped, the hand pulled, the
horse moved away, and I found myself sitting on his lap.

Then it seemed to me that the men in the street had let me go.
And I realised that there were two men on horses, not just one.

'Be calm, dem'selle. Those were the Abbé Soxxal's men. You
are better with us.'

'But – you were collaborating with them!'

'What on earth gave you that impression?'

'They made no attempt to – '

'They were taken by surprise. And perhaps a little intimidated
when they saw who we were.'

'Who are you?'

He smiled. 'We are the Devil's men.'

'The Devil?'

'The Devil of the Vilaine.'

'Devil …' I mocked.

'Sleep now,' he said. 'We have a long journey before us.'

I laughed at him. Too young, too ready with my certainties
and my mockery. 'Do you think you are talking to a child?'

'Sleep.' He snapped his fingers.

And I slept, on his chest.

16

I wasn't simply asleep. I was dreaming.

I knew I was dreaming.

And I needed someone.

Who? Maître Flamel? Nicolas? Such a small man. So unimpressive.

But that hand, that hand!

He couldn't help me, though. He was so uninvolved, so uncommitted. An outsider still.

Nor could Maître Thomas of Pizan. Another small man.

My mind flew to Uncle Yacoub: Yacoub of Murcia. Were all magicians, all great masters, then, little men? Of course not. Albertus Magnus had been a great man in every sense. But I had been taller than Yacoub when I was thirteen. The last time I saw him.

I wanted to see him again! I wanted him back! There was so much I had forgotten, so much I never knew.

Could I get in touch with him? As I had then? As we had then?

I had tried many times when we were first separated, but without success. I couldn't find him, couldn't contact him. I had never been conscious while sleeping, though, as I had when I was a child and we planned to meet in our dreams - and as I was now, sitting on the lap of this fat man who, I suddenly realised, was a priest, not a warrior. I was asleep, my eyes were closed, and yet I could see myself, see him, see the man riding alongside.

'Yacoub!' My cry echoed through the empty corridors of my mind. 'Yacoub! I miss you! I want to sit at your feet once more as I did when I was a child!' And I found myself flying with the cry, I was the cry, echoing down a great tunnel.

The tunnel grew light, opened onto a grey coast. I was standing in the mouth of a cave. Far below me, at the foot of the cliff, was a sandy bay. It was silent. The waves broke but I couldn't hear them. If I fell, I would be killed. Panicking, I clung to the rocky wall at the mouth of the cave.

'Jump!'

The voice was in my mind.

'I'm on the beach. Yes, there, you see me now.'

He was a tiny figure, unmoving, on the far side of the bay.

'Jump, and come to me.'

'But it - '

'Jump. Trust me.'

If I couldn't trust Yacoub, I couldn't trust anyone.

But was it Yacoub?

Or was it the Counterfeit Din, the Evil Urge, tempting me to my death?

The Devil.

'Yacoub!' I cried. My mouth, my tongue, worked, but no sound issued from it. 'Yacoub! What did I play with when I was a toddler still? Play with and give a name to?'

'A stone. Now jump!'

'What did I name it?'

'You had two stones. One named Magnus, the other Mariana. Jump!'

I jumped.

My first - last? - thought was: If you die in your dreams, do you die in reality? Then I was floating, floating, floating down. I landed lightly on soft dry sand well above the tide line. I was thrilled. I tried to do it again, to float - fly - to where Uncle Yacoub was waiting for me.

It didn't work. I crashed forward onto the sand, heard Uncle Yacoub laughing in my head, laughing and calling: 'Walk!'

Yacoub never laughed when I did something silly. Never.

'You are not Yacoub.'

'You called for Yacoub - because you needed help.'

'Who are you?'

'Come.'

I looked back up at the dark hole in the cliff. I looked out across the sand, across the breaking waves, the grey sea. Far out, the sun was shining through a break in the clouds. Gulls swooped and soared. Yet all was silent as a picture, a painted world. A dream world.

Should I walk away in the other direction?

I saw a white horse coming along the beach from that other direction. It veered towards me. It had seen me. It came right up to me. Stopped. Lowered its head.

I put my hand to its neck. It was cool, smooth, and dry.

Let the horse take me where it would. I looked down at myself, realising suddenly that I was not dressed as I had been, would not need a high rock to serve as a mounting block: I was wearing only some kind of hose such as men wear, white, and a short white gypon. I sprang up onto the horse, gripped him with my legs and feet and grabbed his mane. We were away.

As I rode, I could hear the man who was not Yacoub saying, in my head, 'This is what was called in the old days, in your father's country, a Shelti world. Here you find answers; or if not answers, help, and strength.'

'Who are you?'

'You.'

'Me?'

'In another life. Only here in this world may we meet.' There was a long pause while I thought about that. Then he said, 'Yacoub would not have laughed, but Mariana would.'

I bowed my head. It was true.

And then I was there, but it wasn't a man now, it was an owl, a great snowy owl perched on the rock, feathers ruffling in the sea wind.

I still thought that in some way the owl was, or at least represented, Yacoub. I slid down off the horse and sat on the sand, my chin on my knees.

I gazed up at the owl.

'You know little of alchemy, but who can help you? Nicolas Flamel cannot help you.' He stared back at me, blinking wisely. I wanted to laugh. 'All right, laugh,' he said. 'Then when you have finished laughing, listen.'

That sounded like Yacoub.

I didn't laugh, but he waited anyway till I had got used to his disapproving expression, his yellow eyes, the sharp beak and his sheer size, standing there towering over me. He could tear me apart, I realised, with that beak, those long talons all thickly covered with white feathers and ending in shiny black claws like the claws of a great cat.

Was he so big? Or was I so small, in this dream, this dream-world?

He blinked again, and suddenly he was no longer a snowy owl but a little white-breasted barn owl with a beautiful heart-shaped face and I realised he was not a he but a she: 'I didn't mean to frighten you,' she said, and now her face was not disapproving but sad. 'Listen.' The voice was quite different, too. The snowy owl had been a male then, if the voice was anything to go by. Or perhaps all snowy owls speak like that. 'In alchemy,' she said, 'there are three phases: the first phase is practica - the practical aspect, trying this, trying that. Then there is theoria, the phase Nicolas Flamel is starting on now: thinking about it, thinking deeply, attempting to fathom the mysteries of matter and of life.'

She paused, and I said, 'Yes? That is so. And the third phase you mentioned?'

'The third phase occurs when feeling, the heart, enters into it: as it must. I am not sure Flamel can accomplish this phase without help. But he has help there, someone ready to help him, someone who is all heart.'

'Perenelle.'

'Exactly.'

'But she is not a virgin.'

'Heart is not a matter of being, literally, in the body, virgo intacta. It is a matter of innocence, of being uncorrupted by the world, of being naïve.'

'Of being a fool.'

'If you like.'

I thought of Natalie, Maître Guillaume's virgin. She was no fool. Would never be a vagabond, be whipped out of the town. 'Tell me,' I said, 'did Natalie ever get upset, ever cry, over the fate of the mice?'

'I only know what you know of your world, your little world.'

Of course.

She put the question back to me. 'Do you suppose that she did?'

'Yes, I imagine she used to get very upset. And at that time she would have been able to help Guillaume le Breton in his endeavours. But in time she was made callous, became inured to pain – as we must if we are not to remain like children all our lives.'

'What is a fool but a child who has grown but not grown up?'

'Towards the end, she will have been no help to him at all. On the other hand, I think he himself must have been softened by the death of Charlot and by his great love for Lule. When she too died, his heart broke. He became gradually more and more able to be his own source of heart and feeling, his own fool.'

'From a broken heart, the hardness and corruption and the sin may all leak.'

'And innocence seep back in?' Or is innocence simply the absence of hardness and corruption and sin?

Does one become more corrupt or less through successive lives? Is one born innocent – or born in sin, as the Church teaches? If so, is that sin the residue of past lives? Is this owl the

past or the future? Was I her once? Or will I be her one day? And
the man I took at first for Yacoub? Were we all one?

  She smiled. Really. Something about the beak, the eyes,
changed. 'That is not for you to know … Listen. Alchemy is not
the point at issue here. Enough for you to know that Guillaume le
Breton still had much gold when he was murdered, and the secret
of its manufacture, the Divine Tincture which is also the secret of
– not immortality, but such longevity as may be desirable for one
poor body: hundreds, nay thousands, of years. He was not
interested. Lule was lost to him. Natalie, whom he loved as a
daughter, was the daughter of, and had something of the look of,
his worst enemy, his nightmare … What more do you need to
know of alchemy? It is not for you. It will destroy your life and
that of those around you. Leave it.'

  She was right.

  'What you really needed the help of Yacoub with was not
alchemy, or even the devil. You can handle any devil, any
manifestation of the Counterfeit Din, of evil and injustice. No, it
was to ask about Kabbalah and Tarocchi, Kabbalah and alchemy,
and for the comparatively simple problem of deciphering the
esoteric Hebrew in which that other scrap of paper is written. He
is the only Kabbalist you know … Rabbi Yacoub has been in
Lithuania all these years. Is now in some small town in
Muscovy. You cannot contact him because he cut you off, set
you free. You were too close: so close he failed you, he says – '

  NO! my mind cries, but I am silent, silent as the breaking
waves, the wheeling gulls, the wind.

  'But it is nothing, some notes on the preparation of the Divine
Tincture – which, as I say, is not for you. The will is far more
interesting. What does that say?'

  'It's an old one.'

  'It is not. Think about it.'

  I did. Again, she was right.

  'Do you remember?'

'Not all, but he leaves the gold to Natalie, and says the first clue as to where the gold is hidden is where one would expect an astrologer to hide something for her. It also says: To my nephew Jaquet le Breton, I leave my adopted daughter Natalie – if she will have him.' I laughed.

The little barn owl was gazing at me, reading my mind, and carried on for me: 'He adds, "Whoever you are, my lady – for I have seen you take this document, seen you many times – I am almost as good at scrying now as Charlot was, though I still use Natalie's blood – whoever you are, my lady mermaid with the sea-green eyes, and whatever your interest in this affair, beware the Abbé Soxxal …" I think he must mean you.'

The abbé? Was he then the truly dangerous one?

'Your eyes change colour with the sea, now blue, now green, now grey. He is right, I think. Beware l'abbé. Now swim.'

'Swim?'

'You are not called a mermaid here in this world for nothing.'

I stood up, looked round. There was nobody here but the owl and the horse. I took off my hose and gypon, and slipped into the sea as I had so often slipped into the Mar Menor at home, and swam. But I had never swum like this! I ran my hands down over my hips. What had happened to my legs? My first reaction was to panic, but that was only for a second. This was a dream … I swam, hips working, great tail undulating like a dolphin's, then dived, down, down, away from the sunlight, down into a green world, green water, brown muddy sand, seaweed, shoals of little fish come to inspect me: one bit me, but it was hardly more than a touch of tiny cold lips, a kiss. Then more of them kissed me.

Laughing, and remembering the owl, I swam to the beach and put my head out, hands on the sand beneath me, waves breaking gently around me.

The horse had gone, but the barn owl was still there, blinking at me.

'Et le Diable?' I called. 'The devil I go to meet?'

'The end is in the beginning and the beginning is in the end, as it is written, but we poor mortals living here beneath the changing Moon do not see the end until we reach it.'

That certainly sounded like Yacoub again.

I felt myself slipping away, a current dragging me back tail first into the sea.

'Be patient.'

My hands were pulling free of the sand.

'You can come here any time.'

But I was slipping back down into the depths, was in the tunnel again, was back in my body on the horse, on the rider's lap. With two legs, two feet.

I took a deep breath. Realised I hadn't had to breathe while I was underwater.

Then found that I was still asleep.

When I awoke, we were riding along a road through a forest. Heading west, into the setting sun. The two men were staring at me. I gave them a weak smile.

They both instantly grinned back at me.

Well, that was encouraging.

The one I was riding with, the big one who had somehow put me to sleep, said: 'Shall we introduce ourselves? I am Maître Baudouin Herault, Canon of Saint Benoît – '

'Oh, I know! In the rue Saint-Jacques, close to where I live.'

'Yes, and no doubt less importantly, close to the Sorbonne. And this is Père Pierre le Mesurier of Saint Aubin. We all of course know who you are.'

'Do we?'

'Doña Mariana de la Mar, also known as the student Magnus of Orkney, also known to the good Abbé Soxxal as Jack Cutting, Esquire.'

'Wrong on all counts, maître, I am afraid. I am Lady Marian MacElpin of the County of Ross in the Kingdom of Scotland.'

'Ah. That was the one I did not, could not, believe. Though Père Pierre was impressed by it.'

'It was the fact that you have Scottish eyes, my lady,' murmured Père Pierre. 'The sergeant at Le Châtelet agreed with me. That and the perhaps equally salient fact that your woman at home – the Moorish slave, Khadija – informed me that her mistress was Mariana MacElpin.'

'You didn't mention that to me,' Maître Herault reproached him.

'You were so sure she was Spanish, and you may have been right.'

'You were half right, maître,' I said, sorry for him. 'My mother was Spanish. De la Mar is my Spanish name. And Magnus MacElpin is my twin brother's name.'

'Really? You have a twin brother?'

'Really, maître.'

'So "Jack Cutting" was your twin brother? Not you at all?'

I could have said "Yes". It would probably have been better to say "Yes". But this Canon had such a soulful expression (it reminded me suddenly of the barn owl) and seemed so disappointed at the thought of having to go back to Paris and find another more elusive me, that I admitted, 'No. Jack Cutting was me, a creature of fantasy created for the amusement of the one you call "the good abbé".'

They were both grinning at me again.

'You seem very friendly for kidnappers. Surely you realise that you could end your lives on the gallows.'

'We did not kidnap you, señora.'

'My lady,' put in Père Pierre, smugly.

'My lady, yes, sorry. We rescued you. Those men who seized you were the Abbé – '

'Yes, you told me: the Abbé Soxxal's men. You also told me that you were the Devil's men. Which is worse?'

'In this case, my lady, believe me, the abbé's men.'

'Much worse,' agreed Père Pierre. 'L'Abbé est un diable. The Devil is not.'

I was very thirsty. There was una borracha, a leather flagon, on the Canon's saddle. 'What's in that? Wine?'

'Mostly water.' He undid it and passed it to me.

I held it up and squirted a jet of watered-down wine into my mouth. And carried on squirting and gulping till I felt better.

When I had finished, I looked at them. I chose Père Pierre. 'Would you care to explain that about the Devil not being a devil?'

'Our master … Our master …'

The Canon helped him out: 'Our master's attention was drawn to you by – '

'The Sire de Montrouge,' I interrupted.

'I wouldn't say that, no. No. By his steward, in fact.'

'Ah oui. Le Boeuf.'

'Exactement. And he sent me to enquire about you – me because I know Paris. Unfortunately, Paris knows me. So our master sent Père Pierre along with me. He does not know Paris, but Paris does not know him either, so he was able to move around openly asking questions about – ah – a certain ewe-lamb from his fold, "an ewe-lamb which was lost".'

'Me?'

They both nodded and grinned again.

'And did you have orders to kidnap me?'

'No. To pick you up and bring you to him, out of harm's way, if necessary. It was necessary.'

True.

'Tell me about yourselves. How you come to be working for – le Diable – when you are a Canon of Saint-Benoît, and you are the curé of a church. Saint Aubin? Isn't that on Jersey?'

'Oh, not that Saint Aubin, my lady. My village, my church, lies to the north of Rennes. One winter afternoon it was attacked by tard-venus – English soldiers abandoned in France by their leaders. The church was robbed and the blood of those who took shelter there was shed.'

'The church had been defiled. It could not function as a church again till it had been reconciled and reconsecrated,' explained the Canon.

'Which cost far more than we could afford,' finished Père Pierre.

'The Bishop would not help?' I asked.

'The Bishop? He sent men – but not to help: to harrass us for our church taxes. Eventually, after we'd been given a final warning by the Bishop's men, I set out in search of le Diable. I had with me two small boys whose father had been killed defending the village and whose mother had died soon afterwards as a result of – of the brutal treatment she had received at the hands of the tard-venus.'

'I see. And you found le Diable.'

'He found us, sleeping out in the forest.'

'And you, Canon?'

'I was accused of teaching false doctrine. Of heresy. I was warned that my arrest was imminent. That I would be put to the question. Be burnt. They burn heretics now, my lady. As you must be only too well aware if you come from Spain.'

'I spent some months in the south of France, too, which is worse. And is where the Inquisition started, don't forget.'

'Paris itself is almost as bad, these days. There are black friars acting for the Inquisition sitting like great bats at every lecture.'

I had noticed them.

'In what had you erred, maître?'

'You know something of theology?'

'I have attended lectures at the Sorbonne – as young Sir Magnus MacElpin of Orkney.'

They both grinned again.

'But I haven't heard you lecture.'

'I have been with the Devil now for more than a year … Being pressed by some students, I admitted that I thought Origen right on the question of Universal Salvation.'

'He taught that in the end no one would be condemned, not even le Diable,' explained Père Pierre with a grin. 'All would be saved and go to heaven.'

'But it wasn't only that. Under pressure from the Bishop's gang, I said that in his case an exception might be made. After all, Origen had never met our Bishop.'

I laughed. 'You're not going to make friends like that.'

'I have made many good friends just like that. There are a surprisingly large number of good men on the Devil's side.'

'May I ask if this Devil has a name? And what his interest in me might be?'

'He is Jean, Sire de Montrouge – '

'P'tit-Jean!' I almost fell from the horse. 'Then you have kidnapped me!'

'No!'

'Sit still!'

'Please, my lady!'

'Calm yourself.'

'What is it that you have against P'tit-Jean?'

'For a start, he killed a man I knew, Maître Pietri, in Paris on the Pont-au-Change, this morning.'

'P'tit-Jean is not in Paris. He sent us to – '

'To murder Maître Pietri?'

'No!'

'And he was certainly in Paris for the funeral of his brother, Pierre, whom he probably killed. He also probably killed Maître Guillaume le Breton. And that is his interest in me, for I am interested in the murder of Maître Guillaume.'

'No, my lady. He did none of these things.'

We were silent.

Then I said: 'You will tell me next that P'tit-Jean has never killed anyone. That he is a good man.'

They looked at each other.

'No,' said the Canon, 'no, I would not say that. He has killed, but he is not a bad man. We are what some term "routiers" – highway robbers – and others "écorcheurs" – skinners of the rich; the Pope has named us "sons of iniquity".'

'We are men who, faced with the choice between stealing and starving, chose stealing,' went on Père Pierre. 'Many écorcheurs are soldiers, or were soldiers, no different really from the tard-venus who attacked my village and church. Except that Messire Jean would never allow us to attack a defenceless village.'

'We steal from rich travellers. We hunt deer and wildboar in the forest.'

'For the hunting alone we would be hanged,' put in Père Pierre.

'We sometimes kidnap rich or important men and hold them to ransom. What else? Ah yes. The town of Rennes, our nearest sizeable town, pays us money to protect it.'

'Protect it from others like yourselves.'

'As you say. But we do protect it.'

'Are we going all the way to Rennes?' I asked, realising suddenly how far that was. Nearly as far as St Malo.

'No, Messire Jean has a house in Le Mans, where he is known as Evrond du Bois. He will meet us there.'

Le Mans? Where Ferchard was hoping his beautiful widow might still be?

'We shall stop for the night soon. Tomorrow we shall pass through Chartres, and be half way there.'

We never got to Le Mans, or even Chartres. We spent the night at the auberge in one large bed, me in the middle between the priest and the theologian, all fully dressed except that I took my boots off. Herault kept his on: the more orthodox the theology, the smellier the feet, he laughed – but he kept them on, as I say, out of consideration for me.

Père Pierre, who was wearing only sandals, sniffed as I removed mine, looked incredulous, and said, 'You must be a great heretic, my lady.'

Maître Herault was shocked. 'That law does not apply to ladies, Père Pierre. You'll have to forgive him, my lady, he's a complete peasant. Should we make him sleep on the floor?'

'No, on the whole I think I'll feel safer with the two of you on the bed with me, one on each side.'

'You are right, my lady,' said Père Pierre. 'The Canons of Saint-Benoît are quite as bad as those of Notre Dame – '

'I meant safe from attack from outside,' I smiled. 'I am a great admirer of Maître Abelard's. His theology, bien sûr.'

'Bien sûr,' murmured Maître Herault.

We all lay down.

It was very cold.

17

When I woke, I was warm. Each of them had one arm over me, one leg over me.

And someone was knocking on the door. It opened. The landlord looked in. 'My lady! There are people here asking for you and your two companions.'

My companions were still snoring, Herault loudly, Père Pierre softly, contentedly. I removed their arms, sat up. The landlord removed their legs, and gave me a hand. When I was sitting on the end of the bed between their feet, I said: 'Who?'

He passed me my boots. 'Le Sire de Montrouge, Sir Farquhar de – somewhere – and a lady. A fine lady, dem'selle. You have nothing to fear.'

Estelle de Saint-Samson de Montrouge did have a five-year-old daughter called Isabeau, and this daughter had indeed gone missing. When she learned that I had news of the child, she turned pale and swayed, and it was I who caught her. Then she clung to me.

I was reminded of the time I saved the man from drowning in the open sea, he too had clung to me, but this was different: it wasn't her who was drowning, it was her child who had sunk without trace, and whom I, the mermaid, would now restore to her waiting arms.

She was small - I could hold her up easily - and she was dressed all in black. When the veil came off, it revealed a woman still young, still beautiful, with big blue and hazel eyes and, beneath the chaplet, light brown hair.

Then a large man, as large as Ferchard and much younger, attempted to take her. She clung to me. Together, we led her to a bench and sat her down. Would she like to lie down? No, she just wanted to sit beside me, hear all I knew.

'Let us be, Jean. Make sure that the horses are ready for us to leave.'

Jean?

But where was my Jean? P'tit-Jean. The Devil.

'Who is that, madame?' I murmured, as he left.

'My cousin, Jean. Le Sire de Montrouge. He inherited the title when his brother Pierre was - died - last week.'

P'tit-Jean? But …?

'So tell me, I beg you, dem'selle.'

I told her the little I knew. It was enough. Her sobs were sobs of joy.

'And they haven't harmed her?'

'No.'

'She will still be there?'

'Oh yes, I am sure she will.'

'But why should he do a thing like that? Pierre, I mean. Did you know Messire Pierre? No? He was a bad man, it has to be said.' She crossed herself. 'Not like Messire Jean, bad in public and by reputation, but good in private. Pierre was worse in private.'

I had definitely gone astray here. 'Is there someone else? Another brother, or a cousin, but a small man. Maybe living in Paris, and running up debts?'

'No, no. Jean is all we have left.'

'And the next in line after Messire Jean?'

'That will be my daughter – my daughter's husband – when she grows up. Unless of course Jean produces a son before then. Which I pray he will. I swear there is a curse upon this title.'

'And Messire Jean, your cousin ... he is the one known as P'tit-Jean?'

She smiled. 'Yes. You have heard of him. Well, he has a reputation. Not undeserved. Jean was born to be a leader, but had the misfortune to be born the younger son with a fool for an elder half-brother and an even greater fool for a father. All around, the land was being plundered by those who had once been soldiers but were now leaderless and desperate; the peasants, their fields burnt year after year and their pitiful stores raided, were starving; he could do nothing. He went away. He travelled. And when he came back, years later, he found his half-brother Pierre now Sire de Montrouge. He also found that a peasant who had been a childhood friend of his had died at Pierre's hands while attempting to protect his sister from Pierre. Then another woman, Fleur, a prisoner in the castle, appealed to Jean to save her and he fled with her into the forest. That was six years ago. Now he is the leader of a band of routiers. They do live outside the law, yes. They steal from rich travellers. But much of Jean's evil reputation was given him by his jealous brother, Pierre. God rest his soul.'

Six years? And Fleur, now?

I wouldn't ask.

I wasn't going to need to. I caught her eye. She smiled that

angelic smile again. 'Fleur is their Queen.'
   The tall, and very handsome, Jean, Sire de Montrouge,
returned to tell us that all was prepared for our departure.

I rode my own horse now, as did Estelle. Maître Herault and Père
Pierre we had left at the inn. Jean had woken them before we
left, and I had given them each a farewell kiss: they had been
kind to me, and I loved them both.
   'Now will you ever come to visit us in our forest home?' they
said.
   'Oh yes!' And I did – but that is another story.
   We raced back towards Paris, stopping only to change horses
and for something to eat and drink. We arrived, frozen and
exhausted, just before they locked the gates, and went to my
house: theirs was closed up and, they said, unavailable.
   Yahia must have put me to bed, for I remember nothing else.

Next morning, although Estelle was pressing me, gently but
insistently, to go and find the child, I had to agree with Khadija
for once: I needed breakfast. I was exhausted and starving.
   And while we ate, all four of us – Ferchard and Jean, like me,
wolfing the warm sweet-smelling bread, Estelle sipping an
infusion of basil (which Khadija managed to grow in a sunny
corner) – le Cafard arrived.
   I introduced him.
   'A fifth for breakfast,' laughed Jean.
   'He comes too often, eats too much,' grumbled Khadija. 'We
don't have enough.'
   'What does she say?' asked Estelle.
   Ferchard translated.
   'Tell her he can have mine.'
   Ferchard did so. I watched, smiling. It wasn't easy to win an
argument with Khadija, even for old hands like me. Estelle had
done it in six words, first time out.

The boy stood by the door, eating the bread, and some cheese Khadija had put with it, and gazed at us.

Suddenly I realised (I was still half asleep) that he had not come just for his breakfast. 'Do you have something for me, le Cafard? Some news?'

He nodded. Glanced pointedly at the others.

'What does it concern? The house you were set to watch?'

He shook his head.

Then ... 'You've found the page-boy?'

He nodded.

I jumped up, ran over and gave him a hug and a kiss, while Khadija tut-tutted in the background. It was true he smelt, but — oh!

'Ferchard, give me a silver sou.'

He turned to Estelle. 'They've found Pierre's boy.'

'Pierre's boy? But then Jean, you pay him! And if the boy — what did they call him? Coco? — knows anything of what happened that night, of how Pierre died — '

'And how Maître le Breton died,' I put in.

'Yes — then you must give this poor child a gold coin!'

Jean laughed, and beckoned the boy to him. 'You heard the lady — what's your name? Le Cafard? Le Cafard. I like that. You heard the lady, le Cafard. This is for you now. And when you deliver the boy to us and he answers our questions you will get a gold livre. D'accord?'

Le Cafard nodded. 'Oui, messire. But he's frightened. He fears the Albanian. And he fears the family of Messire de Montrouge.'

'But — '

I interrupted Jean. 'He need not fear me.'

'I know that, madame, but he doesn't. You're rich, you're a lady, you have powerful friends, you — '

'Does he know Jack Cutting?'

Le Cafard looked at me and grinned. 'Yes. And he likes what he has seen and heard of him.'

'He has seen him?'
'He was outside La Adriatica when Sire Jacques went in.'
Sire Jacques?
'So because - you know, La Adriatica - he thought Sire
Jacques must be one of the Albanian's men, someone to avoid.
Then he saw the sergeants arrive, and heard who they were
hunting. And he heard that Sire Jacques had got away, and that
everyone was hunting him: the sergeants, the Albanian, l'Abbé
and the Church ...'
'So he likes him.'
'Oh, yes.'
'He also likes me, and trusts me,' said Estelle. 'Which is more
to the point. Bring him here, tell him that Madame Estelle says
he will be safe.'
'He will not come here, madame.'
'Then - '
'Tell him to be outside Les Halles,' I said. 'He will see
Madame Estelle and Jack Cutting together. If he should choose
to speak to them, that will certainly be to his advantage. Hurry
now. There is not much time.'

Estelle and I went to Les Halles alone. P'tit-Jean had wanted to
accompany us, with Ferchard, but the boy would have been sure
to spot them.
'How? We will stay well behind you. And when we get to Les
Halles - '
'He will not be waiting for us at Les Halles, he will follow us
there.'
'From here, you mean?'
'From somewhere along the route,' Ferchard agreed, 'the Petit-
Pont perhaps, to check whether anyone else is following. And if
we try to spot him and catch him, he'll run off and we'll never see
him again.'
So they waited in the house while Estelle and I walked across

to the Right Bank and through the crowds in the rue Saint-Denis
- I as Jack Cutting, elegant in brown cloak over a short cote-
hardie and hose: Coco would know it was "me".

'I hate Paris,' murmured Estelle. "So much ordure and smell,
so much noise.'

'The smell was much worse in the summer.'

'Oh yes, it's worse when it's hot.'

'But there aren't usually so many people. Perhaps they're
performing an unusual execution.' I saw Heloys la lavendière,
who did most of our washing for us - Khadija was too old now,
but of course she insisted that Heloys didn't do it properly. I
asked what was happening.

'They're boiling a forger!' she told me, excited, 'Sire James
l'escrivain!' and pushed her way on through the crowd.

Estelle shuddered.

We got as close to Les Halles as we could, then stood and
waited.

Le Cafard emerged from the swirling crowd and beckoned to
us. Estelle looked at me. I nodded.

We followed le Cafard along the rue des Halles. He turned
into a narrow alley. It was dark and suddenly quiet. He whistled.

A small cloaked figure appeared from a doorway.

Le Cafard performed the introductions. 'Coco, this is Madame
Estelle - you know her. And you also know Sire Jacques. '

A black face showed from within the hood. A smile. White
teeth.

'Coco, qu'est-ce que tu fais ici?' Estelle demanded. 'Why
didn't you come to me?'

'Coco, where can we talk?'

He gazed at me, big eyes, the whites slightly bloodshot. From
lack of sleep? From crying? Where had he been sleeping? I
wondered where he was from, how he coped with this weather.

'Will you come with me to the house of Dem'selle Mariana?
We will be safe there.'

He shook his head. 'Down by the river.' His first words.

'It will be cold down there!' Estelle objected.

'Just for a while,' I said. 'Come on.' I looked at le Cafard, back at Coco. 'Do you want le Cafard with us?'

'No. But you stay, Sir Jack.'

He said "Sir Jack" much better than le Cafard could. I smiled at him and thanked le Cafard, who nodded, and hurried off with a wave and a grin.

I held my hand out to Coco. He stared at it. Took it, gingerly. Then with Estelle on my other arm, I made my way down to the river, leaving le Cafard to watch poor Sire (Sir?) James – was he English? Scottish? – come to his dreadful end.

We went right down to the water. The bridge was high above us to our left, the water swirling endlessly round the piers at the base of the huge pillars. It was Friday, the first of January: the worst of winter was still to come.

'Coco, listen. I'm on your side. Unconditionally. I'm your friend whatever happens, and whatever happened that night you left Messire Pierre and ran away. Though I want to know why you ran away, who or what you ran away from, what frightened you; and also where you ran away from: was it from home, or from somewhere else?'

He gazed up at me, glanced at Estelle.

'Madame is also on your side, just so long as you played no part, however small, in bringing about her cousin's death. Did you?'

He shook his head, silent still. Then suddenly burst into tears – needing to trust someone, tell someone. 'It was the Albanian … ' Then went on sobbing.

'Albanian?' asked Estelle, finally.

'Tell us from the beginning,' I suggested. 'That night. How did it start? What happened first?'

He stared up at me.

I sat down on a big round stone. It was damp and dirty, but it put me at his level. 'Did your master go to the Albanian? Did the Albanian come to your master?'

He nodded slightly.

'Was this before your master called on Maître Guillaume the miser?'

Another slight nod.

'Was the Albanian alone when he called?'

'The - the first time, he was alone, yes. He just appeared in the room where my master was drinking. My master had been telling me he was going into the Cité. "Do you want to come with me?" "Oh, yes! Please!" "You'll have to wait outside in the cold at some of the places, Coco, mon fils. Still, you're used to that." He always called me "Coco, mon fils", when he was sad.'

'And when he was happy?'

'"Sunshine", he called me, "Sunshine". He was good to me, he was kind, whatever other people say!' More tears.

'And then? The Albanian walked in unannounced?'

'Yes. My master jumped up. "What the Devil?" "Sit down, messire. Let's all sit down, shall we?" They both sat. The Albanian was not smiling. He never smiled. But he looked sort of happy today - I don't know - something in his eyes. Sort of pleased. "How are you, messire?" he asked. "I - I am well." "Good. Because your time has run out." "Today?" My master cried, and leapt to his feet, clutching at his throat. "Tonight," said the Albanian. "But you said in the new year! The new year is not - " "Sit down, messire." My master sat back down. His face was pouring with sweat. "It will be New Year very soon, and I am a little pressed. I can wait no longer."'

'Wait for what?' asked Estelle. 'What did he mean? Do you know, Coco?'

I looked from her to Coco. Had Pierre been borrowing money from the Albanian? Surely not. Yet ...

'Oui, madame. He owed the Albanian money. A lot of money. He had written his name on a paper. "I just signed away my life,

Coco, mon fils," he said to me, after he wrote his name on that paper.'

'When was that?' I asked.

'In the summer. He had six months. Half a year, the Albanian called it.'

And, of course, he had no idea who the Albanian really was.

'Did you ever ask him why the Albanian wanted his life?'

The boy nodded. 'He said: "He doesn't. That's just how he makes sure he gets his money back." "But if you haven't got the money?" "I die." "How does that help the Albanian?" "It sets a fine example to the others."'

'And then what happened? The Albanian left?'

'Yes. He said he would be back.'

'And was he? I mean, did he come back?'

'Yes! He came back and he killed my master, as he said he would!'

'Who is this Albanian?' Estelle asked.

'I'll tell you later, at home, in the warm. I know that part of the story, and I understand it now, but I still don't know what happened at Maître Guillaume's house. Coco, did your master go out as planned, or did he change his mind and stay at home?'

'He went out. We went out. He took me with him.'

Ah ha! 'And where did you go?'

'We went to the cockpit in the rue de l'Enfer, and my master staked what gold he had left on a big yellow-skinned game-cock with dark red feathers round its neck where they leave the feathers. Its wattles and comb were all swollen and red, and he said, "You see, Sunshine? Now our luck has changed. The yellow-skins are the toughest, the bravest, and those great red wattles mean passion, mean madness! This beauty will eat the others!" Well, he was brave all right. He never gave up. The more he suffered, the harder he fought. He still wouldn't turn tail even when he had no tail left, no comb left, nothing left. And they wouldn't stop it, not even when he had his second eye pecked out, not while he was still running about looking for trouble and making everyone laugh. "You can't win some fights, no matter how brave you are," my master said. "Bah! Let's hope I can be as much a man as that fool cock was. Did you see the one that beat him, the one that made minced meat of him, Sunshine? Looked more like a hen. And that cock-like-a-hen would still have won, even with one wing removed first. It would have won with one leg! … At least the Albanian is a man. Come on." "You mean you're going to die, master?" "I hope not. There's still one more chance."'

Ah. Now it is coming. 'So where did you go then, Sunshine?'

'We went to the miser's house.'

'Who let you in?'

'A lady. A girl.'

'Had you seen her before?'

'In the doorway only. At a distance. I'd been there two or three times before but he always left me outside, in the alleyway.'

'And this time?'

'I went to the door. But when it opened, Messire Pierre realised I was there with him and he didn't want me with him. He boxed my ear and shooed me away.'

'But you saw her closely? What did she look like?'

'She has hair like – the colour of pumpkin flesh. And green eyes.'

'And have you seen her again since?'

'No … Is she your girlfriend?'

'My girlfriend?'

Estelle snorts, and I look down at myself. Jack Cutting. I blush and grin and say, 'No. Why? You think she's pretty? You think she'd make a good girlfriend?'

He grins back and glances at Estelle as though what he is about to say might not be for her ears. 'Mm. But it's not just that … Le Cafard told me when a man attacked you once, she killed him. Just like that. Is it true? I said it must have been the other way round, but he was sure … '

'It's true.'

'And it was one of Abbé Soxxal's men?'

I nod. 'You know the Abbé Soxxal?'

The smile goes from his face.

Leave the good abbé. 'Her name is Natalie. Dem'selle Natalie to you and le Cafard.'

The grin reappears.

I say, 'What did you think her relationship was to Maître Guillaume – the miser?'

'Relationship?'

'Her position in the house. Did you think she was one of the family? A maid? What?'

'I don't know. A maid. A slave, maybe. My master has a girl like that at home. Tanya. She's a slave.'

Estelle says, 'I don't remember any Tanya.'

'Who do you remember?' I ask.

'He had a whore called Niniane living there years ago, a really beautiful girl.'

'What happened to her?'

'Oh, he threw her out. Strangely enough, the bailiff was talking about her only the other day. Said she still hangs about there sometimes. "The slut still worships him," were his actual words. I don't like such things, but I suppose it must be true.'

What, that the poor girl still worships him, or that she's a slut? 'And this Tanya?' I ask Coco.

'He keeps her shut away. There's a little secret room near his room. Like the other girl, the one before her – the one just before her, I mean. Raquel.'

Raquel? I feel my scalp prickling. These are girls like me. 'How old was this Raquel?'

'I don't know. Tanya's seventeen now, and he's had her for about a year. Raquel was younger than Tanya, I think. She seemed younger, anyway.'

'What happened to Tanya? Wait a minute. Did he keep them locked in that little secret room?' He nods, eyes wide now again with fear, realising. I turn to Estelle. 'We must go there now, at once!'

'Why? What – ? Oh no!'

'Coco? Will you come with us? You're the only one who knows this hidden room.'

He gazes at me.

'Tanya might be in there. She might be dying.'

'She might be dead.' His eyes are enormous.

'Did you like her?'

'She was nice. And pretty, like Dem'selle Natalie.'

'So you'll come?'

This time, despite Estelle's protests, we got a boat across the river, then hurried back to the house where I explained the situation to Ferchard and P'tit-Jean. P'tit-Jean took charge at once. I couldn't go with them, I had to go with Estelle to the Fille d'Or to find her daughter, I had to go and see Jaquet, I had to find Raoul and see what more he had learnt from the Albanian and Natalie, and from Mère Henriette, and – and – I had call on Maître Thomas about the horoscopes the Emperor had asked us to prepare. It was all becoming too much.

'Ferchard, you go with Messire Jean and little Coco. Coco, you can trust Sir Farquhar as you trust me. We are as one. And Ferchard, find out all you can … '

I ran upstairs, taking Yahia with me, to become Lady Marian again.

Estelle and I were shown straight into Madame Mireille's private apartement.

'Lady Marian!' She kissed me on both cheeks. 'Or perhaps I should call you Mariana. I've been hearing stories about you. And you bring your little friend? You too would like to come and work for me, mon ange?'

Estelle raised her veil.

Madame Mireille was taken aback. 'Ah, madame. Non. I am sorry. The face is still beautiful, but the heart is broken, the soul ravaged. What is it, madame? Wait. I know that face.'

'My friend is the Countess Estelle de Saint-Samson de Montrouge.'

'Montrouge, you say?'

'Oui, madame. I think she may be the mother of little Isabeau. She has, had, a daughter, Isabeau, and … '

Suddenly she grasped the situation. 'And if she is not? I would not want to upset the child.'

'Bring her to me,' I said. 'Tell her Lady Marian is here and wishes to say hello to her. Estelle, you stand over there, out of sight. If she is your Isabeau, cry out to her. We shall see at once whether she recognises you.'

So Isabeau was sent for and came running into my arms. 'Lady Marian! I didn't - '

But what she didn't was never known, for Estelle screamed 'Isabeau!!' and ran at me and then the child was in her arms and there was nothing to be said for several minutes.

When eventually Estelle calmed down and could speak to us, she said she realised that Madame Mireille was in no way culpable, that it had been a bizarre and inexplicable act on the part of her late cousin Pierre, Sire de Montrouge, and that if Madame Mireille did not intend to make any difficulties, then …

'Difficulties, madame? I am happy to see the child returned to her maman. Though we have naturally incurred certain expenses …'

I looked at Estelle. She was not coping at all. Not even listening. Her whole mind was on the child.

I said, 'Would a gold livre be sufficient, madame? You understand that nothing must ever be said about this - ah - episode, that there must never be any whisper to the effect that

Isabeau de Montrouge was once a child-prostitute in a bordel in Paris.'

'If there ever is, it will not have come from me.'

'And you will not tell any of the girls who Isabeau really is.'

'I do not discuss such things with the girls.'

I gave her the livre d'or, we kissed again, she kissed the sobbing child, who wanted now to go and say farewell to Seraphina but was not allowed to, and we left, by a side-door.

Outside, the snow was settling thickly over everything. We made our way back across the strangely silent Île de la Cité to the rue Alexandre l'anglois as fast as we could, taking turns to carry the shivering child. When we got there, and were seated by the fire, warm once more, Estelle said: 'Mariana, how can I ever thank you?'

I looked at her. What could I say?

I said, 'By letting me go now, Estelle. I have other urgent tasks.' I explained, briefly, why I needed to hurry round to the Grand Châtelet, and then go in search of Raoul.

'But Mariana, the snow! You can't!'

'I can. I must. Jaquet's situation is grave, and becoming more so with every passing hour.'

I never reached the Châtelet. As soon as I turned into the rue Saint-Victor I became aware of men coming up behind me, their eyes on me. I walked as calmly, as unconcernedly, as I could, given that my feet kept slipping on the frozen snow, but I wasn't fooling anyone: I saw that others were waiting directly in front of me, and more closing in from all sides. I couldn't get to the Place Maubert. I couldn't fight – I didn't even try – but then suddenly a fist slammed into my stomach, another hit my face, knocking me over. I was hauled to my feet, a bag was pulled over my head, and I was led, vomiting and sobbing, down to the river.

The same spot where I had earlier sat with Estelle and Coco? No, of course not. We were on the Left Bank now.

And Coco? Was the girl Tanya dead? Was I too about to die?
I was, it was obvious! I'd be thrown into the icy water with a
rock tied round my neck! I started struggling and screaming.
They punched me, again and again, on my face and my head
inside the black bag and on my body. I fought wildly. They
threw me down, kicked my kidneys, my belly, my breasts, till I
curled up, could take no more. They turned me over and knelt on
me, face down, flat on the frozen mud, and bound my wrists
behind my back, while another bound my ankles, pulling the
cord so tight I cried out at last, cried out to them to stop. I
couldn't help it. Then they picked me up by my feet and
shoulders and swung me … The rock? Didn't they know I needed
a rock or something? "Mariana, they know their job, stop trying
to teach men their job" – my father's voice. Perhaps it was there,
on the ground, tied to my feet – how would I know? I wouldn't
know yet, would I? … They swung me again, and threw me. And
of all things, all people, in that last second as I flew blindly
through space, I thought of Maître Pietri, who had gone before
me, of his medallion, of the me – it was me – I had not let fall
into the river – it was still in my purse, and now both it and I …
Instead of icy water, I came down thud on my face and front on
something hard. Always my face, unable to protect it! Something
hard that rocked – a boat! – and water – my face was in water,
even inside the hood, it was on my mouth, on my lips. I licked at
my lips, licked them clean, spat. It wasn't water. It was blood.
My blood.

Ferchard! I need you! Raoul! Yahia! Anyone! Père Pierre, I
believe you, now! Maître Baudouin! I believe you! Do it again!
Come on your horses, Can we be of any assistance, dem'selle?
My two gallant priests – oh, you can, you can, yes, you can! Pick
me up! Help me! Can't you see I am tied? My bloody head in a
bag like a sheep … Just come, come quickly …

18

This time, there was nothing Père Pierre or Maître Baudouin could do for me. They were leagues away, in the forests of the Vilaine. And even if they had been in Paris? I hadn't shown much gratitude last time.

Raoul searched. He went to Khadija and Yahia. They were worried, but no more than that. They were used to me, and could not understand what he was saying anyway. He asked for Estelle. She told him I'd gone to the Grand Châtelet. He left a message with her for Ferchard that he would be back later, that he feared I had been seized by Abbé Soxxal's men.

And Ferchard? He was at the old Paris home of the Sires de Montrouge, with Coco and the new Sire, P'tit-Jean. The bailiff, it turned out later, had known about the secret chamber, and upon discovering Pierre's body had immediately gone to let the poor girl out.

But Tanya had not been there.

When it happened, she had been hiding under the bed.

It was a neighbour who told them the girl had gone back to the bordel from which she had come, and good riddance. It was a nice neighbourhood. Bourgeois. Even aristocratic. They didn't want her sort around there.

She must mean the Fille d'Or, Mireille's bordel, Ferchard reasoned. That was presumably where Pierre got all his girls.

And perhaps Estelle and I were still there.

We weren't. But when Mireille learnt that the imposing Sir Farquhar was from me, she let him interview the girl – in her presence. She herself had not been able to get the full story out of the girl, even after a good beating at the hands of Seraphina. She had been with Messire Pierre, she said, when the Albanian arrived, and had hidden in the nearest place, but had seen nothing.

Ferchard succeeded, as he would, by kindness. Tanya had
seen everything. Yet even so, when pressed by Ferchard and
P'tit-Jean to make a statement to the prévôt indicting the
Albanian for the murder, she refused. She was terrified of him, of
his son, of his men; and P'tit-Jean had to agree that there was no
way he could guarantee her safety, even in his castle in Anjou, or
in the forest with his écorcheurs: the Albanian had a long arm.
Short of having her put to the question — which he declined to
consider, to the obvious relief not only of Tanya herself but of
Ferchard and le Boeuf — there was nothing to be done.

She would help, though, she said, on the matter of "the
miser". She would give evidence that her master had come home
drunk and a little out of his mind shortly before dawn, and then
had slept. She knew no more. But that would be enough, P'tit-
Jean was sure, to obtain Jaquet's release, taken along with Coco's
testimony that his master visited the miser for an hour or so
immediately before coming home and the testimony already
given that Jaquet was not in fact Guillaume le Grec's heir.

Madame gave her consent, and they set out once more
through the falling snow.

There was no difficulty. Jaquet was released, the
commissaires taking under consideration the fact that it was the
late Sire de Montrouge's own brother who was laying charges
against him for the murder of Maître Guillaume le Grec, and
adding the strong presumption that he must have perpetrated this
crime while drunk and deranged and then gone home and hanged
himself.

Jaquet went home to his mother.

Tanya was taken sobbing back to Seraphina.

Estelle took little Isabeau and went back to Saint-Malo.

Raoul went to my house, and there he and Ferchard, and P'tit-
Jean, with the assistance of Coco and le Cafard, began trying to
come up with a plan for rescuing me ...

I must have passed out in that boat, for I remember no more until I woke up in the abbé's private prison.

Not that I knew for sure whose prisoner I was.

I was lying on a bare wooden bench. My hands and feet were still tied. It was pitch dark.

It wasn't the Albanian. It wasn't P'tit-Jean. So unless it was someone quite new, it had to be the abbé.

And I was trembling.

Fear, but not just fear. I was icy cold. My robe had gone. My pocket. Everything. I was in my shift. And my shift was a chemise of the finest silk. How long would that last?

I should have listened.

The pain in my head was worse than the cold. Was something broken? I couldn't even put my hand to it, to see. My whole body was likely to be broken in the next few hours.

It was over. Time to leave.

I tried. I tried to go to that cave that led to the Shelti-world, that beach where I had ridden the horse, spoken to the owl, shape-shifted, been a mermaid for a while … I couldn't.

I tried yet again to contact Yacoub. I couldn't.

At least I could think warm. I settled into a rhythmic breathing pattern, albeit through my mouth, not my nose … went back to summer in Andalucía. Home. I was lying on the sand of La Manga, the arm of land, of white and silver sand and dunes, that closes off the Mar Menor, our little sea. It was cool still, it was dawn, but it was going to be hot, you could tell: the hottest day of the year, Pedro, the old fisherman said. He had a soft spot for me. 'Come on, I'll take you out where the water's deep and you can dive down and find those shells you like.' So I stood up and walked through the glistening water to where he was sitting in his boat. I stood there a moment, enjoying the water round my waist, then clambered up onto the boat. He didn't help me. He was always very careful not to touch me when I was undressed for swimming. And looking back on it (for I was awake, and conscious of being grown up now, a woman) I realised he did his best, too, not to look at me, and I smiled to myself and loved his memory.

I knelt on one knee up on the prow, looking down into the clear water, one fish here, two there, then a cloud of fish turning together, turning this way then back again, all together, all at once. How did they do that? They must be in touch with each other, thinking as one. And me? I can't even get in touch with Yacoub. 'Now,' he said. 'Dive in here.' I stood up on the prow, balanced there a moment arms outstretched like a carved mermaid on the prow of a great ship, then dived off, sideways, and went down into the water, and swam and swam … and (because I'd been thinking of myself as a mermaid?) it was as it had been in that other dream, the Shelti-world: I didn't need to go up for air, I could stay down there, I could escape and stay down there for ever. If I attempted to go up onto the beach I would be sucked back down and spewed out into the real world, as I had been that time on the horse with the two priests. This time, though, the real world was a prison, and the priest was a very different kind of priest.

I swam on.

I should go up to the surface, check where Pedro was, let him see me. He worried.

But he would see the mermaid's tail. Could his love for me survive that? Or would he denounce me to the authorities, have me – what did they do to mermaids anyway? Hook them up by their tails? Or hang them by the head with the hook through their jaw? It would be something nasty, something – they've caught me! I writhed and thrashed and woke.

A hand was shaking me, gripping my shoulder and arm as I struggled: big hands, a stupid face, quite young, my age, and behind him another, older, with a grey beard and dark eyes shining in the light of the torch he was holding.

'Pick her up, I told you! Carry her!'

'I did! I tried, Captain, but she started thrashing about like a great fish and – '

'You scared her. She's calm now.'

He put one arm under my back, the other under my knees. This time I let him. Carrying me like a child, he followed the captain along a narrow passage and up some stone stairs. At the top of the stairs, in another corridor, was a carved door, closed. Outside it, stood two armed guards. And seated on a bench beside the door was a Jew, a rabbi, from Spain or, no, Portugal, probably.

The two guards looked me over, as did the rabbi.

'He's had to go somewhere, Captain.' said the nearest guard, the fat one, not taking his eyes off me. 'He said to wait.'

'Ah. Right then. Put her down there on the bench, with our Hebrew friend. That's it. Don't worry, boy, she'll be all right.'

The rabbi moved along to make more room for me. His eyes, unlike the guards', seemed full of pity as he watched me try to get into a comfortable position. It was difficult. My hands were still tied behind my back and my ribs were badly bruised, probably cracked.

The rabbi was not an old man – forty, maybe – and his eyes were large and soft and kind, but he was skeletally thin. He smelt horrible.

Not his fault.

He shifted further away from me, to the end of the bench.

Reading my mind? Or perhaps I smelt worse than he did. If I didn't, I would, after a few more days in the good abbé's hell-hole.

The four men moved over to a window further along the corridor, and stood gossiping in hushed tones.

'You are Mariana? Daughter in God of Rabbi Yacoub of Murcia?' the rabbi murmured, in Spanish.

I thought it safer to answer in Djudezmo. One of them might

understand Spanish or Portuguese, or even Arabic. 'Rabbi, you know Yacoub?' It seemed so strange.

'We've met, yes. But he's in Lithuania now.'

So it was true.

'Listen, we have little time. I have to tell you this: what will happen will happen; but when it happens, it will happen to your body only, not to you. When it happens, go to him. Go to Yacoub in Lithuania. He'll be waiting for you.'

I didn't understand. Was it going to be so bad? I quailed, my very spirit quailed.

'You are trembling, girl. Here.'

He wrapped his cloak around me. I glanced at the captain, saw him glance at us, but he didn't interfere.

'Thank you. Yes. More shivering than trembling. They took my gown, my cloak.'

'And you are hurt.'

'I am spoilt these days, no longer used to going barefoot.'

'Paris in winter is very different from Granada – or Lisboa.'

'Is that where you are from?'

'Near Lisboa, yes. Ah, here comes the son of Shaitan. Don't forget what I have told you, girl.'

I looked round, saw the abbé coming along the corridor from the other direction, and heard the captain shout, 'Stand up, you two! Help her up, boy!' I tried to get to my feet, but couldn't. It was the pain in my side. I couldn't push down. Then the "boy" tore the cloak off me, threw it at the rabbi, and picked me up, in his arms, cradling me as he had before.

'Bring them in – both of them, both of them! I haven't time to waste.'

'Oui, mon père.' The captain snapped his fingers at the rabbi, who stood up obediently behind me and the "boy" and, leaving the two guards outside, we followed the abbé through the now open door into a warm, comfortable, candle-lit room. There, taking no further notice of us, he seated himself at a large table, examined a quill, rejected it, inspected another, dipped it in the pot of ink and began writing fast on a sheet of vellum.

We waited, me half-naked in the arms of the "boy", the rabbi and the captain standing patiently to our left, where I could see them.

This abbé was no fool. I was the fool for having thought him one.

At last he looked up at us. 'The young lady. Can she stand?'

The "boy" very gently put my feet down, stood me up. It was difficult to find my balance with my arms tied behind my back and my feet bound together, but ... I stayed upright when he took his hands away.

'All right, you two wait outside.'

They went. The door closed behind them.

The abbé studied me. 'So you thought to deceive me again.'

'D-deceive you, mon père?' I croaked.

'Dressing up, making out you are Sir Jack Cutting.'

What did he mean? Don't say anything. Let him give himself away.

But he too was waiting, waiting for me to give myself away.

I couldn't see properly through my right eye.

'Is it Master Cutting I am after? Or is it you, and not Master Cutting at all …?'

'Could I have my hands undone, mon père, for a moment at least? I need to do something about my nose, my eye …'

He gazed at me.

'Please, mon père …'

He still gazed. Not stared; gazed, incuriously, as one might gaze at a rat in a trap. Before one drowned it, I realised, suddenly. Or gave it to the dogs.

The dogs.

'There seems little point, ma fille. You have sinned. You must be punished. Your punishment has hardly begun.'

'Sinned, mon père?'

'These documents were found in the house of the alchemist –
apart from this one, which was found in your purse.' He had my
purse there on the table, I saw now, and the pages of Kabbalistic
Hebrew from Guillaume's laboratory. 'How did you come by it?
And what do they mean?'

I dropped my eyes, saw again my bare feet, blue with cold
and bruised and filthy. I saw that the two little toes on my right
foot had been crushed – under some man's boot? I hadn't noticed.
But now, having got my attention, those two little ones joined in
the chorus of pain.

'You have sinned, and are still sinning. You know where you
got it, and I think you know what they mean … I have been
informed by one I trust that they are in an arcane form of
Hebrew, used by certain Kabbalists in Spain. In Spain, Doña
Mariana, where you were once the pupil of a Kabbalist … or so I
have been informed by another who has good reason to fear the
stake and is therefore to be trusted. But the rabbi here will
translate the documents – won't you, Mordecai? Here, take it.' He
held them out to the Portuguese rabbi, who had been standing
silent beside me all this time. 'Tell the guards to take you
somewhere you can sit and write, and to provide whatever you
need.'

'But, Abbé, I – '

'Or you can tell them to take you where you can not sit, or
stand, or lie down: the cage we keep for the impenitent, the, ah,
uncooperative.'

We waited. I glanced round at him. He looked at me.

'Will you be needing the documents then, Mordecai?' asked
the Abbé at last.

Mordecai nodded, took them, touched me briefly on the
shoulder as he turned, and left the room.

I was alone with the abbé.

Your mind is free, Uncle Yacoub had told me. Your mind is
always free. When your feet are not free to come and go, or your

hands to make and do, or your tongue to praise and pray, your mind is free to do all these things and more: you can go where your feet could never take you, do what your hands could never do, and speak the words you could never speak out loud …

'If ever I saw Satan's spawn in Lucifer's handmaid, she – or is it he? – stands before me now, flaunting her unnatural charms; alluring to the many, yes, but to those with eyes to see, sold and tainted flesh, fit for nothing but to be cast into the fire. And the stake and flames which await you here on earth will but introduce you to an eternity of torment – smoking dungeons, flails, brands, needles, wheels and chains – till screeching nerves stretched over jagged broken bones are all that is left of your depraved little body, to be roasted on a spit with an apple clenched between lipless, toothless gums for ever.'

It seemed to me he was getting rather confused, that he had the body in Hell, which I supposed reflected his way of life and way of thinking: but this wasn't the time to say so.

Why not?

'If your understanding of politics,' I sobbed, 'and ecclesiastical law, is as – as flawed as your understanding of theology, then it is hardly surprising that you ended up as little more than a slave-trader.'

I should have noticed the riding crop lying on his table. If I had, I might have kept my mouth shut. But my eye, the one I could see out of at all, was full of tears, and I was full of pain and foolishness – the Mariana la puta loca I had tried so hard to suppress since arriving in Paris now coming out with a vengeance – and the next thing I knew he was striding towards me with a look of rage on his face and the whip raised. I screamed as he slashed me across my breasts with all his strength, backhand first, then forehand, but no one heard or no one cared. He lashed me with it again, and again – four times in all – I didn't know then, it seemed more – but the weals on that sensitive flesh took weeks to close and heal, and four faint lines still criss-cross my breasts.

When I could open my eyes, or one of them, again, I saw that it was not the abbé but the Devil sitting before me.

He opened his mouth, a forked tongue flicked out, and in, out … and in. His voice, from a long way off, grated out things I didn't wish to hear, things about Guillaume's writings (horns sprouted from his forehead), that I too would translate them, later, for he did not trust either of us; that he was going to hand me over to the captain and the cabin-boy; that when I left, if I ever left, I would leave as a woman, broken, contrite, a real woman (tiny demons crawled in and out of his nostrils) with no mind of her own, no other thought in her head but to obey: obey God's holy priests, obey the men around her – fathers, brothers, uncles – and obey her husband; that as I seemed to have no father, brother, or uncle, and no husband, he would arrange a marriage for me (he leant back, leant his horned and scaly head back, and up his nostrils I could see white-hot holes and hot, white slime, like lava), he knew many a man who would be only too pleased to take over my property and my person, and use me as a woman should be used: in short to take over where the captain and the cabin-boy left off. He would perform the marriage himself before he released me. 'Captain!' (Demons fell onto the table and wriggled there like tiny mannikins, quick as cockroaches, slimy as slugs. He swept them away with his sleeve.) 'CAPTAIN! Ah, there you are.'

The captain came back in, the cabin-boy ("cabin-boy"?) peering in at me from behind him.

'Captain, take her back down and thrash her. Use her, break her – make a woman of her, Captain. Only spare me the details.'

And I will spare you the details. Suffice it to say that I was hauled up onto the cabin-boy's back (as he had so often, no doubt, been hauled up onto the back of a muscular sailor when he had been a real cabin-boy, and in need of chastisement) and in

this ignominious position, thoroughly thrashed by the captain.
The pain grew with each stroke and became overwhelming.
There was no way I could escape it mentally. Nothing existed but
the pain, the desperate screaming need for it to stop.
    It stopped.
    Then, still on the cabin-boy's back, I realised that I was being
raped. I didn't mind - I stopped screaming - anything - anything
- just so long as the beating, the pain, didn't start again. But it did
start again. One of the other guards arrived, the fat one, wanting
his share of the fun, and the captain said he had to thrash me first
to earn his turn. 'No!!' I screamed. 'No! He doesn't have to! I
don't mind!'
    I was beaten again, then raped again four times, five times, I
lost count. Then they laid me on a bench, on my back. It's over, I
thought. But it wasn't. I understood that when I found myself
being lifted up while my arms, still tied at the wrist, were forced
under the bench, pulling my shoulders right back when they
thrust me down again. Then they cut the cord binding my ankles
and, a guard to each foot, they forced my feet down onto the
floor, one each side of the bench, splaying my legs. I lay back.
Gave up. I don't know how long it went on. This was when I
managed to slip away.

And it was true. Uncle Yacoub was indeed there waiting for me.
    'But this is not Lithuania!' I cried. 'This is La Manga - the Mar
Menor! How …?'
    We were sitting together on the sand, looking not back at the
lagoon and across it to Al Kazar, Los Alcazares, and my home,
but east, out over the open sea and into the coming night.
    'We can go anywhere, do anything, remember?'
    I remembered.
    We sat in silence for a while, hand in hand, looking at the sea.
No one had held my hand like that, like a father, for - oh, for so
long. And it was so comforting. So simple.

'The body, the gross body, has many functions,' he said, at last, answering my unasked question with a question of his own, 'but what can it feel?'

I knew the answer to that. 'It can feel pain.'

'And what else? A coin has two sides.'

Yes. Pleasure, of course. Pain and pleasure.

'In our lives, we all experience both pain and pleasure. The fortunate among us experience great pleasure. The unfortunate, great pain.'

I knew what was coming next.

'You have been one of the fortunate. Will be again. Would you not – ?'

'He can empty me, Yacoub. My very soul. He can destroy me.'

'He cannot. Your soul is immortal. Only you yourself can harm it.'

'He can break my spirit. He intends to.'

'With enough time, and enough pain. But to break your spirit he would need much more time than he has and far more pain than those clowns know how to inflict.'

'And if he himself takes a hand?'

'Let us hope that he doesn't, that he doesn't realise how little time he has until it is too late.'

'And if he marries me to someone like that captain, the pain will go on for ever.'

'He will not. Such was never written on your hand, in your stars.'

'But that is theory! It means nothing when you are under the rod! When you are screaming! When there is only pain, when you can't see past the pain, can't think past the pain … I'm not as brave as you believe. If they beat me again now on top of the other beatings, I don't think I'll be able to bear it.' And suddenly I smiled. 'How am I able to sit here beside you on this hard beach?'

He smiled back. 'The beach is not hard, it is soft as fresh

milled flour, soft as a new fall of snow. And this is not that poor body of earth and water.'

'What that poor body of earth and water – and of fire, believe me! – would give to be sitting in fresh fallen snow!' I gazed at him. How much I had missed him! 'Ah, Uncle, I am but a child still. I do not have your wisdom, your understanding.'

'My child, you have something better. You have inspiration. You remember what I taught you? That in Kabbalah we speak of the three forms of knowledge?'

'Yes, Uncle. There is Hokhmah, which is wisdom, the knowledge that is the fruit of experience. And there is Binah, which is understanding, the knowledge that results from thought.'

'And?'

'And there is Da'at, which is the knowledge that comes direct from God.'

'So. That is Fire, believe me, Da'at, the Fire, the inspiration, that comes down from Heaven; not the pain that your poor body feels. Da'at can be something as seemingly simple as intuition: though you are a logical creature, too logical for your own good, some would say, being a woman.'

'The abbé seems determined to make a real woman of me, at last.'

'He will have a hard job beating that out of you – your capacity for clear thought, for coming to understand. And he may even add to your fund of wisdom, which is already impressive in one so young, so – relatively – inexperienced.'

'If I survive this, will I see you? Really see you?'

'You will survive. Give me your hands …'

Are the hands of the astral body the same as those of the etheric and the material body? Yes, of course, they would be, wouldn't they?

'Look. There is no death here, no disaster or deformity, no marriage … though there is an affair of the heart. More than one.'

I blushed.

'I am not judging you, my daughter. Indeed, I consider it a very good thing that you were not unaccustomed to that which befell you today. Rather providential.'

'I hardly think – ' Then I saw the smile in his eyes. He was teasing me, as he always did, always had.

'Yes, you will see me again. Sometime, somewhere. I have the feeling you will come to me here – in Lithuania, I mean – but it will not be soon. It will be in eight, ten, twelve years, when you are in your prime, a woman of power …'

Suddenly, with a crash and a thud that near broke my head, I was back in my body of pain, on the floor: the bench had tipped over, the guards were laughing.

Then: 'Up, bitch!' one of them shouted, and kicked me, with his boot, from behind, between my legs.

I struggled to get my wrists out from under the bench.

He kicked me again, harder: 'Up, I said!'

I got myself out and up and – my ankles were free, my legs naked and free – and as Ferchard had taught me, exactly as Ferchard had taught me, I flexed my foot and kicked out and up as he came towards me again, his head bent forward, and my foot exploded into his face, smashed his nose, smashed one of his eyes, and in a shower of blood he flew back and cracked his head on the wall and slid to the ground. There was a stunned silence.

The captain went and bent over the man, felt his neck. Then turned and looked at me. 'He's dead.'

I was locked back in my cell, swollen and aching and bloody and sticky all over with semen – in my hair, my eyes, everywhere – why did they do that? Locked in my cell while … While what? While they decided what to do with me? Hardly. No one cared that that man had died. It just meant they had to be more careful with me. The beating would start again soon, if not the rapings. Could you rape a woman with her legs tied together? Of course

you could. And you could tie her legs apart, each foot tied
separately, as wide apart as they would go.

I lost track of the time.

No one came near me.

I needed water.

Were they leaving me to die?

I woke and found them in my cell. I leapt round to fight, and fell
on my face in the filth.
     My ankles had been tied while I was unconscious.
     They carried me out and along the passage again, and out
through another door that led to a courtyard. There, beside the
horse trough, they swung me back and forth, back and forth,
laughing, then let me go. I flew straight into the trough, hit ice,
and smashed through the ice into the water.
     Shocked and freezing, and almost helpless tied as I was, I
floundered and bucked and threw myself out again, and fell with
a final splat to the wet frozen ground.
     More laughter. But no kicks this time. They all stood there,
looking down at me, grinning.
     I gave up, lay still. Now I knew how a fish felt. How a real
mermaid felt.
     To be served later.
     Mariana à la manière Parisienne.
     The cabin-boy wasn't grinning. He grinned at all the wrong

times, grinned when nobody else did. Stupid. A natural. If he'd been Maître Guillaume's instead of the captain's … Maître Guillaume! Jaquet! I'd forgotten about him! Oh God – and me lying here playing mermaids again! God, God, help me now! Or if not me for myself (and I can understand that) then for Jaquet!

How was I to know that God had already helped Jaquet?

At a sign from the captain, they picked me up, threw me back in, and held me down under the water. Then, while I struggled and screamed, they rubbed me, with their bare hands, with handfuls of straw, with stones, with anything hard and nasty and sharp and abrasive they could find.

A window opened somewhere above, I couldn't see where for the hands and arms and the ring of faces grinning down at me, and the abbé's voice called: 'I'm waiting for her! Bring her up now! At once! As she is!'

The grins vanished.

Were replaced by mutters, pouts, bared teeth: dogs, being done out of their treat.

'NOW!' roared the abbé. 'And put some kind of smock on her first!'

The captain nodded to the cabin-boy. 'Take her.'

Then as the cabin-boy picked me up and cradled me in his arms again, the captain put his foul mouth to my face and hissed, 'Have you ever seen a woman who's been flayed? No? I have. And if you ever come my way again, bitch, I will have your skin.'

The cabin-boy carried me to a room in which there was a chest full of old garments. Why? I wondered, as he opened it and pulled out a few. Their original owners no longer needed clothes?

I suddenly realised just how close to death I stood. Despite Yacoub. This priest would need to silence me.

Then why the smock?

He wanted my translation of those documents, which I knew

all along I should never have touched.

And after that …

The cabin-boy looked me in the eye. 'Please?'

What? Oh, my hands. I nodded. I would be good.

He undid them, and helped me into a silk chemise even more beautiful than the one I'd been wearing when I arrived.

He grinned.

I smiled back – he was nice in his simple way – and held my hands out for him to tie them again.

But I didn't think the abbé was going to be as impressed as the cabin-boy was by my new "smock".

Outside the abbé's door, a guard I hadn't seen before was waiting. He led us to another room, and unbolted the door. The cabin-boy set me down and the guard pushed me in.

The Portuguese rabbi was sitting at a table. He jumped up when he saw me, held me by my arms, obviously wanting to hug me, comfort me, but not daring to. I tried to smile.

'There's no need to be shy,' I said, in Spanish.

The door closed behind me.

'Shy? Oh, I see. No, it's simply that you're injured and I don't know where you've been hurt most. Here, sit down.'

Now I really smiled. 'That's where I've been hurt most.'

'Ah. Well, in that case, do you mind if I sit? I haven't been fed for three days and – '

'No, of course not. Please, rabbi …' He was not a young man, and though tall, not a strong one either. 'You've been working on the translation?' I peered at the papers on the table.

'Half-heartedly. I don't know whether – ' He went into Djudezmo. 'I didn't know whether I should … I could refuse. I could translate it wrongly, but he said he would compare my translation with yours.'

'Mine? But I … How important is it? How dangerous is it for him to know what it says? Does it matter?'

'It's meaningless unless you're already a skilled alchemist.'
'Then it doesn't matter.'
'No.'
We looked at each other.
'He's listening to us,' I said, switching to pure Hebrew.
'I know.'
'They'll come for me now.'
'I know. The Lord bless you and keep you, my daughter.'
'And you, rabbi. And thank you for the message. It helped. Without that I don't think I - '
The door flew open.

The cabin-boy stood me in front of the abbé again, as before, and backed out of the room.
    And as before, the abbé gazed at me for a while. 'It appears that the King is searching for you. Does that surprise you?'
    I shook my head.
    'That the Emperor himself is impatient to grant you an audience. Now why should that be?'
    He waited.
    'I suppose he wants an answer to the questions he asked me last week.'
    'Last week? What questions?'
    This was my salvation.
    'I was with him and - and his children. His daughter, Anna, is a friend of mine.'
    'You mean the Princess Anna.'
    'I - yes, of course, to you, but we are on first name terms.'
    Another long stare. Then: 'After further reflection, I have decided the married state might not be your, ah, avocation. I am beginning to wonder whether it might not suit both of us better were you simply to ... disappear.'
    Salvation? No, he was going to silence me. He had to. Stupid, Mariana. What is a Scorpio doing jumping to the easy, optimistic

conclusion?

I wonder what his Sign is. Ask him. Distract him. Get a moment to decide which way you want this conversation to go.

'I'm an astrologer. I've been – I'm supposed to have been – working on Princess Anna's horoscope. What Star Sign were you born under, mon père?'

He's thinking about what I told him, not what I've asked him.

But I know. He too is a Scorpio. Unlike me though, he has chosen the forces of darkness, whereas I at least try to work with the forces of light.

'You're a Scorpio,' I say.

He looks up.

'You're a Scorpio. Born sometime between the twenty-third of October and the twenty-second of November.'

He smiled. 'And that means?'

'It means you have a choice: darkness or light.'

'We all have that choice, my daughter.'

'True, but others walk a straight path most of their lives, with only the occasional fork in the path, only the occasional choice to make. The symbols of Scorpio are the scorpion and the eagle. People born when you were born face a continuous choice: Down or Up? Down into darkness with the scorpion, or up into the light with the eagle.'

Still that cold gaze.

'To side with the forces of light? Or the forces of darkness. That is your choice.'

'You are insolent, girl. It is you who have chosen the forces of darkness, I who am trying to save you … '

'By murdering me?'

His eyes flick up and down, up and down. 'You too were born under the Sign of Scorpio.'

I realise how foolish I am being, that he is succeeding, that I am being turned into a proper woman – proper girl – standing there before him in my silk chemise, beaten and used and helpless, and losing the argument. And blushing.

'I shall save you; not by letting you have your life to live as you will but rather by letting you spend it in a penitential cell – the deepest, darkest penitential cell – in a convent run by a certain Mother Superior of my acquaintance.'

He lets that sink in.

Watches me realise that marriage even to the captain would have had its charms.

'They … they know I am here.' My last shot.

He smiles. As well he might. If they know I am here, why are they searching?

'Thomasso di Pizzano knows.' They would kill him. Others, quick. 'Others know. My man, Sir Farquhar de Dyngvale, knows. Oh, and the Sire de Montrouge knows, and his cousin, Lady Estelle.'

'I think your experiences of, ah, being a woman have all been too much for you, my dear. You forget. You came here involuntarily. No one knows of your intention to come here because you had no such intention.'

'I may be in pain, mon père, I may be a woman, but I am not stupid. All four of those people I mentioned – and they are all important people – know of my interest in you. And of your implication in the murder of Maître Guillaume.'

He gazes, debating in his mind. He could have my tongue torn out to stop me speaking; he could have my hands cut off to stop me writing; but neither of those moves would be as good as the tiny penitential cell beneath the convent … somewhere … And, of course, they could be combined, thus ensuring that no one at the convent ever heard my story, ever took pity on me. But a chain and a heavy boulder at the bottom of the Seine would be simpler and safer.

The tongue flicks, the eyes blink.

He is without feeling.

L'Albanien.

'And then there are others who know, less important men, perhaps, but still men to be reckoned with. Men like my eunuch.'

He laughs.

'From what I hear, you didn't laugh last time you came face to face with him, father.'

'I'll have him brought in, too. The captain and the cabin-boy can have some fun with him before I have him garrotted for the infidel he is.'

'And then there is the Albanian.'

The blood drains from his face. Ah ha!

'Natalie is his niece. She is with him now. And they await me. They know you were involved in that murder, and they know I know, for we discussed it the other night when I was present at the Court of Miracles of Saint Antoine. And they know you will want to silence me.'

The snake was cornered.

'My dear, you have dangerous friends.'

'I do indeed, father.'

'They could get you into trouble.'

'I manage that quite adequately by myself.'

'The Albanian will end his days in chains on a gibbet. You would not wish to join him there before you burn in hell.'

'He has the means – and the imagination – to make you suffer more while he puts you to the question regarding my whereabouts than he or I will ever suffer – on earth or in Hell. And as for Heaven: if that is where you – '

'Silence. You are just a little whore. You will be cast out, for the dogs to eat. And if somehow you survive even that … remember to remember nothing of what happened here. If you mention my name to a living soul, ever, then all those you love – the Scottish knight, the Moors you live with, will die. As of course will your brother, Jack Cutting, thief and spy. You see? I know who you really are, Lady Jane. An English whore who has long been resident in Spain. You are the property of the Scot, and

the old fool, of course, indulges you, lets you pass yourself off as
a lady. Lady Jane Cutting, Doña Mariana de la Mar. Did he find
you in Spain and buy you there? Or did he pick you up here or in
London before he ever set out on his travels and take you with
him?'

I needed to sit down, lie down, and his whiny voice droned on
and on.

'Or did he buy you recently, here in France? From your
brother, perhaps … Was it your brother who brought you back
from Spain? I'm surprised your brother didn't sell you down
there, in the south of Spain. He'd have got a good price for you
from the Moors.'

What was he talking about? That wasn't my brother, it was my
father.

Then I heard him shout: 'Guard!' and knew no more.

I am in pain. I'm in pain, therefore I'm alive and awake and ... it's
dark and cold and wet. Where have they put me?

I open one eye.

Not so dark. That's sky above the roof-tops.

Sky? Then …

I am lying on a strand by the river, on the Left Bank, opposite
Notre-Dame. This must be where I was thrown into the boat.

Was I brought back here in the same boat?

All I remember is the abbé calling the guard.

I try to move. Pain lances through my head and eyes. As it
recedes, lights flash and fade.

I try again.

It is dawn. Too quiet for evening.

Gulls walking among the flotsam.

A cat watching the gulls.

A boy watching the cat watching the gulls.

And all very aware of me.

Suddenly, we all looked at each other.

The urchin got up.

The birds took off, circled, landed a few yards further up the strand.

The cat stretched, yawned and lay down again.

'I thought you were dead,' the boy said. 'Drowned … Then when I saw you I thought you'd been beaten to death.'

Saw me?

I didn't have to look. I could feel. They'd removed their precious shift – probably the men who threw me down here took that – and now I feel my bare skin pressing down on cold wet mud and slime. At least I am lying on my front, one leg drawn up, and not flat on my back. But seeing me like that, no wonder he thought I'd been beaten to death.

'I was going to stick the point of my knife in you, see if you were alive, but then … I didn't want to. So I held your nose and mouth shut, and after a moment you jerked your head and gasped for breath. So then I sat here to keep the gulls off you.'

The gulls?

'They would have gone first for your eyes. Then the dogs would have smelt blood, and come and driven off the gulls. But if the river had frozen and the wolves had come …'

If the wolves had come, there would have been nothing he could do. It would have been too late even to save himself.

I tried to sit up. 'Help me.'

He did so. I turned and sat and squawked and leapt to my feet, my hands on my bottom.

The boy laughed.

I laughed too, or tried to. It hurt even to smile. Then I remembered my face and put my hands to it. It was swollen and tender but the nose didn't feel broken.

Then I saw the direction of his gaze.

I had been standing there, my hands on my bottom, my hands on my face, oblivious of the fact that I was completely naked.

Now though, I put my hands down where, in the circumstances, they should be. But why? Why was I bothering. I was freezing. Literally. I threw my arms round myself, hugged myself, jumped up and down – it hurt – then ran my hands down over my aching bottom again and held them there.

'Help me. You will be well rewarded.'

His eyes came up, met mine. He was still on his knees down in the mud.

But the look in his eyes.

What had I said?

Ah.

'Do you know le Cafard?'

He nodded.

'Le Cafard is a friend of mine. Still, he's not too proud to accept a reward when he does me a service.'

He gazed at me. My eyes. Then: 'Yes. I'm sorry, dem'selle.'

'I'm sorry, too. I know you've been watching over me with no thought of reward.'

I was shivering. Trembling. But the icy wind that had been blowing through Paris for the last two weeks had dropped, and the air was still. If it hadn't, I would be dead, I realised. Food for the dogs indeed. I wasn't finished yet, though, far from it. I certainly wasn't finished with the abbé.

'Please, get up.'

He stood up.

'Go to the sign of the crescent moon in rue Alexandre l'anglois. Tell them where I am. Tell them I have no cloak and I'm cold, so cold. And please – hurry!'

He nodded, ready.

'Oh, and if you see le Cafard, send him here.'

We looked at each other. No, this was special, between this boy and me.

I changed my mind, shook my head.

He smiled.

'What's your name?'

He blushed. 'Le Pitre.'

The clown. 'You don't seem like a clown to me.'

'No?'

'Pas du tout. Tu es un jeune homme sérieux, et très gentil.'

'Non! Moi, je suis rien, dem'selle! C'est toi qui es gentille, et –
'

Shivering, shaking, I laughed – ouch! my ribs! – and cried,
'Run now, please, le Pitre! We can pay each other compliments
another time!'

He ran. Turned back. Took off his little tunic, offered it to me.

It was filthy.

I was filthier.

I pulled it on.

We both burst out laughing – I clutched my ribs again – but I
couldn't help it.

I took it off and gave it back to him. 'Go!'

He went.

I looked round. The sun would soon be rising. There were
people about, though no one showing any interest in me as yet.

I went and stood more out of sight, up against the
embankment. Then got down on my knees. I found I could kneel
fairly comfortably if I had my feet slightly apart. I bent forward,
pressed my breasts to my thighs, my face down between my
knees, my hands in front of my knees, under my face. Like that I
was warmer and, I hoped, if not invisible, at least less obvious to
a casual glance. It was a good thing my back was covered with
wet mud. Le Pitre must have taken me for one of his own, one
who could have been his sister, his cousin, his friend, and had
got herself into trouble, as no doubt so many of the girls he
knew, especially the pretty ones, did. And had sat there cursing
the rich, who had done this thing to her. Then found I was one of
the rich …

I must have slept, for next thing I knew I was screaming and struggling in the arms of the cabin-boy as he picked me up to take me back to my cell, only it wasn't the cabin-boy, it was Yahia, and Ferchard was there with him, and the boy le Pitre. They were trying to put a big cloak round me. Then I clung to Yahia. There is great comfort, sometimes, in big men. And they carried me home.

20

It was morning again next time I woke. I was lying on my front. My nose was hurting on the pillow. My ribs hurt when I tried to move.

But I was at home. In my own bed.

Someone was touching my bottom, gently, soothing it, smoothing cool unguent into it.

Khadija must have noticed my eyes flutter and open, my head move. 'Oh, Mariana! Thanks be to Allah! What a fright you gave us all! What happened? Where have you been? Who did this to you?'

'Shh. Later.'

'Later? You need food, you need – '

'That, too, later.'

There was a brief moment of silence. The hand continued its ministrations, but it was less gentle now she knew I was awake and well: the touch conveyed her pent-up anger as well as her relief. Finally, she exploded. 'What did I tell you? Well, what did I tell you?'

I smiled to myself. Things could be much, much worse. I (which meant we, not only me, but Khadija, and Yahia too) could

all belong to the captain now. The captain. That was a man
Khadija would respect. And the cabin-boy would come and live
with us …

'Still, it was no more than you deserve, than you've been
asking for. Allah is merciful.'

If she was younger – twenty, forty, years younger – I'd have
Yahia take the cane to her, see how she liked it. Then tell her it
was no more than she deserved.

No, I wouldn't.

'Send me Yahia,' I murmured, contentedly. 'I want a gentler
touch. And a gentler tongue.'

'Tongue? If you want your bottom licked better, I'll send in
that young Raoul – '

'That wasn't what – oh, just send me Yahia. And some water, I
need water. Then some food.'

Yahia had been waiting outside the door.

He stroked and soothed and caressed in silence. Not quite
silence. I could hear steady, half-stifled weeping. And feel
something … dripping.

'Your tears are falling on my bottom. The right cheek.'

'I'm sorry, Lalla Maryam. It hurts me so to see – '

'If it hurt you half as much as it hurts me, we'd have to swim.'

There was a knock on the door. Ferchard put his head in. 'May
I?' He had a tray of food with him.

'Yes! Oh, come in, come in! You've seen a girl's bottom
before.'

He peered at me – at it.

'Aye, and I've seen a girl's bottom when it's been beaten
before, too, but I've never seen one quite as well beaten as that.'

'Trust me to stand out. I suppose Khadija's been telling you I
got what I deserved.'

'Aye, but she exaggerates – a bit.'

'I'll kill you when I get up.'

He sat by my pillow, holding the plate, wondering whether he should feed me.

'Tell me what's been happening! I want news – news of Jaquet le Breton, of Raoul, of P'tit-Jean, and that poor girl – what was her name?'

'Tanya. Aye, well, after we left you …'

While I ate, he told me the story and I was so relieved, I started crying again. I stopped eating. I couldn't go on.

'Ferchard, listen,' I croaked, when I had got control of myself and was able to concentrate again. 'There's something wrong. I don't know, but … Look, for a start, I hear no mention of blood in the description of Pierre de Montrouge.'

'Blood?'

'He had supposedly committed murder by repeated stabbings, and there was blood splashed everywhere in Maître Guillaume's house, yet he was seen by Coco and Tanya and there is no mention of him or his clothes being in any kind of a mess.'

'No. That's right. I should have thought of that.'

Ferchard had become involved. I loved that. It made him more interested, less authoritarian.

'He was seen by the Albanian after he returned from Guillaume's house, so I must go out to the Court of Miracles and talk to – '

'You're not going anywhere, lass.'

'Ferchard – '

'I'll tie you to your bed if I have to. And Yahia will help me. Won't you, Yahia.'

'He won't. He wouldn't.' I looked over my shoulder at him, catching sight of my swollen bottom as I did so.

Ferchard asked him, in Arabic: in such circumstances, would he still obey me, or would he obey Ferchard?

The question was too much for him. He started wailing.

'Stop! Stop, Yahia,' I cried, heart-broken. 'I won't go, I promise!'

Slowly, he got control of himself.

Eunuchs are worse than women.

'I'll bring people to you here, lass,' Ferchard said. 'Those we believe you need to see.'

'Ah, Ferchard … All right then, I'll stay one more day. Will you see if you can find me Jaquet and Mère Henriette? And the boys - le Cafard and le Pitre, and Coco - where are they?'

'All waiting downstairs.'

'You go for Mère Henriette then, she'll listen to you, and I'll send the boys on other errands.'

When he had left, I told Yahia to cover me and leave me with the three boys, who filed in, all very grave and concerned.

I smiled at them. 'Don't look so worried. I'll be all right, thanks to le Pitre here. Now, I want one of you - you, le Cafard - to go in search of my friend Maître Raoul.'

'He was here last night. He's waiting for news.'

'You know where he lives?'

He nodded. 'In that alley by the Sorbonne.' And he sped off.

'Will you wait downstairs, le Pitre? I shall need someone to run another errand for me very soon.'

Alone with Coco, I beckon him closer: 'Coco - Sunshine - I want you to think back very carefully to when you went with your master to the miser's house, that night, the night both of them died.'

He nods, eyes enormous.

'What was he wearing?'

'Boots and a cloak, dem'selle. It was cold.'

'And under that? What colour were his tunic, his hose? Was he wearing a belt? A sword?'

'Oh, yes. His short sword. He was wearing his red and gold tunic, with the fur collar, and his hose were dark yellow - ambre, he called it.'

'And afterwards? When he came out of the miser's? And when

you arrived home?'

'The same.'

'You're sure of that? You saw them?'

'I … Not when he came out of the miser's house, no. He was wearing his cloak and it was windy and cold. But when we got home, he took his cloak off and I saw his clothes. Yes, they were the same.'

'And were they dirty at all?'

'Dirty?'

'Did they look as though they needed washing?'

He looks at me blankly.

'And himself? How did he seem?'

'He was upset, dem'selle. He'd been drinking. He had no money. And he had to face the Albanian.'

Anyone would have been upset.

'And did you, while you were standing there in the rue Saint-Pol that night waiting for him, did you see anyone else? Anyone at all, doing anything at all.'

He shakes his head.

'And did he say anything at all after he came out?'

'No. Only something about Dem'selle Natalie.'

'About Dem'selle Natalie?'

'Mm. He thought she should be a nun.'

'What?'

Did he know she was his daughter? Was he taking a last-minute interest in her? But a nun? Natalie? Why would he of all people want to impose that on her of all people? In an attempt to save his own soul?

'Do you remember his exact words, Coco? Think carefully. It may be important.'

'I can't remember … But he was angry with her. That's right – and I said – no, that was afterwards … but he said something about shutting her up in a convent and throwing away the key.'

He could have been talking about me.

'Then I said, "But she's pretty," and he stared at me, so I said, "Sorry, messire," and he pulled me up behind him. After that I stayed very quiet because when he's been drinking, and especially if something's gone wrong and he's in a bad mood, he, you know, takes it out on me.'

I smile. He looks so indignant. 'All right, Coco, you go and wait with le Pitre, will you? I must rest.'

But I didn't need to rest, I needed to think …

My teacher, Uncle Yacoub ben Amar, had been taught by one who had actually sat at the feet of Moses ben Shem Tob de León, author of much if not all of the Zohar, the Book of Splendour. The Zohar is a vast, mystical interpretation of the Torah (the Pentateuch, the first five books of the Bible). And the Zohar is Kabbalah. From Yacoub, I have as good an idea as it is possible – and rather more than is permissible – for a young woman to have of Kabbalah, to be a Kabbalist, "one who understands".

In Kabbalah, they speak of the sefirot, the nine attributes of God. But those nine attributes are seen in human terms; and humans, likewise, can be seen in terms of the nine attributes, especially as they, the humans, relate to each other in a story or situation or case like the present one. Or so Yacoub taught me.

And it seemed to me that Tiphareth – the hanged or crucified god, whose astrological symbol is the Sun – was in this case neither Guillaume le Breton nor Pierre de Montrouge individually, but both, as it were, together; and what killed them is what stands above and before them on the zig-zag lightning flash, namely Gevurah or Din: judgement, severity – and power. Kabbalists consider Din to be feminine, and from it not only good (judgement) but evil may emerge. Indeed, evil originates in justice, according to the Zohar. It is Sitra Ahra, the Left Hand power, the power of the Other Side.

That is what I am up against.

Battle has only just been joined, and already I am flat on my back. Or rather flat on my front.

I have no idea yet who represents Sitra Ahra. It cannot be the abbé, he is too weak, too ineffectual. Devil he may be, but not … the Devil.

The Devil. Perhaps I should be thinking rather in terms of Tarocchi. After all, the Hanged Man and the Magician are Tarocchi symbols. In that case, we might say that I, the Fool – yes, all right – having faced Death and The Devil – oh, and the Emperor! – now come up against ... The Moon? The Priestess?

All my intuition tells me the Devil in this case is a woman.

Khadija broke into my thoughts to tell me that Raoul had arrived. Should she send him away, tell him to come back in a week or so, when I was better?

'No!' I screamed. Or tried to. What had they done to my throat? It sounded as though my voice was breaking. Was I turning into a man? The good abbé had said they were making a woman of me. Well, if my voice did break, I'd be my brother Magnus permanently. Or Jack Cutting, he was more exciting. Like that girl, now a boy, Thomas of Pizan had been telling me about. But she was a poet. Like Raoul. 'Bring him in here at once!'

Tutting furiously, she showed him in and left us alone together. And the door ajar.

Raoul was kissing my temple, my cheek.

'Raoul, close the door. Properly.'

He closed it and came back, and by kneeling and placing his head on the pillow next to mine managed to kiss me on the lips. 'I was so worried. I thought they might have hurt you.'

I stared at him. 'They did hurt me.'

'Yes, but I mean – I mean, look at you! You are beautiful! I thought you might have been really hurt.'

'I was really hurt.'

'But – '

'Take this cover off me. Go on! Pull it down!'

He did so, shuffling sideways on his knees.

Oh, that was better, the cover off, cool air getting to it.

'Mariana …'

I peered over my shoulder at him. As I did so, he kissed my
bottom. Gently. Both cheeks.

'You see?' I murmured.

'But that's nothing, Mariana. I thought they might have spoilt
you.'

'They don't believe in spoiling girls in that place.'

'I meant spoilt your appearance, your beauty.'

'Yes. I know what you meant.' I forgave him. He was a man.
'So I look more or less presentable, do I?'

'Oh, yes. As long as you keep your skirts down.'

'I intend to keep my skirts down, Raoul – for the rest of my
life.'

He was still kissing my bottom.

'Raoul, be serious.'

'I am being serious.'

'Listen to me!' I squawked. 'Go and find your friend Philippe.
Tell him I need to, I must, get in contact with Thomas of Pizan. It
is extremely urgent.'

'Mm.' He carried on kissing.

I had been cold, so cold, in that cell, and in that horrible horse
trough, and down by the river, but now I was warm; and I had
been in pain, so much pain, and now the pain too, like the
coldness, was becoming a memory.

'Raoul, that is truly wonderful, but please, go. Now. It really is
urgent.'

Next, Khadija announced that Mère Henriette and Jaquet were
waiting to see me. She pulled the cover back up over my bottom
– then on second thoughts pulled it back down and said,
sarcastically, 'But perhaps you want all the world to see your
shame?'

'Shame? I didn't do anything! This was done to me! It is the men who did it who should be ashamed! Oh, cover me up and show them in. And close the door after them.'

Mère Henriette came in first, followed by Jaquet. 'Dem'selle ...' she said, but he pushed past her and knelt beside the bed and took my hand and kissed it. Just kissed it. No words. As he had kissed it when I visited him in prison.

'Demoiselle,' she began again, eyeing Jaquet disapprovingly, 'I want to thank you personally for trying to help my son. You did your best, I know. And fortunately, the Sire de Montrouge, Messire Jean, was able to help clear Jaquet's name when you got yourself into trouble …'

'Maman! Dem'selle Mariana didn't do anything. Any more than I did.'

'I heard she dressed up as a boy and – '

I didn't believe this. 'Madame, I did not ask you here to thank me – or to discuss me.'

'Then why did you ask us here, dem'selle?'

'To answer a few more questions.'

'Why? It is finished. We no longer need your "help".'

Poor Jaquet.

'It is not finished, madame, very far from it.'

'But – '

'Messire Pierre de Montrouge was no more guilty of that murder than Jaquet was.'

'What? You dare to say – '

'I intend to discover who really killed Maître Guillaume, and would prefer to do so without announcing publicly – yet – that Pierre de Montrouge could not be the murderer, as such an announcement would no doubt result in poor Jaquet's being reincarcerated in the Châtelet.'

'But Messire Jean himself believes that his brother did it.'

'He won't, not after I have had ten words with him.'

'I see … I thought you said she was your friend, Jaquet.'

Jaquet gazed at me.

'I am your friend, Jaquet. Now help me as I have helped – excuse me, madame, tried to help – you.'

'But of course we will, Mariana.'

'Then I wish your mother to answer me this: why did she deny the very possibility that Natalie might be Maître Guillaume's daughter?'

'I – he – but she – but – ' she stammered.

'Madame, tell us the truth. Was she born after they arrived in Paris?'

'Yes.'

'Long after?'

'Oh, yes. Long enough, certainly, for Guillaume to have been the father. And it is true, her mother claimed always that she was Guillaume's daughter – to me at least, if not publicly. But she would, wouldn't she. She used to entertain men downstairs while poor Guillaume was busy upstairs in his laboratory. And there was one just like her, could have been her sister, probably was, they never introduced her to me, and she was a putain if ever I saw one. So … Who knows?'

'She entertained men even then? As soon as they arrived in Paris? For as I understand it, Natalie was born about nine months after they settled here.'

'Mm. Well, perhaps not. But all the same, the kind of woman she was …'

'What did Maître Guillaume himself say?'

'He never said. He did not treat her as a daughter, though … But then perhaps he did not wish to be accused of incest.'

Elle était incroyable. Unbelievable. 'Madame, Natalie is certainly a virgin.'

'Nonsense.'

'Believe it or not, as you wish, but it is true.'

She stared at me in open hostility, while her son continued to kneel by the bed, holding my hand.

I decided to play a little. Embroider. 'On the other hand, there was a woman, one who used to visit le vieux Guillaume at home, at night, alone.'

'How do you …?'

'Natalie told me. Maître Guillaume had few, if any, secrets from her. Unlike her mother, she was even permitted to enter his laboratory.'

'I am quite sure that on the occasions to which you refer she did no more than open the door and show the lady in. You imply, too, that these visits were frequent, even regular, while to the best of my knowledge, they were infrequent in the extreme.'

'Please share that knowledge with me, madame. At once.'

'Maman! Please!'

'Oh, very well. I know a woman who lives in the neighbourhood. She – '

'Your neighbourhood? Or that of Maître Guillaume?'

'The latter, bien sûr. I know her as a customer. Our apothecary's shop in the rue du Dragon is after all not far from the rue Saint-Pol. She comes and she gossips. Can I prevent her? And knowing that her mysterious neighbour is, or at least was, once, many years ago, my brother-in-law, she tells me of his visitors, all of whom she manages to see. She has for years. She took a great interest in l'Albanienne – Natalie's mother.'

'Well, I do not. My interest is purely in Maître Guillaume, and in those who called on him during the last few months.'

'Apart from the religieuse who, it seems, came in a litter which she would then dismiss – '

'Religieuse?'

'Religieuse, yes. When she emerged after an hour or so, she left on foot, in the direction of the Pont-au-Change. Apart from her, as I say, there seem to have been two women. One rich, one poor – but not so rich or so poor.'

'Their ages?'

'No longer young.'

'And that is all you know?'

'The rich one was well dressed, but veiled, always. Tall. Slender. What else should I know?'

'And the religieuse, the nun? '

'Also tall.'

'Was she on occasion accompanied by the good abbé?

'No.'

There was nothing else she could tell me. I promised Jaquet I would ask Natalie to contact him, and that I myself would keep in touch; then they took their leave.

The truth was, of course, that Natalie had never so much as hinted at the existence of these women. Apart from some woman who could control the virgin-stone. And that silence of hers was both strange and curious. Whatever was terrifying Natalie concerned one of them.

Ferchard knocked and put his head in. 'You want to rest, lass, or you want to talk?'

'Talk.'

He came in, sat on the edge of the bed. 'Tell me.'

'Ferchard, it was not Pierre.'

'Aye, you said that. No blood.'

'Mm, but there's more.'

He waited.

'Natalie's fear is too great, too irrational. Her refusal to give evidence in order to obtain poor Jaquet's release remains quite inexplicable. Pierre was dead, she had nothing to fear from him. Even the abbé, who is, I grant, extremely unpleasant, blanches at the mention of the Albanian, who is Natalie's uncle, and is therefore hardly likely to fill her with terror. No, there is someone else, someone who does terrify her. And someone – a woman – was in Guillaume's house that night, still in that house when Pierre came out and went home.'

'Have you any evidence of this?'

'Wait. There is also the manner of the murder. The Death by a

Thousand Cuts is not the kind of death Pierre would inflict. Or you. Or any real man. It is the mark of a eunuch or a priest – '

'Aye, or a sodomite. Or a woman. Well, we have a eunuch to hand, though I hardly think poor Yahia is a serious contender. We have a priest, too, of course – '

'One quite capable of ordering, if not of inflicting, such a death. Oh, yes. But it wasn't him.'

Ferchard agreed. 'So. A woman. We have several. Natalie herself, for one. She was there.'

'Right. She can be very cool, very calculating. And very hard. She is also an expert, believe me, in the use of a dagger.'

'Then there's her mother.'

I looked at him. I hadn't thought of that. Was Lule still alive?

'You mean, did she not so much die as run off? Guillaume and the Albanian would, of course, have colluded in keeping this secret. To them, she would be dead. And Mère Henriette did say that Lule had many admirers whom she did nothing to discourage. Interesting.'

'There is Mère Henriette herself.'

'She wouldn't terrify Natalie. On the other hand, Natalie would be very unwilling to divulge her mother's secret life.'

'So. Natalie or her mother. But no evidence.'

'Wait, Ferchard. There are other women.' I told him about Guillaume's nocturnal visitors. But were they nocturnal, I wondered, even as I said it? Mère Henriette had not said so. 'And this is interesting,' I continued, 'because it relates directly to one of the abbé's plans for me … I haven't told you about his plans for me yet, have I? The first – his favourite, I think – was to marry me to one of his henchmen: he himself would perform the ceremony, and as soon as I was well and truly wed I would be rudely relieved of all my rights and all my property – '

'Oh, lass … What made him change his mind?'

'I told him the Albanian would widow me within hours of the wedding – not to mention giving the abbé himself a most painful death.'

'I would.'

'Oh, I know. But he doesn't know you. He does know the Albanian.'

'And his other plans?'

'The one that concerns us now was to send me to a convent run by a certain Mother Superior of his acquaintance, a convent where they have underground penitential cells which are in effect oubliettes. There I would be incarcerated in the smallest and deepest and darkest – sans hands and sans tongue, if need be, to prevent my gaining the sympathy of anyone or attempting to smuggle out a message.'

'He's a devil, and I will kill him, whatever you say. Only think! If you hadn't put the fear of Hell into him with your stories of the Albanian, you might be there now, and not one of us with any idea where you were or what had become of you.'

Suddenly, I realised that time had gone by unaccounted for. He was looking at me as though I was not there with him, in that room, having that conversation.

In a sense, I wasn't.

Nothing seemed right or real since I woke at dawn down by the river with the eyes of the boy and the cat and the birds all upon me. It was as though I knew I was dreaming, that this was a dream, and I would wake at any moment back in my cell, or perhaps even bent over backwards on that bench having blacked out for a moment while I was being fucked.

'Are you all right, lass?'

'What? Oh. Yes. I'm fine, Ferchard. Just …'

'You should rest now. Sleep. Sleep another day – sleep a whole week.'

'I know, but I can't. Not yet. I was saying … I've lost the thread.'

'You were telling me about a woman of whom Natalie is terrified, a woman who might have been Guillaume's slayer. But

you hadn't got to her yet.'
    'I had. That Mother Superior.'
    'Lass … Oh. I see. Yes.'
    'What I'd like you to do is put le Cafard and le Pitre on watch
outside the abbé's residence. They are looking for a tall, slim
woman, probably a religious, but maybe not. They are to follow
such a woman, see where she goes, and report back to one of us.'
    'Right. I'll do that.'

21

I slept again.
    And was woken by voices outside my door: Khadija saying in
Arabic that no one could enter my room, I was sleeping, I was ill,
Raoul insisting in French that I was perfectly all right, I was
simply resting, Ferchard interpreting for them – then another
voice, a deep, male voice: I knew that voice, that Italian accent!
Dottore Thomasso di Benvenuto da Pizzano – here!
    I croaked.
    No one heard me.
    I got up with a groan, and went to the door. Stopped. I was
naked. I picked up a white shift and tried to pull it over my head.
My ribs! Any second that door would open. But I couldn't get my
right arm up, get it into the sleeve, it was impossible. In
desperation, as the door seemed about to burst open judging from
the noise, I pulled my fur wrap round me, took as deep a breath
as I could and opened the door myself. Sudden silence.
    'Dottore. Forgive us. Come in.'
    'Doña Mariana.' He bowed over my hand while I desperately
hung onto my fur with the other hand. 'This is my daughter,

Christine. She was anxious to meet you.'

'Come in, please. Both of you. Thank you, Raoul.' I closed the door on him, and on everyone else.

'Sit down, dottore – there, yes. And you, Christine, come and sit on the edge of my bed.' I managed to get onto the bed myself without losing the fur. Shyly, she sat beside me. I wanted to take her hands in mine, but could not. 'You have a beautiful daughter, dottore.'

'Thomas, please. Yes, she takes after her poor mother fortunately, in that respect. But she has my interest in all things pertaining to science and history.'

'You teach her yourself?'

They both nodded.

'She is indeed fortunate.'

'Ah, she reads widely. Too widely, it may be, for a maid of thirteen. I tell her, wisdom is not to be found only in books but in nature, in life.'

I looked at her.

She smiled – laughing black eyes, and such full, smooth cheeks, soft lips, such white little teeth. She was very sweet. And she had dark wavy hair and the longest, thickest eyelashes I had ever seen, even during my time in Granada among the Moors. They would have loved her.

'When my father says "too widely", he means the poems and songs, the romances that I love.'

I waited. She was shy, but she was full of thoughts, full of words.

'Are not people nature and life? Just as soon as my father told me he had met one of the brightest, cleverest women living in France today, and that she was beautiful, too, with the cold green-blue beauty of the north and the dark golden beauty of the south distilled into one person, I knew I had to meet you.'

'Dottore! Thomas! Did you really say all that?' I tried to adjust my uncomfortable position, my fur wrap slipped, I grabbed at it

– and gasped as the pain shot through me. The poor girl jumped up but Thomas just patted her on the shoulder and moved her to one side and calmly took her place on the edge of my bed.

'Mariana, I am a physician. Tell me. Show me.'

Ah. Yes. That's right, of course. He was to all intents and purposes the King's physician.

'It is your ribs? This side?'

I nodded.

'Allow me … ' He took the fur from my shoulders then tried to lower me onto the bed.

I tensed and cried out.

'Relax, let me take the weight. That's it. Good. There now … '

I was lying on my back, naked to my waist. Christina was staring in horror at the four glaring purple weals across my breasts. But they were not my problem. It was the first time I had lain on my back and it hurt and –

'Now what hurts? This is something different, isn't it?'

I blushed. 'It's my bottom. I've been beaten.'

He looked shocked – then more surprised than shocked. Then he grinned.

'It is not amusing, dottore!'

'Father!' cried Christina.

'Yes, yes, I'm sorry, of course it is not amusing, Mariana, but, ah, it is hardly a serious matter, either. Whereas your ribs – '

'Doña Mariana is quite right to protest, Father. I too have noticed that a beating strikes all the world as funny – when it's a girl or a woman who is being beaten.'

'You have never been beaten!'

'Yes, I have! You just weren't told, because the once that you were informed you teased me about it unmercifully.'

He stared at her, obviously trying to remember. Then said, 'Hm. Well, perhaps you are both right.'

'Perhaps?' we chorused – then laughed, which caused me to gasp with pain again.

'Enough! I'll look at that later. Now I need to examine your chest, make sure the ribs are all in place and simply bruised or cracked, not actually broken …'

He knew his job. Within half an hour – Khadija was called in to help – he had my whole chest thoroughly swaddled in bandages made out of torn up sheets (and had made a joke about me having no trouble now passing as a boy at the university, which had earned him another glare from his daughter) and this binding gave me so much support I was able to move almost freely, though I was not able to laugh, even when Christine said that in her opinion the reason women were excluded from universities was that their presence would show most men up for the fools they were: easier to keep women uneducated and go on pretending.

I liked her, obviously.

'And now for that bottom,' he announced, rubbing his hands together.

Even Christine, my ally, grinned.

Khadija had never been my ally, but she had found to her delight that she could communicate with them, she in her Moorish Spanish and Thomas in a mix of Spanish and Italian, while Christine's Spanish was perfect. Now Khadija helped him lay me down again, this time on my front, while they all ignored my protests that my bottom was fine, it was just a matter of time, it had had the right salves applied to it …

'Mama mia!' He sat down again on the edge of the bed and put his cupped hand gently over it and stroked it. He did have the healing touch.

I saw Christine turn pale, her eyes wide, incredulous.

Khadija, of course, immediately began telling them how I'd been asking for it, how I would never listen, how I needed a man to keep me –

'Out!' I said.

'But – '

'OUT!'

Thomas nodded towards the door, and Christine took the poor old thing by the arm and led her firmly from the room.

She came back and stood beside her father. They both gazed down at me. I thought they were criticising my treatment of her.

'I'm sorry,' I said. 'She's probably right. I just couldn't listen to her any longer.'

'Do you want to tell me who did this to you?'

I hesitated. I didn't, no. I much preferred, as always, to do things my own way.

'I have great influence,' he went on. 'And as the King knows you, the influence will be that much easier to bring to bear, that much more effective. Even the Emperor himself, who was so taken with you, is still in Paris – '

'The Emperor?' gasped Christine.

'Oh yes. The Emperor was fast falling in love with Doña Mariana. In fact, to judge from the number of enquiries I have had about her during the last few days, I do believe she has him quite enthralled.'

'Oh no! Oh, Mariana! May I call you Mariana? It's like a dream!'

'Yes, you may call me Mariana. And no, Thomas, you may not mention this assault upon my person to anyone, least of all the King or those in his entourage.' I glared at him, then added, 'As for the Emperor, I'm quite sure he would fall out of love again very rapidly if he could see me as you see me now.'

'I'm quite sure he would not,' breathed Thomas of Pizan.

'My father is right. The Emperor is a man. He would – '

'Mariana, why do you not want me to – '

'Because I shall handle this as I always handle things – in my own way. I haven't relied on a man since I was a child and I don't intend to start now. That goes for the King – and the Emperor, too.' You hypocrite, I thought to myself, even as I said it. The Albanian is a man: and if he had not existed, you would have been only too ready to mention any man whose name might have saved you, king or emperor – or street urchin. In fact, you did mention all the men you knew, including the Emperor. They all failed to impress, save the Albanian: who, in his own words, has balls.

I was getting tired, confused. 'Could I please have the cover over me now?'

'Yes, I think I've seen quite enough to make a diagnosis.' He smiled. 'You are suffering from the after-effects of what the world would call a good beating.'

'Thank you. And what would you recommend?'

'I would certainly recommend staying out of trouble. Other than that, time will be the best physician.'

'You have been most helpful, dottore.'

'Mariana, he is laughing at you again.'

'I know.'

'Oh, what shall I do with him?'

'I know what you can do for me, chérie: you can cover me up.'

She did so.

Her father looked disappointed.

Time for a change of subject.

'So you are an avid reader, Christine. Tell me what you've been reading these last few days.'

'I've been reading the Roman de la Rose. Have you read it?'

'Yes, when I was a child, in Spain.'

'You see, Father? How old were you, Mariana?'

'Oh, eleven or twelve.'

'It's beautiful, isn't it? I haven't read all the part attributed to Jean de Meung …'

'Jean is long-winded. And much is boring.'

'But is he really so against women? I heard he so upset the ladies of the court that they – '

'Christine!'

'Oh, Father – do you really think anything could shock

Mariana?'

He looked at me, eyes twinkling again. 'No, probably not; though I'm not at all sure that is a compliment to her.'

'Only when something is meant as a compliment, is it a compliment, Thomas. But go on, Christine, chérie.'

'The ladies of the court cornered him in some small antechamber, where they proposed to strip and flagellate him, in order to teach him to speak well of women – '

'How would it?' demanded her father. 'I mean, how would that teach him to think better of women? Completely illogical.'

'It would at least teach him not to speak ill of them,' I laughed. I felt better already.

'Would it? Then listen to what happened next. A clever man can always get the upper hand. He – '

'You tell me, Christine.'

'He said a man should always be given a hearing before being condemned and punished. Laughing, they agreed. After all, how could he change what he had written? Was he going to claim he had not written those vile lines? Oh, he had written them, he admitted, but they were not intended to calumniate all womankind, only the immoral and debased – certainly not such models of virtue and beauty as he saw before him. However, if any lady there present truly felt that the lines might be applied to her, then he would strip and submit to well-deserved chastisement.'

I laughed, or rather grunted. 'Clever indeed,' I said. 'But I don't think he would have got away with that if your daughter and I had been there.'

'Oh no, he certainly wouldn't,' she said. 'To insult one lady is to insult all.'

'And to punish one man for doing so is to punish all, I suppose?' added Thomas, sarcastically.

'Yes!' cried Christine, and simultaneously I croaked, 'Yes, in a sense.'

'Mariana?'

'Yes, Thomas, for men are men and the sons of Adam, while women are women, and the daughters of Eve. And their origins are quite different.'

'As you say, Mariana: quite different. Eve was created from the flesh of Adam, dependent on and subordinate to him. Without him, she has no existence.'

I looked at Christine, and smiled.

She smiled back. She could handle this. 'But, Father, it says quite clearly that man was created from mud, outside Paradise, while Eve was created from flesh, in Paradise. And when they were expelled, he was sent back where he came from, while she, poor thing, had to accompany him, and give up the joys of her native world.'

'Hm. But it also says that Adam, man, was created in God's image.'

Christine glanced at me: my turn. 'In Kabbalah,' I said, 'we learn that it is the soul of man which is created in God's image, not the corruptible and ephemeral body. And as Jesus said, the soul, in Heaven, is neither male nor female, but like an angel.'

Christine liked that. She beamed at her father, and asked, brightly, 'So what have we established? That the soul of man and the soul of woman are indistinguishable; and that the body of a woman is much superior to that of a man; and that she is on this earth, this world of toil and pain that men call home, an exile from her own home in Paradise.'

Thomas, who had been listening to all this and covertly admiring his wonderful daughter, now said: 'Mariana, will you glance at Christine's hands for me?'

I looked at her and raised my eyebrows. Would she like me to?

She smiled and nodded.

I raised myself up a little on my elbows and she put her right hand on the pillow in front of my face.

She had a long, impressive thumb which stuck out at a right angle from the palm as it lay there.

'Shall I read just your thumb for today? Then another time, when I can do so more comfortably, I'll read your two hands and interpret them in conjunction with your horoscope.'

She glanced at her father.

'Yes, I've heard of this reading of the thumbs,' he said, 'but have never seen it done.'

'The thumb is normally thought of as having two phalanges only, unlike the other fingers. However, this, the ball of the thumb, the Mount of Venus, is in reality the third phalange of the thumb. Move your thumb – waggle it. You see? It is all part of what we call the Pollax. The limit of the thumb is this long line here that runs right round the Mount of Venus.'

'The Life Line,' she murmured. 'I know that one.'

'Yes, though sometimes it is called the Venus Line. Now, the top phalange of the thumb represents volition, the second or middle phalange represents logic, and the bottom or base phalange represents love – as one might expect, it being the Mount of Venus. So you see, we have everything here: the Life Line, love, logic, and volition. We also have the angle of the thumb, and its flexibility, both of which yield us yet further information … Shall I go ahead?'

'Oh, yes! Please!!'

'Right. So the thumb is long and flexible. The length indicates the ability to rise to any challenge and to triumph no matter what the circumstances, while the flexibility means just that: flexibility.'

'I don't find her very flexible,' muttered Thomas.

'Oh, she is, in the sense that she can bend with the wind. What you are coming up against is her will-power and determination, indicated by the long top phalange. The angle the thumb makes here with the rest of the hand, a full right-angle, shows qualities of leadership, and also a desire to bring about reformation.'

'She certainly has that. She'd reform me if I let her.'

Christine grinned. 'And this? The Mount of Venus?'

'It is full and well-formed. You have a loving nature. And the Line of Life is interesting. You see where it starts, right up here under your index finger on the Mount of Jupiter?'

'Is that unusual?'

'Very. And it indicates ambition, the drive to succeed - a drive you were born with.'

'And will I have a long life?'

'Long enough. Look. The Life Line stretches unbroken all the way round here … '

'That's wonderful. And did you read the Emperor's hand?'

'She did. And Princess Anna's. And it is her reading of Princess Anna's hand that concerns us now. It is urgent, Mariana.'

'It's ready. You can take it.'

'No, I can't deliver it for you. The Emperor wishes to see you personally.'

'You mean now? Today?'

'Yes. Tomorrow there will be a great banquet at the palace. Then on Thursday, the visit to the Louvre. His message to me said Today, and it implied Today or Never. He is, as you know, not in good health.'

'And you think I will be all right? I mean, will I look all right? My nose …'

'You will be, as always, bellissima.'

'But will I be able to move? My ribs still ... '

'The bandage will support you. It will hurt, of course - and so will your bottom - but you will smile and pretend …'

It had taken a lot of arguing, and demonstrating my fitness, but finally I had been permitted to dress - or rather be dressed by Yahia and Christine, with Thomas supervising - and go to the palace with Thomas and Christine. When an emperor summons even Ferchard – even Khadija – is impressed, though she was still sulking.

When we got there, Thomas was called straight in for a private audience. Christine and I were left outside.

This lasted only a few minutes, then the doors opened again and Thomas beckoned. 'Christine, the Emperor wishes to meet you.'

The girl grinned at me, pushed at her hair (her cap was in her hand) and stepped past her father in the doorway. The door closed behind them.

This interview took longer, which was hardly surprising when I thought about it. Christine and the Emperor were made for each other, but this was the only time, in this life anyway, that they would meet.

I waited patiently. There were some chairs in the corridor, but I preferred to walk up and down. I smiled at the footman/guard whose eyes had been following me, but the only effect this had was to make him gaze straight ahead once more. I had stood outside my mistress's room like that, hour after hour, unmoving, while I was a slave in Granada. And no doubt would be doing so still, had I not had the good fortune to be sold to ibn Khaldoun.

Eventually, they emerged, Christine flushed and excited, Thomas looking grave. 'The Emperor will see you now, Mariana.'

I hesitated.

'Well, go on.'

'Alone?'

He nodded. And smiled.

I went in. I, of course, had my cap on my head and a veil down over my face.

He was lying propped up on a couch with his feet on a cushion. I knelt beside him.

'Mariana?'

'Your majesty?'

He laughed. 'I made your name sound like a question because you are hidden behind that veil. You could have been anybody. Whereas I …'

'Your majesty.'

'You would know me anywhere. Mariana, stand up. Sit down - here, on this stool. That's it. And would you mind very much removing the veil, and the cap?'

'Of course not, your majesty.'

He gazed at me while I did so, then said: 'It would please me, also, if you were to consider me a friend, as you do my daughter, and - we are quite alone - call me Charles.'

I gazed back at him. The black eyes were so bright in that tired face, that failing body. This was a man I could … I had thought, whimsically, that he and Christine were made for each other. Now I realised he and I had been made for each other.

Did every woman feel that in his presence?

'Charles,' I said, softly. And it sounded, Deo gratias, like a murmur, not a croak.

Then, struggling to return to practicalities, I added: 'My reading for Princess Anna ... '

'I have it. Thomas gave it to me, along with his own. Is there anything you wish to add to it, in confidence?'

'Only that … she is not very strong, your - Charles. She will need a father-figure when ... '

'And you don't trust my son, Prince Wenceslas.'

Oh dear. 'He is very young.'

'As you say.' He thought about it. 'I will do my best for her. She will be married quite soon, of course.'

'To Richard of England?'

'You tell me.'

'It seems very likely.'

His eyes rested on me for a moment. 'Mariana, are you all right? Are you comfortable? Thomas told me of your, ah, misadventures.'

'Told you everything?'

'Enough to know that it might not have been quite thoughtful of me to tell you to sit on that hard little stool.'

He didn't grin - he was a gentleman - but his eyes had taken on an extra sparkle.

'Would you prefer to stand? I would invite you to lie beside me, here, on the couch, but I am hardly able to make room for you, and from what Thomas told me about your ribs you are hardly able to lie down. I should like to think, though, that we might meet again under what might be for both of us happier circumstances.'

'In another life …'

'I would like that.'

'May I kneel back down, here?'

He nodded, and I knelt beside him, my hands on the edge of the bed. He took one in his and held it, caressing the fingers. 'At least they didn't spoil your beauty, Mariana. Your face … you are still ravissante. But when you came in, I thought I should have known you by your walk … They have spoilt your walk.'

The way he said it, it sounded like: And for that they shall die. I laughed. 'That is temporary. In a week or two - '

'I shall not be here … Who were they? Do you know?'

'I do, but not everything, not yet. It has to do with scrying and Tarocchi, and with alchemy.'

'Alchemy? Then Mariana, you must be very careful, or you may find yourself in real trouble.'

I looked at him. No one was perfect. But when he said Tell me, I told him. The whole story.

Then I waited.

At last, he said: 'There are three points to consider. First, Maître Guillaume's will: clearly you must work with this girl Natalie; you must look for some hiding-place marked by her Sign - which is?'

'Capricorn?'

'Capricorn, then. I 'm sure that between the two of you, you will find whatever he may have left for her, in papers or in gold. If there are papers, and I'm still in Paris, I would dearly love to see them. Second, the murderer of the Sire de Montrouge: this Albanian is Natalie's uncle and only remaining blood-kin, and there do seem to have been mitigating circumstances. You must decide what to do about that.'

'He would be a difficult man to bring to justice, Charles.'

'Just so. And quite apart from that, both Natalie and, more importantly, you, seem to owe your continued existence to his. Third, this abbé: I could have him arrested and incarcerated deep beneath some monastery in Bohemia, and there forgotten.'

'That sounds perfect. If he lives long enough for you to get to him. However, he is no longer my problem. The woman is.'

'I know of many women in France who may be described as witches (and of a few who are) but I know of only one who has been called a witch and shown an interest in alchemy and sometimes appears as a nun. We do know that she is tall; and we do know that she has been in touch with both Maître Guillaume and Maître Flamel.'

'You know them?' I had had no idea.

'I know of them. I have a network of agents who keep me informed.'

'You have?'

'All monarchs have. Mine is better than most. And mine is the only network that interests itself in alchemy and alchemists.'

'Apart from the Inquisition.'

He smiled. 'As you say. Are you quite comfortable like that, on your knees all this time?'

'No, but any other position would be worse.'

'You must be used to kneeling.'

I looked at him.

'I mean, you bear the marks of a convent girl.'

'I bear the marks of many things. It is true, yes, that I was a

convent girl, as you put it, for a while, but since then, since I was
fifteen, I have preferred not to kneel when I could possibly avoid
it. However, these are exceptional circumstances. I don't often
find myself at the bedside of an emperor.'

'Very exceptional. I am not used to finding myself helpless, a
cripple.' He gazed at me.

He wanted to caress more of me than my hand.

'Kneel closer to me, Mariana …' He put his other hand slowly,
tentatively, to my face. 'Your poor nose.' His sensitive fingers
brushed over it. 'Twice I have seen you, and on both occasions
… Mariana, stay out of trouble. For me.'

Tears welled up and ran down my face. He wiped them away
gently with his fingers.

'I'm sorry, Charles. I do believe that your feeling sorry for me,
feeling concerned about me, is making me feel sorry for myself.'

For a moment, we did not speak. I was wondering whether the
woman who sometimes appeared as a nun might be the abbé's
friend. I said, 'Do you know anything more of this woman who
sometimes appears as a nun? '

'To the world, she is known as Niniane des Sept Soeurs.'

'You don't think there are six more at home like her, do you?'

'That wouldn't surprise me. Mariana, tomorrow, after the
banquet, there is to be a great entertainment in the Hall of
Parlement. Be there. Come with Thomas and his daughter. At
some point, I will send for you and I will tell you what I have
been able to discover about Niniane des Sept Soeurs. Meanwhile,
I should like you to make contact with one of my agents. Let me
see. Do you know the Chaire?'

'On the Petit-Pont, yes. But I'm surprised you do.'

'I grew up here in Paris.'

Ah yes. I remembered hearing that.

'Enter the Chaire at any time between tierce and sext
tomorrow morning. Be alone. Look around you, as if expecting
to meet someone. A small man will say: "Bonjour, dem'selle.

Maître Guillaume could not be here today. I am Gabriel. Follow me." You will follow him. He will help you.'

'Who? Gabriel? Or Maître Guillaume?'

'Mariana, Maître Guillaume is dead. That is simply a phrase by which the agent you will know as Gabriel will introduce himself. And you will be known as – let's see ... Demoiselle d'Écosse.'

'Ah. Yes.'

Silly me, I wanted to say. But he stroked my eyebrows, and all my embarrassment melted away.

'Mariana, I have to rest now, and much as I should like … My daughter is waiting. She wishes to talk to you again, and she would enjoy meeting Thomas's Christine ... '

'Thomas! Oh, don't tell me they're still waiting outside that door?'

'I should be exceedingly surprised if they are not.'

'But we have been talking for ages.'

'That is your fault. Now go. The footman knows. And I'm afraid Thomas will have to wait outside yet again.'

I kissed his hands, both of them, then got to my feet with a groan.

'Mariana, be there tomorrow when I send for you.'

'I will.'

22

Once outside, I told them Princess Anna was waiting for us, then added that only Christine and I would be allowed to enter. The smile slid off Thomas's long, mobile face. He opened his mouth, closed it again.

We followed the footman along the corridor. He stopped at

the third door, and knocked. A voice called: 'Enter!' The footman opened the door and showed Christine and me in. Then closed it behind us.

Anna was sitting at a table, reading. She jumped up and ran over to me. We kissed on both cheeks, while Christine curtsied and stayed down.

'This is Christine de Pizan, Anna, Thomas's daughter. The Emperor, your father, thought you might like to meet her.'

'Of course! I should love to! Christine, stand up. You are beautiful!'

'Your highness.'

'Not here, not while we are alone. Maître Thomas is the King's astrologer?'

'Yes, your - er - '

'Anna.'

'Anna.'

'Maître Thomas teaches Christine himself,' I said. 'And she is a great reader.'

'Oh, that is wonderful. I adore books. My father teaches me, too - when he has time.'

'He does?'

'And he has time, these days, usually, though here in Paris everything is rather hectic. For him, at least. I just sit quietly, waiting, but Sigismund - my brother, Prince Sigismund - tries to join in and do everything as though he were grown up already. Now there is an argument going on over the banquet. There will be tableaux vivants for the diners to feast their eyes upon, but Father says we are too young for them. And afterwards, there will be some kind of spectacle in the Hall of Parlement.'

'We're already invited to that, ' I said.

'And me?' cried Christine.

'Yes. You, your father and me.'

'If Sigismund were here, he would cry "That's not fair! If Christine can go, why can't we go?"'

'And you?' I asked her.

'Life is rarely fair,' she said. 'But I should adore to see those tableaux vivants.'

'From what I know of tableaux vivants, they would hardly interest girls like you. They seem almost always to depict naked women.'

'Oh, I know,' said the princess. 'My father told me that once when he entered some city they had a portrayal of Eve and the serpent set up for him in the main square outside the cathedral, but there was a cold wind blowing, and he felt so sorry for her!'

I smiled; then told them about one I had seen in Avignon. 'It was for the procession to mark the arrival of some cardinal-archbishop, I don't remember who. There were three naked girls in the fountain, and they were there for hours. They didn't seem to mind, though.'

'But who are these girls - these women?' protested Christine. 'I mean, can anyone do it?'

We laughed.

Anna looked at me.

'They're prostitutes,' I said. 'But chosen ones. The most beautiful.'

Christine said, 'I imagine business must be good after a performance like that.' She, too, was looking at me.

I would know, they thought.

Suddenly Christine laughed. 'Mariana, you were one of those three girls!'

I wasn't, but I could so easily have been, and the princess's excitement at the thought, her sparkling eyes and parted lips, made it clear what she wanted to hear, to believe. What Christine obviously believed about me already.

So I smiled enigmatically and said nothing. Tantamount to an admission.

'And you didn't mind?' Anna asked. 'Being - being naked like that, I mean.'

I remembered standing up on the block in Granada in front of all those hundreds of men, all those beards, all those gleaming eyes, and being sold to the highest bidder. 'Being naked, like anything else, is something you become accustomed to when you are given no choice. And it will often turn out to be the least of your problems.'

'Like standing there in that fountain in the cold and wet hour after hour!' crowed Christine.

I shivered and smiled and they laughed, then I withdrew into myself and watched and listened as they relaxed together and chatted of this and that.

The blonde Anna, though the younger, was the more serious, the more conservative, the more aware that in her life she would have few choices; that a path was laid down for her, and had been since her birth.

Christine, dark and vivacious, had done more and seen more, perhaps; would always be able to do more and see more, for though she would never be a queen, she would, at least to a limited extent, be free. Anna, on the other hand, would live in a cage, a golden cage that would pass from her father to her eldest brother, and finally from her brother to the man he chose to be her husband.

They had begun to talk about Jean de Meung, and Christine was telling Anna the story she had told me. The princess clearly found it shocking, if also amusing. 'And yet he was right,' she said. 'There are good women and there are bad women.'

Suddenly they were both looking at me again.

They had so much to learn about life. So did I; I was only twenty. And though my halter was longer than that which held Christine secure, it was nevertheless a halter.

'I think the problem is telling which is which,' I said.

'You mean …? Ah yes, I think I know what you mean. There are bad nuns.'

'There are indeed.'

'Of course,' said Christine. 'But can a bad woman, be "good"?'
She was beginning to annoy me.
'Many a prostitute, forced into it by men or by circumstances,
retains her natural innocence, her kindness, her ability to dream.
One of the problems of Guillaume de Lorris' view of women is
that no woman can live up to it, that it's not true: we disappoint.
But Jean de Meung is more realistic. Only he could present
Reason as a woman. And she is a real woman. What she offers
the Dreamer is real love, natural love.'
The princess, unlike Christine, had read all the Roman. She
nodded, wide-eyed.
'Natural love,' I repeated. 'Nature, in Jean de Meung, is
completely opposed to such notions as virginity and celibacy.
And he is right. Such notions are completely unnatural.'
Now they were both gazing at me, Anna wide-eyed, Christine
with a shocked grin.
It was Anna who spoke. 'My father would agree with you
about that, I am sure. But he says the most interesting, and most
important, difference between de Lorris and de Meung is their
concept of The Garden: de Lorris' Garden of Love, which is an
earthly paradise, becomes in de Meung the True Garden, a
mystical paradise, a place outside time where the sun always
shines …'
I nodded and smiled. 'A country meadow on a day in May,
green grass, white flocks grazing – flocks that will never be
shorn or slaughtered. Peace. Sunshine. That is heaven.'
'And my father says the Garden of Love is an imitation: all it
does is to seduce us away from our search for the True Garden.'
A serving-lady knocked and entered.
Anna arched her perfect little eyebrows at the poor woman.
'Your highness, forgive me, but we must prepare you for
dinner.'
Leaving her standing there, Anna turned back to Christine and
me. She sighed. 'No one is free. I am probably the least free of

all. Do you not agree, Mariana?'

'I do, absolutely. You have all my sympathy, and all my love.'

'And mine,' murmured Christine.

'But shall I ever see you again? I was so enjoying our conversation. If I get the chance and if I send for you, will you come?'

'Of course, your highness,' I murmured, and Christine said: 'Of course. At any time.'

We all stood up. (Yes, I had been sitting. Why did I find it easier to discuss such things openly with the Emperor than with a girl? And that reminded me of poor Gwyneth. How free was she?) Anna came with us to the door and showed us out herself. She opened the door, and there was Thomas, glowering. Never did a glower flick so quick into a smile of awe. She extended her little hand to him and he bowed over it. 'Maître Thomas. I do hope you have not been too bored out here.'

'No! No, of course not. Waiting outside your door is a pleasure in itself, your highness.'

'Though not to be compared with the pleasure of passing through it. Yes, I recognise the allusion. Unfortunately, no man is permitted to enter this room. No man at all. Farewell, Christine. Mariana. I do hope, and do believe, that we shall meet again.'

As we walked away down the long corridor, I rehearsed to myself beneath my breath the way she had said "Unfortunately". She was a girl I could come to love.

Would my Life Line lead me to England? To London? Why should it? But then, why shouldn't it? Paris stank, and everyone agreed that London was far cleaner, far more wholesome, and the countryside around London idyllic, unlike the barren waste that lay for miles in all directions around Paris. Of course, it had been the English who had laid waste to it time after time, decade after decade, until there was nothing left; but for me and Ferchard (and of course for Khadija and Yahia) England and France were

quite the same, as indeed they were for Sir John Froissart and so
many others.

"Unfortunately …" I chuckled. Perhaps my chuckle sounded
like a gasp or croak, for Thomas and Christine both peered at me.

'I'm all right. Really I am. Will you drop me off on your way?
There is someone I - '

'Not that young islander, the one with the English
sympathies?'

'Islander?'

'Philippe de Saint-Helier. Saint Helier is on the Island of
Jersey, one of les Îles Normandes. You know it?'

'I know of it … No, it's not Philippe I want to speak to, it's a
friend who lives in the rue des Écrivains.'

'We have to take you home. You are not well. You - '

'If you take me home, they will never let me out again, not
today; and you needn't wait for me.'

'Of course we shall wait for you,' protested Thomas.

'If you're not too long,' Christine grumbled. She was tired
now, and hungry, I could see.

'Two minutes,' I promised.

'And then we shall take you home.'

Perenelle herself opened the door and peered out at the waiting
coach. 'Mariana?'

'Perenelle, I cannot stay. I must ask Nicolas two questions,
that is all.'

'Come in. I heard that poor Jaquet has been released.'

'Isn't it wonderful? I hope this visit is not too inconvenient.'

'Nicolas is here and free, though he thinks he's busy. Come
through.' She led me to the kitchen, where the master was
busying himself not with preparing the divine tincture but with
preparing what looked like vegetable broth.

'Mariana! Are you hungry? The finest soupe de légumes in
Paris, though it won't be ready for another two hours.'

'Two hours?' cried his wife.

'It takes time and thought to convert the base vegetables into the philosopher's dinner.'

'I'm sure it does,' I laughed. 'You must teach me sometime. I know no more of the culinary arts than I do of the black arts.'

'Less, I imagine, my lady.'

'Tut tut. Listen: I have two questions, and two minutes only to ask them in. Thomas of Pizan and his daughter are waiting outside.'

'But you must bring them in!'

'They are in a hurry. I promised them I would be no more than two minutes.'

'All right. Your questions,' he said, wiping his hands.

'I wish to know about a woman who has been showing an interest in alchemy. She may be an alchemist herself.'

'I am afraid I know no such woman.'

'She has visited you here, I am told.'

'Nicolas!' said Perenelle.

I glanced at her, but she was joking. Nicolas was hardly a coureur de femmes, and nor did Perenelle strike me as the jealous type.

'Her name is Niniane des Sept Soeurs.' That meant nothing to either of them. 'But there may also be a nun.'

'The only nun who ever comes here,' Nicolas said slowly, 'apart from one or two friends of Perenelle's who show no interest whatever in me or my work, is Mère Athanasía.'

Ah ha. 'And what did she show a particular interest in?'

'The Book of Abraham. Those same pictures that I showed you last time you were here.'

'Was there anything distinctive about her?'

He cast his mind back.

Perenelle said, 'She has strange dark green eyes. I've never seen eyes that colour before. It's a colour of the forest, of plants.'

Nicolas looked surprised. 'I didn't notice.'

'With you, she kept her eyes properly lowered. You wouldn't have.'

'I don't remember. I remember that she was tall and slim and – ah! That one! When she forgets herself, she walks like an angel.' He laughed suddenly, and blushed.

'Ah, you noticed that, did you,' murmured Perenelle. 'Yes, there was a swish when she turned.'

Just one "swish" and it engraved itself upon the brain of this man who probably never noticed a woman in the street.

'I must go,' I said. 'Thank you both so much.'

'So, the nun's name is Athanasía, and she has dark green eyes and a walk that a blind man would notice,' I summed up later. I was back on my bed, prone, propped up on my elbows, and had been telling Ferchard and Raoul of my visits to the Emperor and the alchemist.

'Hard to create such an effect wearing a nun's habit, wouldn't you say?' murmured Ferchard.

'Let's dress Mariana up in one and see,' said Raoul with glee.

Ferchard regarded him balefully. 'Mariana does not walk with a swish.'

Raoul returned his regard, incredulous, while I too peered over my shoulder at Ferchard.

He looked at us both.

Raoul said, 'I saw a blind man following her up the street one day, not so long ago.'

Ferchard laughed.

But a blind man? 'Where exactly, Raoul? And when?'

They both stared.

I blushed. Then pretended annoyance. 'There are blind men and blind men. The Albanian's blind men are not blind at all. Was one of them following me? If so, I want to know when, and why.'

'I don't remember now. It was in the snow one morning, over

on the Île somewhere, coming off the Petit-Pont, behind the
Hôtel-Dieu. I smiled to see it and went on my own way. I was in
a hurry.'

'You didn't speak?'

'I waved, but you were in a hurry too … He saw me. No, he
wasn't blind, you're right.'

'There may be "blind" beggars who answer to men other than
the Albanian,' said Ferchard.

'I'm sure there are.' It could have been anyone taking an
interest in me. 'So. What about tomorrow morning? Can I go?'

Ferchard hesitated. 'All right, lass. But we will follow you.'

Raoul grinned.

I smiled back at him, I couldn't help it, then said to Ferchard,
'He'll know at once. He's a professional.'

'We'll see,' said Ferchard.

We did see. As Gabriel and I emerged from the Chaire, the
tavern on the bridge, into the snow that had been falling lightly, a
flake here, a flake there, for hours, and turned towards the Hôtel-
Dieu, I remembered Raoul's story of the blind beggar; then
became aware of a scuffle behind us at the gate onto the bridge. I
took no notice. However, that was as far as Ferchard and Raoul
got that day. They were simply not allowed onto the Île de la
Cité.

Meanwhile, Gabriel hurried me round to the Parvis Notre
Dame where even in the snow the homeless were begging, the
crippled and starving alongside fat friars appealing for "bread"
with which to buy themselves pies and pasties, women and wine.
The whole city hated them it seemed, and yet the whole city gave
to them – to be on the safe side.

In fact, I prefer Paris frozen, Paris under snow. The filthy
stinking mud no longer stinks, no longer splashes over
everything when horses gallop by. Everything seems clean. Of
course, this is the view of one who wears warm clothes and thick

boots. The frozen mud forms sharp ridges which must slice into
bare feet, bare knees. I had been naked too, though, at least for a
while.

Then I found that we were passing through the gate into the
Hôtel-Dieu, the great hospital of the Ile de la Cité. I had been
here before with other students of the École de Médecine, to
watch and assist in attending the sick; but that had been with
Jaquet and other young people I knew and who knew me (albeit
as Magnus MacElpin). Now I was a woman, injured and
helpless, and alone here with a stranger who was in all
probability little more than a cut-throat.

I glanced at him.

He didn't seem very dangerous.

He took me down to the huge underground chambers where
they did the laundry. A branch of the river came right into the
chamber and two nuns and a lay sister were kneeling beside it,
wringing out sheets in the icy water. We stood and watched for a
moment, then the lay sister looked round and saw us. She
finished the sheet she was holding, stood up and came over to us.
She glanced round nervously.

'What's wrong?' asked Gabriel.

'The Prioress. She was here a moment ago. I was in trouble
yesterday. I don't want to get in trouble again.'

I knew how she felt.

'Has favourites, does she?' Gabriel guessed. 'And you're not
one of them?'

'It's not that. She's fair. At least she doesn't put us on bread
and water all the time like that other prioress used to.'

Gabriel smiled and nodded. 'They need their food,' he said, to
me. 'Especially in weather like this.'

'At least it's not frozen,' I said.

'Not yet.' She grimaced. 'It makes the fires of hell seem like a
dream of heaven when this lot ices over.'

'You have that to look forward to. Like this young – ah –

lady? – at my side.'

Moi? I peered at him.

'Dem'selle d'Ecosse.' He grinned, then grew serious. 'And this poor creature is called Lyse – of Strasbourg. You may tell her all your secrets, dem'selle. She is a listener, and a putter-together of what she hears; but she is not a talker. If anything she learnt from us or one of ours was passed on, she would lose her tongue.'

It suddenly occurred to me: Demoiselle d'Écosse? I had been presented to the Emperor as Doña Mariana de la Mar, from Spain. He had certainly checked up on me. Still, what he learnt must have satisfied him if he opened his own network of spies and intelligence to me as a result.

'I'll go and keep watch for the Prioress, and waylay her if necessary.' He went.

The poor woman looked at me.

'We'd better hurry,' I said.

'No, no, dem'selle. He could waylay her for a week, that one, if he chose to.'

'And those two others?' I nodded at the two nuns who were still kneeling there washing and wringing out sheets.

'Oh, they don't mind. One is soft in the head, the other pities me. I work longer hours, down here in the days on the sheets and up on the wards at night, than those two put together.'

'Just sheets? Ah yes, I remember: the patients are kept naked.'

She nodded. 'It's the only way. It's bad enough that they soil the sheets when they can't get to the privies. If we had gowns as well to wash and dry, I don't know where we'd be. Drying is the worst!'

'And the clothes they come in with?'

'They're washed, yes, and kept for when they leave. If they leave. Many don't, of course; but then their clothes are sold, or used to clothe others who do recover, grace à Dieu, but who arrived in rags. You wish information about some woman?'

'How do you know?'

'It's usually a woman when Gabriel comes to me.'

'You're right, yes. There are three women. All have shown an interest in alchemy, and one may be acquainted with the Abbé Soxxal. The first is a nun, perhaps: all we know of her is that though she goes under the name of Mère Athanasía, she has striking dark green eyes and does not always walk with the gait of a nun. Then there is a tall, elegant lady known as Niniane des Sept Soeurs. She and Mère Athanasía may be one and the same.'

'And the third woman?'

'I know nothing of her except that unlike Niniane des Sept Soeurs she is not a rich woman; she is in her thirties or forties and is known to have visited the murdered miser, Guillaume le Grec.'

'I see. And some background to this enquiry?'

'Is that necessary?'

She nodded. 'It concerns the late Pierre de Montrouge if I am not mistaken.'

I looked at her with sudden respect. 'It does indeed.'

'Then tell me all.'

I did so.

'Come back and see me tomorrow, dem'selle. I will listen on the wards tonight.'

I found Gabriel at the top of the stairs. There had been no sign of the Prioress.

'She wants me to come back tomorrow.'

'Will you need me?'

'Oh no, I don't think so.' I was going to tell him that I was quite familiar with the Hôtel-Dieu, but decided to keep my masculine alter ego to myself for the moment.

He studied me. 'No, nor do I, but … Come.'

He led me out into the Parvis Notre Dame. It was still snowing, flake by flake. There was no wind. Everything was strangely clean, and strangely silent. But I caught a wonderful smell of –

'Look,' he said. 'There. Hot chestnuts. Would you like some?'

'I'd adore some.'

We stayed close to the charcoal brazier while we ate, blowing on the chestnuts to cool them and our fingers to warm them. He smiled at me. Laughed, suddenly. We were happy.

'Tell me about Lyse. She comes from Strasbourg, you said? That's in Alsace, isn't it? In the Empire.'

He nodded. Considered me. Ate another chestnut, and said, 'She was a whore. Still is, at heart. A clever one, too. Knew everyone – and everything.'

'And that caused her downfall?' I wondered. Then wondered at my choice of the word "downfall". He didn't seem to notice anything odd about it, though.

'No, strangely. It was something else. She was simply unlucky. A man tried to kill her. A client. A drunk, you know, shouting "All women are whores!" And in defending herself she killed him, quite by accident. But the magistrates, who like to feel safe when they visit the stews or their favourite maquerelle, are hot on things like that. She was condemned to be whipped through the streets of the city as an example, then boiled in oil. The Emperor intervened, granted her a pardon – on condition she agreed to remain immured within the Hôtel-Dieu in Paris for the rest of her days. And continued as one of his agents. Yes, continued.'

'I see.'

He had finished his. He tried to pick another direct from the brazier but the chestnut man rapped his knuckles with his tongs and he burnt his fingers and jerked his hand back with a howl of pain.

I laughed. And held my own hand out for one more. The chestnut man obliged with a grunt and a half-smile.

Gabriel was not amused.

It was a big one, a beauty. I bit it, gave him half.

'Do you think she'll be able to find out anything for me?'
'If I hadn't, I wouldn't have brought you to her.'
'Wasn't it the Emperor's idea?'
'Yes, but I went along with it. She has a way of asking the right questions. Not even asking. Just pushing the conversation, oh so gently, with a word here, a word there, in the right direction. You will know more tomorrow than you know now.'

I asked where and when we could meet again.
'I will contact you, should that be necessary.'
'And if I wish to contact you?'
'There's no reason why you should. Adieu, dem'selle.'
'Adieu, Gabriel.'

He went one way, I the other, back towards the Petit-Pont, but as I went I turned and distinctly saw him wave a finger at a man who had been standing unobtrusively watching the snow as it began to settle all over again on the steps of Notre Dame.

And when I looked back as I stepped off the Petit-Pont, the man was just coming onto it.

Protection?

Probably. He was making no great effort to avoid being seen. By me, anyway, though there was no reason why anyone else should connect him with me.

I hoped so.

I was beginning to feel very vulnerable on the streets of Paris.

Then I saw Raoul. I hurried over to him and hugged him. He was frozen.

'Let's go into the Chaire,' I said. 'Have something to eat. Get you warm.'

'Oh, please, yes, that sounds wonderful. But they wouldn't let me onto the bridge, me or Sir Farquhar.'

'They may now.'

They did.

We sat down and ordered his usual bean soup for Raoul. I was still dithering between a hot pasty (the Chaire did very good ones) and pulpa en su tinta (cuttlefish cooked in its ink, to remind me of my home on the Mar Menor) when I saw my protector slip in behind us. I caught his eye and he smiled. He had been standing in the snow for at least as long as Raoul had.

The bread came, and the wine, then the soup, and soon Raoul was warm again. He watched as I finished my pasty, cutting it into small pieces and eating it daintily rather than picking the whole thing up and biting it, which was the custom in Paris taverns. Today I was a lady, and I was foreign. When I was dressed in my black student's gown or any other of "Magnus's" clothes (I had various jerkins and tunics at home and full length hose in a variety of colours) I too picked up my pasties whole – and great chunks of pie.

'I have to pay another visit to a certain house in the rue Saint-Pol.'

'Mariana, you are incorrigible.'

'And I thought you were pure de Lorris.'

He grins. 'I am. To me you are a goddess, high on a pedestal, far out of reach – '

'You managed to reach very well the other day, I seem to remember. Perhaps Jean de Meung is simply post-copulative.'

'My mood is pre-copulative – adoring – '

'That's the bean soup.'

'I've been reading Boccaccio. The Decameron.'

'Then you can read me one of his stories next time I visit you.'

'I know just the one.'

'If there is a next time. Raoul, what happened when you went out to the Cour des Miracles with Marc?'

'Nothing. We weren't allowed into the area. When we told some of the others this later, they said we were lucky. Normally, everyone is allowed in. Only the chosen few are allowed back out.'

I smile. 'Raoul, as I said, I have to go and search Maître Guillaume's house again, this time for something quite simple.

But I want to change into boy's clothes.'

'Not Jacques Couting again!'

'No. Well, all right. And it's not "Couting", it's Cutting. Jack. Magnus then, if you prefer. But I don't feel safe any more out on the streets here as myself and in these skirts, hardly able to move.'

'If I come with you?'

I look at him. He is no fighter. But his presence would be a deterrent. And I would have another protector following along behind. 'D'accord, Raoul. It's getting late, and we'll lose a lot of time if I go home and change.' Not to mention another argument with Ferchard or Khadija, or both.

23

We use Natalie's key, go in through the back yard again. The whole house smells empty and damp, but from the laboratory now there comes the smell of death. The mortal remains of Chuvar the snake, symbol of immortality, are still on the floor where we left them. Raoul opens a window: it's the one that was banging on our previous visit. He looks at the snake, looks at the window. The snake is longer than he is.

I nod towards the door and he follows me out. We go to Guillaume's bedroom, take the sheet off the bed and return with it to the laboratory. We manage to get the sheet under the snake, then lift it up, carry it to the window and drop it out, sheet and all, into the yard.

Then we go back to the bedroom. In the corner devoted to the wash-stand, the wall behind the basin and jug is covered with tiles, each bearing one of the Signs of the Zodiac. That must be it. Raoul raises his eyebrows. The smell is still too disgusting even by Paris standards to open one's mouth and speak. I point to the sea-goat that represents Capricorn, a beautiful representation, half fish, shy, tail curled out of sight like a mermaid, the other half a goat, leering and hairy. I want Raoul to prise it off the wall.

He takes out his knife, taps it in carefully behind the tile, and the tile falls away from the wall, revealing a narrow cavity.

I push my hand into the cavity. It is surprisingly deep. And it is empty. How can it be empty? We are the first to open it. Raoul goes to push his hand in.

I glare at him. Does he think I'm stupid?

He ignores me and thrusts his hand in, in, right up to the shoulder. And smiles.

All right, so his arms are longer than mine. There was no need to make the hole a symbol.

Perhaps I am over-sensitive at the moment.

'There's something – a paper, folded, I think – tucked into a crevice, but I can't … ah.' He withdraws his arm slowly and gives me the paper. It is small and folded in four. It says simply, and in plain French, 'Natalie knows which is her card now.'

'What does it mean?'

'It means we have successfully passed her Zodiac sign, the sea-goat, Capricorn; now we must consider her Tarocchi sign.'

'Ah, Tarocchi again. And will she know?'

'This says she does.'

'I see. Where is this "virgin-stone" you told me about?'

Back in the laboratory, I take it out of the drawer where Guillaume kept it, hold it between two fingers. It is clear, almost colourless, slightly yellow. I close my hand around it. 'When Natalie held it, nothing happened. When Yahia held it, nothing happened. When I hold it …' I wait a while, then open my hand: the stone is blood red.

Raoul takes it, holds it. When he opens his hand, the stone is pinkish. He blushes.

'Hold it longer.'

After a moment, he opens his hand again. The stone is, if anything, paler - though pink rather than yellow. 'It doesn't work!'

I hold it again. In seconds it is deep red and seems to be throbbing.

He holds it. Slowly it loses its colour, becomes pinkish.

Like his face. I must be tactful here. No jokes about being almost a virgin - not even in revenge for that act of penetration a moment ago. 'It works, Raoul. What is interesting is that it clearly does not test virginity. At least, not in men. Does it in women? Is it only meant for women? Or does it in fact respond to something else altogether?'

I open my pocket and slip it in. Was Mère Henriette right, and Natalie not a virgin after all? No, that is not possible, she was too convincing. But still … A small experiment would do no harm.

An hour later, Thomas and Christine and I were in the Great Hall of Parlement among the crowds invited to witness the spectacle of the Taking of Jerusalem by the Knights of the First Crusade. And it was spectacular. It was the first time any of us had ever seen the re-enactment of a historical as opposed to a Biblical or mythical event, and it was done on a huge scale. A ship "sailed" through the hall and knights leapt from the ship to attack the city, while up on the turrets a muezzin chanted suras from the Koran - and chanted them correctly. Saracens fought Crusaders, swords clashing, arms and even heads flying, and we all jumped and screamed as loudly as any of the soldiers or the Muslim maidens trapped in the city.

Finally, it was over, and we found ourselves surrounded by bodies covered with gore, all horribly realistic: the blood and intestines came from hundreds of pigs, specially slaughtered that morning. I glanced at my two companions. Thomas smiled wanly. He seemed a little queasy, but Christine was enjoying it hugely.

'Shall we - ?' he began, but at that moment the message came from the Emperor summoning me.

Christine, grinning, said, 'Really, Mariana, I do believe you and the Emperor - '

'Be silent, you foolish child!' snapped Thomas. 'I shall never take you anywhere again.'

'Don't be hard on her. No one is listening.' I turned to Christine. 'It's not at all what you think, sweet. I'll tell you all about it next time I see you.'

'Oh, will you? Will you really?'

'I promise. Now I must go.'

The Emperor is alone. 'Mariana. Please excuse me - once more. I sat through all that. Now I have to put my feet up.'

Without being asked, I lean over and kiss him on both cheeks.

He closes his eyes, lies back, smiles contentedly. 'Perhaps I too died in that bloodbath, and this is heaven.'

I wait.

He opens his eyes. 'Mariana? Is something wrong? You do not speak.'

'I do not like to see you in pain.'

He regards me sagely. 'Nor I you. If it is not an indelicate question, can you sit down today?'

I laugh, and sit on the edge of his bed.

He holds both my hands. 'Mariana, I have only a few moments. Listen. I obtained two items of information for you - neither of any great worth, I fear, though the second at least is amusant and may turn out to be significant … So. First, I have a name: Athanasía. No death - deathlessness. Which to my mind is further evidence of her interest in alchemy and the philosopher's stone, though not so much for the purpose of converting base metal into gold, as for converting this short and worthless life we

know now into immortality.' He pauses, and smiles. 'Believe me,
I understand that. Sympathise with it, even.' He pauses again,
and stops smiling. 'Be very wary of that one, Mariana …
Mariana? I'm serious.'

   'I will be wary.'

   'Good. And now for something a little less serious that,
nevertheless, I must whisper in your ear: come closer … The
King had a mistress, years ago, when he was still the Dauphin,
another tall slender woman with a "swish" when she walked, and
her name was – still is – Niniane.'

   'No!'

   'Yes. And she can apparently still be found from time to time
at Beauté-sur-Marne, the King's favourite retreat. Do you know
it? It is at Vincennes, a village to the west of Paris, and I myself
have been invited there on Sunday. In four days time – my last
day in Paris … It is said that he named the chateau for her.'

   'And you think she will be there?'

   'No. I think she won't be there. He keeps her out of sight these
days, apparently. Though she is still of great beauty.'

   'You've seen her?'

   'No. Yes. I'm not sure. I may have seen her once when I was
here on an unofficial visit, oh, years ago, and he and I met
informally: there was this – lady – sitting silent in the
background. You might have thought he had forgotten her except
that she was unforgettable. A little like you.'

   I smile tolerantly.

   'I'm serious. Green eyes, but not blue-green like yours, a
darker, deeper green, the green of emeralds. And her hair, dark
like yours, but redder than yours, yet not red – or brown or black
– but as it were all three at once, competing, as the blue and grey
compete with the green in your eyes.'

   'And she was tall?'

   'Yes. I saw her walk away from me when he remembered her
and ordered her out of the room … and she walked like – like – '

I know he is going to say it before he says it.

'Like you used to walk before those brutes misused you.'

Misused me? But I am thinking that this way of walking is becoming a theme here, a link, a series of links. Natalie has this way of walking, according to Mère Henriette, as did the woman who visited old Guillaume. They all walk with a "swish" - or like a putain (Mère Henriette's word). And so did the nun who visited Nicolas Flamel, though she tried not to show it.

'Mariana, I will send for you. Meanwhile, go back to Lyse. Go in the morning, she may have something for you then. And remember: tread carefully.'

'I will.'

Being more than a little nervous about making my way back to the Court of Miracles unaccompanied, I decided to go first to the Adriatica and see if Marie-Élise was available to hold my hand.

A large bordel might anyway be a good place to test the so-called virgin-stone.

I gave up on the abbé for the moment and took le Cafard and le Pitre with me (on the principle that two small protectors must be as good as one big one).

The same pair, the Spanish-looking midget and the blond giant, let me in - both of them much chastened since last I saw them. As of course, now I came to think of it, was I. Very politely, I said: 'May I have a word with Mère Veronique?'

Equally politely, the midget said: 'Of course, milady.' And somewhat less politely snapped her fingers at the giant, who jumped nervously then hurried off up the stairs with me scurrying after him as if it was me he was running from.

'Mariana, this is a pleasant surprise.'

'Mère Veronique, I won't take much of your time.'

'Nonsense. I'm curious. I hear your investigation has had its ups and downs.'

I smiled. 'I should have taken your advice.'

'You should have taken more than that. I offered you a nice quiet job here, pleasant working conditions.'

I liked her. 'One day, it may come to that,' I laughed. After all, it had in Avignon, quite out of the blue. 'If it does — '

'When it does,' she interrupted me, 'you will choose the Adriatica. The Albanian likes you.'

'He does?'

'And it would be much nicer if you were here, and him coming here each day, angry at the thought that I might be letting other clients use you, than if you were there at the Court of Miracles, his prisoner. He quickly tires of those he possesses. You must be mine, not his. Do we have a deal?'

'We have a deal.'

'Only look after your face, or the deal is off. Your bottom I don't mind about.'

What did she think? That whenever I was attacked I would cover my face, turn round, and bend over?

For all I knew, she was right. Some animals do that.

Another woman was sitting in the shadows. I could hardly make out her features even now, but Mère Veronique said: 'That is Mère Malina. Bien …'

'Mère Veronique, I should like to borrow Marie-Élise . I have to visit the Court of Miracles again, and I'm nervous.'

'That shows sense. Yes, you can have her for a few hours … And?'

'You're right. There is something else. I'd like to do a little experiment. Could I speak to one or two of your younger girls? The youngest you have who are no longer virgins.'

'Why?'

I opened my pocket, took out the virgin-stone. 'Do you know what this is?'

She took it. 'I can guess. And you want to test it?'

I nodded.

'They are notoriously unreliable. Any man worthy of the name will simply up-end the girl and look.'

'Of course. However, this stone is important and it does show something.'

She closed her hand round it. Waited. Smiled, and opened her hand again. The stone was blood red. 'And when you hold it?'

'The same as that.'

'Good. I should say it tests suitability for working at the Adriatica.'

I laughed. 'You may well be right.' I thought of poor Raoul.

She rang a bell, and passed the stone to the woman in the corner.

The giant entered.

'Bring me Gwyneth, here, now, immediately.'

Gwyneth. Yes, I should like to see what happened when Gwyneth held the virgin-stone.

The woman opened her hand. The stone was crimson. She closed her hand round it again.

'We don't have any very young ones,' Veronique was saying. 'Gwyneth, though, is about as pure in heart as it's possible for a prostitute to be. Perhaps you'd like to spend some time alone with her. As I recall, last time you paid a silver sou for that pleasure but were rudely interrupted.'

The woman – Mère Malina – opened her hand again: the stone was clear, as colourless as water. She passed it back to Veronique.

I stared at her.

But just then, Gwyneth knocked and entered, and bobbed to us both. She kept her eyes down.

'Yes, I should prefer that,' I said, and held out my hand for the stone.

In her room, she kept her eyes down, shyly.

I said, in English, 'Gwyneth? What's wrong?'

'I've never had a lady in here before. I don't know what to do, what to say, how to behave.'

'Yes, you have. You've had me in here before.'

Now she raised her eyes, looked at me. 'My lady, I think you must be mistaken. Only tell me what you wish of me. If I fail to please you, Mère Veronique - '

'Last time, I was dressed as a boy. The sergeants of the Watch came.'

Now she recognised me. 'Oh! It's you!'

We hugged each other and she cried a little. 'I didn't think I'd ever see you again.'

'Nor did I,' I said, with feeling. 'But now there's something you can do for me. Two things. First, hold this stone. There's nothing to be frightened of. Just close your hand round it. That's right.'

She gazed at her clenched hand, then looked at me and smiled self-consciously. If this was a test of innocence, then she should have no effect on it at all.

'Now open your hand.'

Nothing. It was as though she had never touched it.

'Don't look so worried. That's perfect.' I took the stone back. Then, to be kind and talk a while, but also fishing (one never knew) I said: 'Do you ever get men up here who speak English? Or Welsh? Something you understand?'

She smiled. 'Mostly, they don't say much, they just - you know - do their job and go. Sometimes they tell me I am belle, jolie, gentille, comme une ange,' she blushed, 'easy things I understand. And sometimes they say nasty things, but then I don't listen, don't try to understand … Yes, there are one or two who speak English. I think they send them to me specially. And of course I understand Bretons when they speak. Breton is very like Welsh.'

'Is it? I didn't know that.'

'Usually we would never realise that we might have another language, one we shared, but … There's a Breton boy who works in the meat market, Samson – '

'Samson?'

'Not because he's big and strong, though he is, but it's a
common name in Brittany and Cornwall. And, yes, there was an
old man who died a week or two ago, but he had a French name.'

What was this? 'Oh dear. Tell me about it.'

'He'd been coming here for years, the girls said. When Mère
Veronique said she was sending him to me to see if he liked me,
she told me he was a friend of the Alb- – the man who owns this
house – and I was to be very accommodating with him. Well, he
was old, as I say, but he was sweet. It took him a while to – you
know – get ready. He was shy with me, I was so young, he said.
Then he asked my name and where I was from. When I told him,
he started speaking Breton to me. We had a long talk. It was
nice. We didn't do anything that first time and I was frightened –
of Mère Veronique, I mean – but she said he liked me, and not to
rush him. And I liked him. He had a nice smell. Really. With my
eyes closed, I would have chosen him in a room full of men. We
eventually did it on his third visit … Then somebody killed him.
But, oh, my lady! I knew before it happened!'

'You knew?'

'He told me. He said, "Goodbye, sweet Gwyneth. We shall not
meet again." And he gave me a gold piece. They all said he was
a miser, but … "Why? Have I not pleased you?" "Would I have
given you that, had you not pleased me? No, it is … it is that I
am one who knows. I am to die, as my poor brother died. " "To
die? But how? Why?" "They will kill me with their knives, as
they killed him." "Who?" "I cannot tell you that." "Can we not
stop them?" "No, we cannot. All is prepared." I didn't believe
him. Not really. But it was true.'

I held her to me, comforting her, as the ready tears flowed
down her pale cheeks.

To learn this, and to learn nothing new!

'And he said no more?'

She shook her head.

He had seen it, using drops of Natalie's innocent blood. As they had seen his brother Charlot's death in the magic mirror, using drops of Charlot's blood.

'Did he ever ask for a few drops of your blood?'

'My blood?' She looked horrified.

'Oh, it's nothing. Don't worry.' Probably, it would never have occurred to him that she was innocent, just as it would never have occurred to him that Natalie might not be a virgin. And why should it? He was managing very well with Natalie's blood.

'Do you know that woman who was with Mère Veronique?'

'Mère Malina? Oh yes. Malina's mother was a friend of Mère Veronique's. And Malina used to be one of us, or so they say, but now …'

Time to go. 'Keep your gold pieces well hidden, and if you are ever in trouble and need more money, or need help, come to me. Lady Marian MacElpin. Though I am half Spanish, and sometimes I am known as Doña Mariana de la Mar. You will find me.'

'Oh, my lady …'

'Come now, stop getting upset. When an old man knows he is going to die, and prepares for it, that isn't bad, it's good.'

'He didn't die, he was killed.'

'He died.'

She thought about that, then nodded, wiping away her tears. 'I'm sorry. I'm being silly.'

'I must go now. Sweet Gwyneth – is that what he called you?'

The blush came to her cheeks again.

'It suits you so well.'

24

On the way up-river in the boat, I ask Marie-Élise about
Guillaume. She hadn't known him, can't help me. After that, we
don't talk. We are both cold, both thinking our own thoughts.
And when we get to the Court of Miracles, she is taken one way,
I another, and I quickly find myself shown into the same room as
on my last visit.

He doesn't keep me waiting long.

We greet each other with a kiss this time, then I sit while he
stands and looks at me.

How strong are his positive principles, such as loyalty,
compared with negative ones such as the need for revenge and to
silence opponents?

'Well, Mariana?'

'I have been able to establish that Pierre de Montrouge was
not responsible for the death of Guillaume le Breton. I have also
been able to establish – for in many respects the two are one –
who did kill Pierre de Montrouge.'

He keeps his clear, grey eyes on me.

I ask him: 'Was there blood on his clothes when he arrived
home?'

If he says "No", he answers both questions.

Today, there are flecks of green in the grey; the other day the
flecks had been blue.

'No, there was no blood on his clothes, not when he arrived.
And not at any point. The death he died did not involve bleeding
him like the pig he was.'

As he says it, I suddenly think of all the pig gore and guts
spread over everything and everyone that afternoon, and see
Pierre's blood and intestines among all the rest, and feel sick.

'Are you all right, Mariana?'

'Mm? Oh. Yes. Thank you. Just tired.'

'And not well yet. What exactly did they do to you while you
were being held at the abbé's residence?'

'You really want to know?'

'I do.'

'And need to know?'

He nods and the skin beneath his eyes twitches in what is the nearest he ever comes to a smile.

I tell him.

When I finish, he says simply: 'They are dead.'

I must have looked puzzled.

'The abbé and all who took part in that beating and rape. They are dead men.'

'Dead?'

The eyes twitch again. 'They do not yet know that they are dead.'

I understand. 'There was one called the cabin-boy.'

'A boy?'

'No. A man. But simple.' Innocent? I remember the stone. 'And not unkind. I would forgive him.'

'I would not.'

Then he says, 'You took a great risk coming here accusing me of murder.'

I didn't accuse him, but that hardly matters. 'Not really. Everyone knows you're a killer. One more, especially when that one had raped your sister and murdered your niece, is neither here nor there.'

'And?'

Everyone keeps saying "And?" to me today. 'And I consider us friends.'

'Because I fed you a sausage?'

'That and other things.'

He can sit in silence, waiting, this man. Not an easy thing to do. I remember that one of the things I wanted to discuss with him was the will. 'He leaves Charles le Grec to you – you are a rich man and have been a father to Charles. He leaves Natalie to his nephew Jaquet, if she will have him.'

'She won't.'

'She might.'

'Wager?'

'No. Just promise me you won't try to influence her against him. I think she will do very well with him.'

'And the gold?'

'To Natalie, and to her mother, Lule. Shall we call Natalie in?'

'Of course.' He fetches her.

She seems glad to see me, though she shows little response when I give her a hug and a kiss. 'Mariana, what's happening?'

I tell her about Jaquet being released (she knows) and Pierre de Montrouge being blamed for her master's death; tell her I do not believe that.

'What does it matter?' she cries. 'He is dead anyway.'

'It matters,' her uncle responds before I can, 'because until the murderer of Guillaume le Breton is dead, you will not be safe on the streets of Paris.'

'Natalie, he's right.' And then I tell her about the will.

'You mean he left everything to me? But why?'

'So far as I remember, he says that while he has been less than a father to you, you have been more than a daughter to him and, for several years now, all the "family" he has had.'

The Albanian nods. 'That is true, and makes sense, as does what you say about le Grec being my son now and me being a rich man. But why does he mention Lule?'

'Lule was my mother,' Natalie says. 'She's dead, I told you that.'

'I know, but … he certainly doesn't write as if she were dead. Either that is a very old will, or he had reason to believe she might be alive still somewhere.'

'But she's not! She – '

'And if it was an old will,' I insist, 'how does he come to speak of your being more than a daughter to him, and all the family he had all these years? And of you having been a father to le Grec?'

There is a moment's silence. Natalie is shocked, and her mind is racing. Even the Albanian is shocked, that is obvious. Neither of them had any idea she might still be alive.

I say, ruthlessly: 'Did either of you see her buried?'

Natalie looks at her uncle. He says, 'No. It was the Death. The children – Natalie here, and le Grec – were kept right away from her. I visited her, but the last time I was there I was not allowed near her. She sobbed at me to go and never come back.'

'It was her voice?'

'Oh yes. And I was just outside her door. Two days later, I heard that she had died and been taken away.'

"Taken away" on a tumbril for common burial, as always during outbreaks of the Great Mortality.

'Maalot was probably the last one to see her alive, apart from Guillaume, that is.'

'Maalot?'

'A woman who used to be there. There were two women. The other was her daughter. Are they still about, Natalie?'

'No.'

The Albanian sighs. 'Guillaume would have known.'

Meaning it can hardly have happened without him knowing? He was there with her all the time.

Or meaning Guillaume, being a scryer and "one who knows", could hardly have been kept in the dark all these years?

Or meaning, simply, "and now it is too late".

'Someone else might know,' Natalie says.

He looks at her. He does not look pleased.

She means Lule's sister, or one of Lule's sisters, I guess.

I do not have to guess that they are not a subject for discussion. His icy eyes say it all.

I decide to change the subject for the moment, and tell them how Raoul and I found the note behind the Capricorn tile.

'You have that with you?' asks the Albanian.

I take it out of my pocket – touching the virgin-stone as I do so – and pass it to him.

They both study it.

I remember that she cannot read. Was that too a lie?

'Tell me,' she says.

He makes her wait a moment. He likes the fact that she cannot read. 'This, too, mentions Lule,' he says.

'Tell me what it says!' she hisses.

I want to tell her, but prefer not to interfere in his little games.

Le Grec knocks on the door and peers in. 'You're needed, Papa. It's urgent.' He waves to me.

I wave back. He is no doubt the only one who would dare interrupt the Albanian.

When Natalie and I are alone, I say: 'He doesn't mean to be unkind.'

'Yes, he does.'

She is right. He does. 'It says "If Natalie doesn't know which is her card, her mother will tell her."'

'My mother again?'

'Your card. It must be the tarocchi cards. Which would you say was your card?'

'Strength.' She smiles. 'That's what Mère Córbala said. I've been studying it with her.'

'You changed your mind about it?'

She shrugs. 'There's nothing else to do. I'm used to being busy.'

'Does that card, Strength, mean anything as regards the will?'

'No, I don't think so – but what do I know? We should ask Córbala.'

We will. Though he says ask her mother. But for now, it's time to change the subject back again. 'Tell me about the women who visited your father.'

'He was not my father.'

'I know, but …'

'My master.'

'All right, tell me about the women who used to visit your master.'

'So you found out …'

I wait, on tenterhooks.

Natalie outwaits me.

'Only that one is your aunt,' I say, temptingly.

'She runs the Fille d'Or. But you know that. You told me you'd been there.'

'Oh. That. Yes … Well?'

'She visited sometimes.'

I watch as she invents the story. She's good at it; but not good at concealing the fact that she's doing so.

'My master had been making love to her, you know – occasionally – since Maman died.' She hesitates. 'I think my aunt thought it was her duty.'

'And I think you're not telling the truth.'

'I am! They were very alike. She used to come heavily veiled so the neighbours didn't start gossiping about Maman being alive and living apart from us.'

'I know they are very alike. I've seen the picture of your mother. But I think there is another sister, another aunt. And I think, too, that when you said "Someone else must know," you had one of your aunts in mind: Mireille or – or the other.'

She stares at me.

'Might her name be Niniane?' I hazard. But just then the Albanian returns and not even either of us would dare discuss his sisters in front of him. Instead, I say: 'I need Natalie to help me in my search for her inheritance.'

'She is confined to her room in this house until I say she may leave.'

'But – '

'No buts. I have spoken.'

'But the streets of Paris will be safe for her very soon.'

He looks at me.

I may leave; and it is definitely time I did.

25

When I get home, Mari-Élise having elected to stay at the Court
of Miracles for the night (she went straight back once she had
guided me out through the narrow, pitch-dark alleys to the
landing-stage) I leave the boys with Coco and Khadija and take
Raoul upstairs. I need to talk.

'Raoul, it all seems to hinge on Lule and her sisters. What do
we know about them so far? Lule was sold as a slave, then later
lost her baby after some kind of confrontation with Pierre de
Montrouge. I am not at all sure, though, that I accept the
Albanian's version of the story. He wasn't there. He had it from
Lule years later, and she would have made herself out the victim.
Also, I suspect that Pierre was obsessed with her, with Lule, not
with Tarocchi and the Hanged Man.'

'Might he have known she was alive?'

'Quite likely. But again, it is too late.'

'And the sisters?'

'Let's start with Mireille. She was set up in business at the
Fille d'Or by Pierre. But prior to that, she "and her sister" were
with Pierre on Ibiza. That sister was not Lule. Who was it? And
who is this Niniane? "Niniane des Sept Soeurs." Is she an
alchemist? Is she the King's mistress? Is she a nun?'

'She can hardly be both. A nun and the King's mistress, I
mean.'

'With some kings she could easily be, but with this king, no, I
agree. Though the nun does sound, from the eyes and the gait, as
though she could be the King's mistress. She, also, seems to be

taking an interest in alchemy. Niniane – our Niniane, or another? – in the habit of a nun?' You need to have lived among nuns, to have been at least a novice, to be able to pretend to be one convincingly. I know.

'There is Lule, too. She could be a nun, Mariana. Or disguised as a nun.'

'Perhaps the Albanian knows she's alive but to him she is dead, because she played the whore. By all accounts she did.'

'But he owns a whore-house, traffics in women.'

'Not his little sister.'

'Another sister runs the Fille d'Or.'

'That's true … He and Guillaume could have put her in a nunnery – and she could be the murderer. After all, the murderer often turns out to be the husband or wife. Or another member of the family: such as the daughter. Let's think about Natalie for a moment. She too has this distinctive gait, at least according to Mère Henriette.'

'Oh, she has,' Raoul agrees, rather too enthusiastically.

'Was she also playing the whore? Was that why she had the key? And she seems very familiar with La Fille d'Or.'

'But she's a virgin.'

'Is she?' I tell him about Sweet Gwyneth.

'Ah, so it's not only me …' Then, casually, 'And where is the Adriatica, exactly?'

'We were talking about Natalie.'

'Ah. Yes. Natalie.'

'Perhaps her father had been abusing her. Or her master had been using her.'

'It does rather depend how you view their relationship.'

'It comes down to the same thing,' I say, surprising myself. 'Either way, that could be a motive for her to kill him. Or for the Albanian to have him killed.'

'Natalie couldn't have done that – not the Thousand Cuts.'

'No, you're right. Though she is very handy with her dagger.

Raoul, I must sleep. No. Alone. You go downstairs with the rest of the boys.' And dream of Carroty Natalie and Sweet Gwyneth, I think, but do not say. 'Send Yahia in.'

'In? You mean he's outside the door all this time?'

'Of course he's outside the door. In case. In respectable households, while there is a man here with me he would be inside the door.'

'A Spanish custom?'

'No, a Moorish custom. In Spanish homes it would be the duenna, a woman, not a eunuch.'

'And why do you want him inside now? I mean, I'm going.'

'To put me to bed.'

'To put you to bed?'

'He always gets me ready for bed. It's his job.'

'But - what will happen when - ? '

'Raoul! I have no intention of marrying anyone born north of Granada! Yahia!'

The door opens instantly.

'Escort this young man downstairs. Fairly gently. Then come straight back. I'm tired.'

'Yes, mistress.'

In the morning, accompanied by le Cafard and le Pitre, and with my protector, I notice, back in attendance, I call first at the Hôtel-Dieu.

'There seem to have been several sisters,' Lyse informs me. 'The abbess of a bordel, a nun, a royal courtesan, a fortune-teller.'

'Names?'

'Mireille, who was Mirela; Lule, who became Fleur; Niniane, who, if I'm not mistaken, was once called Natalya, but became known to the world as Niniane des Sept Soeurs.'

'That is three names, but four sisters.'

'Seven sisters, dem'selle. But we don't know yet how many are involved in this affair.'

True. 'Does this royal courtesan reside by any chance at Beauté-sur-Marne?'

Lyse has a lovely smile still. 'She's to be seen there occasionally, but she works for her sister, Mireille, at the Fille d'Or.'

Next I call on old Guillaume's neighbour, the gossip in the rue Saint-Pol who keeps Mère Henriette so well informed.

She does not invite me in. And looks askance at my companions.

The two boys at least (if not my anonymous protector) are experts at becoming invisible, but this woman would notice a grey slug playing dead on a path of small, grey pebbles.

I ask the question which has been bothering me: whether it is possible that the nun and one of the other women who occasionally visited Maître Guillaume were one and the same. 'No,' she informs me, 'it is not. The nun walks like a nun, the other walks like a whore.' She almost spits the word at me.

Right. That clears that up, for she is the only person, apart of course from Natalie, who has seen the two women on several occasions.

'Merci, madame.' I turn to go.

'Wait. That is not all. There is another woman, another nun.'

'Another?'

'Two others.'

'Two others?'

Her eyes say You are foreign, you are stupid, how can I talk to you, me, a Parisienne? Which was a refreshing change from the way she had been looking at me. Hold your tongue, Mariana. Let the gossip gossip.

'The woman is another putain, bien sur. But younger, and more arrogant. And she doesn't care.'

'And the nun? You say there is a second nun, as well?'

'If she is a nun, then the abbés and bishops and spiritual fathers must be having a fine time.'

I laughed, to encourage her. 'And who does she remind you of? Who might she be, dressed up in the habit of a nun? The first woman? The second?'

'More the second than the first, but … now you mention it, and I hadn't thought of it before, she walks - not all the time, but when she forgets herself, you understand - like that little slut who lives there.'

'You mean - ?'

'The maid-servant. And she has the key to the back door.'

'I see.'

I didn't see at all.

I walked along the rue Saint-Antoine deep in thought, with the two boys behind me, then heard Raoul calling. He was outside the Grand Châtelet.

'Raoul! Where have you been?'

'Nowhere. Waiting for you.'

'Raoul, go back and talk to her again for me. Le Cafard, take him, show him the house I went to just now, but keep out of sight. I don't want that woman to associate Raoul with me.' Le Cafard gave me his little salute, and I turned back to Raoul. 'Ask the gossip there about the women who have been calling at the house of Maitre le Grec. Grace à Dieu, you're wearing your robe.'

'I'm ready for the ceremony at the Louvre.'

'Tell her you're there on behalf of the abbé. Keep your hood well up over your face. She will tell you of two women, a nun and another. She may go on to tell you of further women. If she does not, say "We have observed one other, one who dresses like a nun but does not walk like a nun." Then come and tell me what she says.'

'Where will you be?'

'I'm on my way to the Fille d'Or, but I haven't much time. I

have to go home and change for the ceremony. I'll meet you at
the landing-stage beside the Petit-Pont, then we can go down to
the Louvre together.'

'D'accord.' He gave me a kiss.

'Raoul, if she doesn't mention Natalie at any point, then before
you leave her, say "What about the little slut who lives there?"
Just like that. See what that produces.'

'Little slut? Mm, I suppose she is really.' He took the
opportunity for a second kiss, and strolled off up the rue Saint-
Antoine with le Cafard.

'Mariana!'

'Excuse me, Mère Mireille.'

'How are you, ma fille? And how is little Isabeau?'

'Isabeau? I haven't seen her since that day. I'm still on my
original quest.'

'Ah ha. And you return to me.'

'There is some information you haven't shared with me. For
instance … Will you let me speak for a moment? Then when I
finish you shall say whatever you will.'

She nodded, her lovely hair floating with the nod. As always,
her shoulders and breasts were bare, the white flesh powdered,
the nipples rouged to match her lips. But it was not cold in here.

'Mireille – Mirela – I know, you told me yourself on my first
visit, that Pierre de Montrouge set you up in business here, and
that prior to coming to Paris you were on Ibiza with him and
your sister.'

'I think on the whole I prefer you to address me as Mère
Mireille. And not to use the name Mirela at all.'

What was this? 'Oui, d'accord, madame. You did not,
however, tell me who that sister was. You didn't tell me that
Natalie's mother, Lule, was – '

'It was not Madame Lule.'

'Please. No, Madame Lule was not on Ibiza with you. By that

time, she was settled in Paris. So there was another sister, and as far as I have been able to ascertain, that sister's name was Natalya. Was it Pierre who changed that name to Niniane. Niniane des Sept Soeurs. Was it the King? I do not know. I don't even know how many of you there are in France. But I do know that Madame Lule is still alive, and that Madame Niniane at least is here in this house with us at this moment. I should like very much to speak to her – and to you, together.'

She regarded me with a half smile. 'Mariana, I don't have that feel for the future that my sisters have (and perhaps you share) but I knew this would happen and we have nothing to hide. I told you of my relationship with Pierre. But Natalya was not here then ...'

'I understand that.'

'I'll fetch her. Oh, and Natalya – Niniane – you don't need to address as madame. The very idea is absurd.'

Why absurd? What was different about her? Was I about to meet the crazed woman who had slowly and pitilessly killed Maître Guillaume, stabbing and stabbing until he could be stabbed no more?

A lady came into the room. A great lady. Who was this? I stood up, hastily.

'Mariana, this is my sister, whom you know as Niniane.'

'Sit down, child, sit down.'

We all sat.

Her voice was slightly huskier than Mireille's, her French slightly less French, slightly more accented. Why? No reason, I suspected. She liked it like that. As she liked her eyes like that – a little sleepy – and her hair like that – a little tousled.

I looked back at Mireille. Beside this darker, slenderer version of herself, she still seemed a rose, but a rose that has bloomed too long, been cupped in too many loving but ungentle hands, been felt and sniffed at and admired till the petals began to droop and fade and fall.

Niniane, despite the emerald eyes, was a creature of the south, a goddess of honey and oil, and of wine. Only something about her face reminded me of Mireille – and of course the way they both moved.

She was still perfect.

I must have been staring, for they both laughed.

'You are wondering about Madame Lule,' Mireille observed. 'Where she would fit in. In the middle here,' she laughed. 'She was like me superficially, but, too, like Natalya – Niniane – in some ways. The lady of the family, and the most beautiful of us all.'

I doubted that.

So did Niniane. She laughed.

'Shh.' Surprisingly – or perhaps not in view of that "madame" thing – Mireille seemed very much in charge. 'So, Mariana. How can we help you?'

'I've seen a portrait of her. Madame Lule, I mean.'

'Ah, yes.' Niniane grew slightly less languid. 'Charlot, Guillaume's brother, the fool, painted that. He was no fool. Guillaume was the fool.'

'It depends what you mean by "fool", madame.'

'It does. In one sense, all men are fools. I like a man wise enough to know he is a fool, like poor Pierre, not fools with pretensions to wisdom like Guillaume le Breton and the Abbé Soxxal.'

'Maître Guillaume may have done some foolish things when he was young, but it seems to me that before he died he became a true Fool.' The complete outsider. The one the kids throw stones at. The one the dogs go for. Prey.

'You are very observant. Unfortunately, one cannot undo what one did when one was young. Lule, too, was a fool, of course.'

'Mariana knows that Lule is alive,' Mireille snapped. 'And guard your tongue.'

'Ah, she knows. Then yes, it's true: Lule never died. It is her story you want?'

I nodded. 'But I should like yours too.'

'Mirela's and mine? Will that be all right, Mirela?' Mireille nodded, and Niniane continued: 'When Pierre couldn't get Lule, who was, and still is, as Mirela said, the lady of the family, the queen, we were the next best thing. He came all the way to Thessalonika looking for others like her, and there he discovered that she had sisters, six beautiful sisters. Four had been taken in the raid, and had been sold. But there were two others still living in their village in Albania. Us. We had hidden and not been caught.'

'I don't understand? How did he learn this?'

'He asked around, offered gold. And it was an Albanian, not a Serb, who sold us to him. He guided Pierre and his men to the village and showed him where we hid, in my little bothie behind the house. I wasn't allowed in the house with the family, and they weren't supposed to talk to me, but Mirela was so terrified she'd started joining me out there each night.

'Anyway, this man was a neighbour and he knew about me and my bothie — all the men did, of course — and that was that. Pierre took us west to an island called Kerkyra, and from there by ship to Ibiza, where he had other business to conduct. Then, when he'd finished, he brought us to France with him. By that time he'd already decided to set up the Fille d'Or for Mirela, the clever one, the femme d'affaires of the family and to keep me for himself. I didn't mind. I liked him, as I say. But his heart was always with Lule. And Lule, who looks down on me as a mindless whore, was — all right, I'm not going to call her a fool, Mirela, but in this case she certainly behaved like one. Men will be men. Pierre was an aristocrat, used to having his way, and he was obsessed with her. Why did she fight him? Why did her foolish husband refuse to sell her on to him? Pierre offered three times, five times, what Guillaume had paid for her. But no, she didn't like Pierre, so Pierre couldn't have her. But Pierre was a man. He had her anyway. And even then, she had to go on fighting. She knew he was drunk, she knew he was crazy with lust, but no, instead of being honoured, she had to be difficult. Honoured, yes! Pierre was a nobleman, he was on familiar terms with the Dauphin himself.'

She gazed at me. I had never seen eyes like that.

'Her baby died, Charlot died, and Guillaume almost died. All because she couldn't lie still and do what she was told. And this nonsense with the Hanged Man. She's good with cards. She's not good with much else, but she can make a card come up in any position she wishes. And now, because of that, Pierre has died the Hanged Man's death at the hands of our unspeakable brother … I shall never forgive her.'

'I see.' It was true. I did see. There are two ways of looking at anything. At least two. 'And Natalie? She is Pierre's daughter?'

'She is. And she was named after me, poor thing. Lule believed she was putting a curse on the child.' She looked to Mireille, who took up the story.

'Lule has the power in her but she fears and hates it, as our father feared and hated it – and our brother at least pretended to fear and hate it. Lule adored them both, and believed everything they said and did was right, even when they joined in the hunting and burning of witches. However, our mother maintained the old ways, in secret, and when she discovered that Lule could read the future in hands and on cards, she arranged for an aged aunt of ours to teach her more – in secret, of course. Lule only did a few lessons, then she told our father about it, and that was the end of that.'

'And poor Mama got a beating,' put in Niniane.

'Did she? I don't remember. But she often got beaten. She was just like Niniane. Papa should never have married her. Anyway, me, she kept at home to do the chores, and Niniane, who was the youngest, but whose talents were obvious, she sent to a famous whore in the next valley to be trained. Only that famous whore

was also an infamous witch, and she taught Niniane things no
girl, expecially no whore, should ever be taught. Like … like ... '
    'Like how to travel in the spirit world. Don't worry,' Niniane
told her sister. 'Mariana travels in the spirit world herself.'
    The bells outside were ringing for Sext (midday) and I had to
go. But first … 'I understood that you were once – still are,
perhaps – the King's mistress.'
    She gazed at me, her eyes still soft, but did not speak.
    I went on. 'And that you were also – still are? – a nun?'
    The eyes still soft.
    'I believe that in some sense you – or another nun, or some
other woman who passes as a nun – may be at the heart of this
mystery.'
    Now she smiled, but still did not speak.
    Then in a flash it came to me. 'Does Lule mean flower in
Albanian?' Fleur. P'tit-Jean's woman, the Queen of the Vilaine;
but I wanted Niniane to say that, not me.
    I had been looking at her hands, which were lying on her lap,
palms up, the fingers of her right hand resting loosely on the
fingers of the left. I wanted to hold them, to open them, to run
my eyes and my fingers over those soft palms.
    She had been watching me, watching my eyes, and now she
nodded, then she spoke. 'I will tell you a little more of myself;
there can be no harm in that – can there, Mirela? – as you already
know so much.'
    Mirela nodded her permission.
    'May I hold your hands, read your palms, while you do so?' I
asked.
    She held them out to me.
    I moved closer and took them in my own. They were smooth
and well kept, with the fine, silken skin of the lazy and luxury-
loving, but they were not small, and neither were they as soft as
I'd imagined: they were large and firm and practical, the palms
long, longer than the long middle finger. All the fingers were

long and straight, and the flexible thumb with its wide, open
angle reminded me of Christine, Thomas's daughter.

'Pierre named me Niniane, then Niniane des Sept Soeurs. He
already knew of my six sisters, and he wanted a name that caught
the ear, just as he liked me dressed to catch the eye. I was his
mistress publicly, and he needed to be proud of me. Then one
afternoon in 1363, the Dauphin Charles saw me; and liked what
he saw.'

The Mount of Venus and the Heart Line were as one would
expect of such a beautiful and sensual woman. Of course Charles
liked what he saw. My Charles had glimpsed her too, once, and
never forgotten it.

'Pierre gave me to him, of course. And a bag of gold changed
hands, along with certain rights and privileges. The following
year, the Dauphin became King. Life went on with little change.
Years went by. When the King tired of me – '

Mireille snorted.

Niniane laughed. 'No, perhaps not. But the Queen grew very
tired of me. And the King is afflicted with religious scruples
which he succumbs to from time to time: a surfeit of me seems to
bring on an attack … Anyway, this was a bad attack: he gave me
a bag of gold and despatched me back to Pierre. Pierre, by then,
of course, had no interest in me at all. He liked his women young
– who can blame him? – and was ready to sell me. Overseas,
bien sur. It would never have done for the poor King to come
face to face with me again one day. But I pleaded. I pointed out
that he had now had two gold purses for me from the King, and
couldn't he possibly shut me away in a convent? I would be
Sister Marie Saint-Pierre – named after my benefactor's patron
saint,' she laughed, 'like all reformed prostitutes. He liked that,
but he wanted more. Would I submit to fasts, vigils, strenuously
strict discipline, and other good works of charity? I would, I
would! So he did. He was always a kind man, at heart. He took
me to an abbess he knew – he even paid her to accept me as a

novice – but on one condition: that she lock me up and he never hear my name or see my face again. Poor Pierre. After a year, I felt I'd been disciplined quite enough. By means of a friendly Father Confessor (very friendly – they are quite right in the Arab world only to let eunuchs near the women, aren't they?) I sent a message to the King who, by then, I knew, was missing me dreadfully. Don't ask me how I knew.'

The Head Line started well above the Life Line, indicating independence; it was clear and long, even more so than Natalie's Head Line; she was a risk-taker, and capable of immense achievements.

'When a message came back for me to meet him at Beauté-sur-Marne, the priest smuggled me out and I came here to Mirela. I threw off my black habit, and with it my name – Sister Marie Saint-Pierre – and was Natalya-Niniane the whore once more. And Pierre? When I met him, he sighed and said: "A convent used to be a place where girls who were not wanted, and women who were no longer wanted, could be safely shut away in the knowledge that they would be kept under lock and key until their hopefully early demise. But now, nuns wander in and out … I don't know what the world is coming to." Poor, dear Pierre. Now I'm no longer a nun in any real sense (if I ever was) but I wear my old habit sometimes when I don't wish to be recognised. I am summoned occasionally to Beauté-sur-Marne, but I live here at the Fille d'Or, just one of the girls.'

Did she have money of her own? Pierre had apparently taken everything she'd ever received from the King. Yet her Sun Line clearly showed success and wealth in old age. How? She was still in touch with the King. Was it that? Was it alchemy? Her hand was not the hand of a murderer – or even the hand of a mercenary woman: whatever she had done in her life, she hadn't done it for money.

'For now that is all I can tell you,' she said. 'Come back tomorrow, and we will see.'

She withdrew her hands gently. As gently as she might
withdraw from a lover. She had been the King's secret mistress
for fourteen years, as well as being an adept in the magic arts.
The well-defined Mystic Cross between the Head and Heart
Lines and the triangle on the middle phalange of the middle
finger would be a clear indication of the latter, if I did not
already know.

'Don't look so upset. Mirela, do you think you could persuade
La Dame de Montrouge to join us tomorrow?'

Mireille shrugged, and snapped her fingers to send Nininae
back out of the room the way she had come.

Niniane winked at me but I couldn't watch her go because
Mireille's fingers snapped again, this time at me, and she said,
'Niniane has a big mouth. Well, all whores have – ' she was
studying mine – 'but you must keep yours firmly closed when it
comes to what you heard here today and may see or hear on
future occasions. Do I make myself clear?'

'Oh, yes! Yes, of course, madame!'

She snapped her fingers again. It was my turn to be dismissed.

'Le Pitre!' I called, beckoning him over. 'Stay here. If a nun
comes out of that house, follow her and let me know somehow.
I'll be at home, then at the Petit-Pont landing-stage. After that, it
will be too late.'

I wanted to see what Niniane did next.

Then I went home and changed into my student's gown.

26

Raoul no longer knew how to behave with me when I was
dressed as a boy. I pushed him away – and noticed someone

watching us. No, it was nothing. He was simply amused. Was
there a pretty boy beneath my robe, and did Raoul, the young
theologian and ordinand (you could tell by his gown. a soutane)
like pretty boys? No one would have been surprised. He grinned
and nudged his neighbour, while I moved further away and
Raoul followed me.

Raoul, unaware of all this, was bursting with his story. 'It was
so funny, Mariana! She said the second nun was you … You
don't seem surprised. It wasn't you, was it?'

'Of course it wasn't. Though I'm not surprised to hear she
thought it was. What did she say, exactly?'

'She said - forgive me, Mariana, these are her words, not mine
- she said: "There's a foreign woman, hardly more than a girl,
who's been hanging around here. And though she gives herself
airs, she's no better than that other little slut - the one who lives
there. Both foreigners. Both putains, though this one's the worse.
I know her walk. She came dressed as a boy: I knew at once it
was her. And she got into trouble, spoilt her pretty face. She
thinks I'm blind? I saw that nose - even today it's still bruised,
still swollen. She can try to disguise her walk, but - " "She is not
disguising her walk. She has been beaten." "Grace à Dieu. Who
by?" "The Abbé Soxxal." "A man of God. Ah, so that is why she
walks now as if she had an icicle in her bottom." "I expect she
wishes she did have an icicle in her bottom." She laughed. "Ah,
you too are a man of God, my son. Or will be soon. And does the
good abbé know she dresses as a nun?" "No. No, I think that will
be news to him." "Tell him, my son. And tell him to have her put
in the pillory at the Porte Paris or the Place au Chats for a
morning so we can all enjoy making her mend her ways - "'

'Raoul, that is more than enough.'

Le Cafard sidles up to us. 'The nun came out and le Pitre
followed her. He sent me to tell you she is inside the Hôtel-Dieu,
down in the cellar. He's keeping watch at the top of the steps.'

I can't believe it. Lyse ...? 'Raoul, I must run. No, you stay here, go to the Louvre if I don't - '

'Stop giving me orders!'

'But I must go down into that cellar among the nuns!'

'You are dressed as a boy!'

'Oh - merde.'

He laughs.

'Don't laugh at me, Raoul! Help me!'

He looks round. Then in front of everyone, he pushes my
hood back off my head, loosens my hair with his two wonderful
hands, and still holding my head, tilts my face up and kisses me.
He says, 'Take off your belt and give it to me.'

I do so. The gown hangs loose, flows free.

'Now you are a woman.'

'Thank you, Raoul.' I kiss him again, quickly, and turn to
follow le Cafard, who has watched all this without so much as a
smirk.

As we go, I glance at the man who grinned. He grins back.
And he winks. But he does not nudge his neighbour. He has
forgotten all about him.

I pass le Pitre, touching him on the shoulder to stay where he is.
At the bottom of the stairs, I pause. A nun in formal habit is
talking to Lyse. At the other end of the chamber, three nuns in
working dress are on their knees scrubbing away at large
washing-boards. Their eyes are down in the presence of this
strange nun who might be anyone.

I can hear nothing. I decide to risk moving closer. Suddenly
there is a brief scuffle, the nun falls backwards into the river, and
is swept under the weir. Lyse is left there, holding a bloody
knife.

The other three nuns, clearly very well disciplined, still do not
so much as glance.

Once again I am about to move forward; this time, a man
steps from behind a vault.

It is the Albanian.

He takes the knife.

Lyse drops to her knees before him.

He studies the knife. 'It was hers.' He throws it into the river after her. 'She was my sister.' He looks at the kneeling woman. 'Your life is mine.'

Her head is bowed.

'They say you are curious about … my family.'

Still kneeling, head bowed, she gives a despairing nod.

'Then tell me: is Lule alive?'

'Sir, I am another's.'

'So?'

'It is written that no man can serve two masters.'

'A woman can. If that is not written, it should be.' He waits.

She says: 'Lule is alive.'

He waits.

She says: 'She has returned to Paris.'

'And where will I find her?'

'Ask Madame de Montrouge.'

He realises that he will get no more out of her.

I think for a moment that he is going to kill her, but he does not. He turns and comes towards me – and walks straight past me and up the stairs without a glance.

I wait, lest he turn back.

He does not.

I come up behind Lyse. Had she known I was there? Had they both? She shows no surprise.

'So Niniane is dead,' I murmur. 'But why did she – ?'

'That wasn't Niniane. It was someone much younger, a girl with light green eyes and freckles on her nose. And she was very fast. It could have been me in there. It should have been. Why wasn't it?'

I clasp her arm, then her shoulder. She is trembling. I stroke her back.

'And, dem'selle … ' She looks up at me. 'She wasn't dead.'
'What?'
In a second I am flying up the stairs past le Pitre crying
'Come!' and across the Parvis Notre Dame to the bank of the
river. 'It flows that way!' And we race along past the Hôtel-Dieu
with the current and look down from the bridge. Nothing. Which
side would she be?
'Dem'selle!' Le Pitre points. She is there, caught at the base of
the bridge – not caught, hanging on.
I kick off the boy's boots I wear with my student's gown and
dive in. By this time Raoul has seen us from the jetty on the
other side, and I hear him scream 'No! Mariana!' as I plunge
down into the icy water.
I remember fighting my way through the current towards her,
and being unable to reach her, and thinking I should have dived
in from the other side, gone with the current, and should have
thrown off the black gown as well as the boots, and that I always
did everything the hard way – the gown was dragging me down
but there was no way I could get it off now – then I was in front
of her and screaming 'Let go! Let go!' Her body hit me, I grabbed
her, and we both went under, weighed down by her and the gown
– the two gowns! – she too was wearing a heavy black robe! –
and I remembered the sailor I had saved off the coast of Spain.
Oh, that lovely, warm, blue water. I want to go home, I want to
go home …

Then nothing, till I found myself wrapped in a blanket in a warm
room somewhere, and Raoul standing beside me, and a fat
woman I thought I knew; and Natalie, also wrapped in a blanket,
lying on the floor.
'Is she all right?' I tried to say but coughed and retched, and
gasped.
Raoul said, 'You're full of river water.'
'Is she …?'

'She's breathing. Thanks to you.'

'And the knife wound?'

'Nothing serious. But what happened?'

'Later. I'll tell you what happened before, and you'll tell me what happened afterwards.' I looked round. 'Where are we?'

'The Chaire. I thought – somewhere warm, where they know us. And it was just overhead. Almost literally.'

I looked at the fat woman again. Of course. I smiled, and she smiled back.

'Could you eat some nice hot soup now?' she said.

Soup?

'Soup, Mariana. I insist,' said Raoul.

Ugh. 'Raoul, are the boys out there, either of them?'

'All of them. Coco is there, Mâchefer.'

'Ask le Pitre to come in.'

He brought the boy in.

'Dem'selle Mariana …' There were tears in the boy's eyes. 'I prefer you in the mud where I can help you.'

'I think on the whole so do I. But at least I had some clothes on this time.'

His eyes flicked down. The wet clothes had been removed, of course, and the blanket I was wrapped in was not very big. He tried not to smile through his tears.

A huge bowl of soup arrived.

'Would you like this soup?' I said, to Le Pitre. The thought of having to eat all that was putting tears in my eyes.

'Mariana!' Raoul was determined. 'Eat it. Or do I have to feed you?' His eyes lit up. 'I know. I'll send one of them to fetch Yahia. He can feed you.'

'No, I'll eat it.' Yahia I didn't mind, but if Khadija came too I would jump back in the river.

I spooned some into my mouth and swallowed. Not too bad.
'Le Pitre, run to the Hôtel-Dieu and find Lyse. Go halfway down those stairs and yell "Lyse!". When you have her, say "La

Dem'selle d'Écosse pulled the girl with green eyes out of the river. Now she needs two sets of dry women's clothes." Can you do that?'

'Of course, dem'selle.' He hurried off.

'Don't think you are leaving here, Mariana.'

'Raoul, you like soup. How about …?'

'Mariana! Anyway, I've had mine.'

For some reason, half-way through my soup I slept again. And when I woke, the room was full of people. My head was on somebody's lap – it was Raoul, who else? – and he was stroking my forehead.

'Marian. Oh, lass …' Ferchard was holding my hand. It had never struck me before, but Ferchard was the only person in France who called me "lass", as my father always had. The only person in the world. I gazed at him. 'Say "lass" again.'

'Marian, lass – I should never let you out of my sight.'

'Natalie?'

'She's fine. She woke up, went back to sleep.'

'And the wound?'

'It's nothing. The poignard passed through her arm, in the arm pit.'

'Oh, thank God.'

'What happened, lass? Nobody knows except you and her.'

And Lyse, I thought. And the Albanian. Better that way, unless … Though why Natalie should have tried to kill Lyse was another question altogether. As was what she was doing dressed as a nun. And where she had got the outfit. And whether or not this was the first time. She'd come from the Fille d'Or dressed like that. Niniane again … And it couldn't have been the abbé who tortured Guillaume to death in his own home. He would have tortured him to death at his Paris headquarters.

While I'd been lying there thinking, a large man with a loud voice had caught my eye – the only person there I didn't know. He was talking to Henri, a friend of Raoul's, and they were speaking English.

'Who is that?' I asked Raoul.

'Henri le Fou.'

'No, not him. The other.' And even as I said it, the man moved and I saw that he had only one leg. One-legged Jack, the soldier who had been left behind to die.

'Le Cafard brought him.'

Le Cafard was called over. 'What's he doing here?'

'Le Pitre told me to bring him.'

I beckoned to le Pitre, whose eyes never left me. He knew who we were talking about. 'Lyse told me you should speak to him. That it was urgent. When I went to get the clothes for you and Dem'selle Natalie.'

The clothes? I realised someone had dressed me while I was sleeping. I was wearing some kind of skirt and blouse under the blanket now.

'Lyse didn't say why I should speak to him?'

'No, only to tell you that Maître Guillaume's first love was imp-implicated in his death - that she was there.'

His first love?

'Ask One-legged Jack to come here.'

He came, grinning. 'You must be young Magnus's sister, Lady Marian. Good evening, my lady.'

Ah yes, he knew me only as Magnus.

'Though as I heard it, young Magnus dived into the river today and you came out.'

Ferchard's pale eyes turned to ice. 'Perhaps those who saw that were as drunk as you clearly are, man. I would advise you to guard your tongue.'

'Ferchard, let him speak. Aye, Jack, we are very close my twin brother and I. I've been told I should talk to you. Urgently. I'm not sure what about.'

'I heard tell you were interesting yourself in the murder of the miser in the rue Saint Paul.'

'That's right.'

'So maybe it's to do with that … May I sit down?'

'No, you may not!' snarled my self-apponted father-substitute.

'Ferchard! Please.' I was still lying on the floor, my head up on Raoul's lap. 'Sit here, Jack, beside Raoul. You know Raoul?'

'Raoul, yes. And Sir Farquhar – '

'How do you know my name?' Ferchard snapped.

'It's well known – in certain quarters – '

'Ferchard! Both of you! Ferchard, you are that side of me, and you, Jack, this side. My body is no man's land. It must not be so much as spoken across. Do you understand me?'

'Yes, my lady,' said Jack, still grinning.

'So, Jack. Tell me.'

'All I know about that murder is that it took place on the night after Christmas. It was a cold night – aren't they all, this time of year? – but that night I was outside, in a doorway close by the bordel they call the Golden Girl. And she is that.'

'Who is?' But I knew.

'Wait, my lady. Let me tell it my own way. It was cold and getting colder, so cold I was praying the river wouldn't freeze over and the wolves find their way into the city with me shut out for want of a denier, having drunk the last one without thinking, it being Christmas. Then I saw two women coming along the road, one a nun, t'other in a cloak with the hood up. The moon was shining so I saw them clearly. And the lantern was lit over the door of the bordel, so I saw them again. The nun was no nun; she was the one they call the Golden Girl – the Filly Dore herself.'

'Her name?'

'Miss Natalya.'

Natalya? But that could be either … 'And the other one?'

'T'other was a youngster with carrot-coloured hair.'

'And her name?'

He shrugged.

But I knew. 'The time?'
'Time? I don't know.'
'Before midnight?'
'Oh yes. Some while before.'
Natalie.
Jack followed my eyes, recognised her suddenly.
I put my finger to my lips.
He nodded.
I gazed at her sleeping form. She was suffering from shock –
and from a guilty conscience: didn't want to wake up. Somehow,
though, I had to get the truth out of her. It wouldn't be easy. She
was a born liar. It would be easier to get it out of Niniane.
Natalie's problem, I decided, was that she had grown up without
anyone showing her any real affection.
Wasn't it Jalal ud Din al-Rumi who wrote "A person who has
never been caressed regards violence as normal"?
But Natalie? Could it be?
I should have remembered that al-Rumi also wrote: "If you
want to see the truth, close your eyes to what appears to be true."
Then Jack said, 'Nun she may not be, but saint she is.'
'Saint?'
He wasn't looking at Natalie. He was looking inside himself.
'Let me tell my story. I haven't finished yet. And tell you who
you ought to speak to next.'
I nodded, contritely.
'You know Disappearing Guilly?'
I shook my head. Such strange names they have. 'Another like
le Cafard who can become invisible?'
He shook his head.
'Mariana, he is …' Raoul tried to explain. 'You know how
they punish people by amputating various parts of their bodies – '
'Of course, Raoul.' Then suddenly I realised what he was
going to say. 'Oh, no.'
'Oh yes. Disappearing Guilly has lost so many parts there's

not much left.'

'No arms,' said Jack, 'no legs, no ears, of course, no nose – '

'He has his eyes still, and his tongue, that's all,' said Raoul.

'One eye. Lost t'other by order of someone he looked at a bit cheeky like, just before Christmas.'

'That's awful. But what has it to do with me?'

'Christmas night, Disappearing Guilly was unlucky. His mate got drunk and forgot all about him. Left him lying there in the cold in the rue Saint Paul. He was unlucky – but you was lucky. Because then he got lucky. The Golden Girl in the nun's garments hadn't noticed him when she went into the miser's house, but when she came out again, through the back entrance this time, she did. And she did what any – any saint – would do: she picked him up in her arms – he's tiny, he started as a dwarf – and took him home with her. And there he is to this day. He's the one you need to speak to. But do it quick. I know for a fact that certain parties are after his other eye and his tongue. Especially his tongue.'

His tongue? Oh, because of what he saw that night, because of what he can tell me, tell the authorities.

'One of those "parties" wouldn't be an abbé?'

'More than my life's worth to mention names, but … I did hear that a certain captain was searching for him, and asking if he had spoken to Lady MacElpin or Doña Mariana de la Mar or Magnus MacElpin or Lady Jane or Sir Jack – I like that, Sir Jack – Cutting.'

'I see. Ferchard. Raoul. I must go now. And Natalie must come with me.'

This time no one argued.

We had come off the bridge onto the Île de la Cité and were rounding the Hôtel-Dieu when we were attacked. The litter in which Natalie and I were riding crashed to the ground. Natalie, battered back into consciousness, moaned 'My life used to be so peaceful till I met you.'

'Now wait a minute!'

But then the litter tipped over and we found ourselves rolling
in the mud. I was getting used to it. She looked as though she
wished she were still unconscious. Two struggling men landed
on me, squashing me flat, then rolled off, each intent on killing
the other. I realised I had never seen either of them before and
was wondering about that when I saw someone grab Natalie –
and it was as though he had grabbed a sleeping cat. Her nails
ripped open his face and when his hands flew up to protect his
eyes she took his knife, almost casually, and killed him, and
looked round for more.

I was still sitting there admiring her, and feeling that I had
probably done my share for the day, when I noticed all was quiet.
The fight was over. We had won. But who were "we"?

Then a handsome young man offered me his hand and helped
me up out of the mud in which I seemed to have become
embedded. It was le Grec.

'Merci, Charles.'

'A votre service, demoiselle.'

He shouted some orders, our litter was put back together, and
in no time at all we were on our way as if nothing had happened.

I suddenly realised that le Grec had spoken only to me. Why?
Of course. Natalie was not supposed to be here. It was not us
they had saved, but me. She had slipped away from the Court of
Miracles without telling anyone. Why? And how?

She was pretending to sleep again.

I pushed my head out through the curtain. 'Ferchard! Raoul!
Come here … What happened?'

'We were attacked by the abbé's men. The Albanian had been
expecting it. He's had someone following you.'

'Ah.' My shadow. 'He's not very good at his job.'

'Not very …? He saved your life, and the other lass's. You
don't think the abbé would have let either of you go again, do

you? Your very visible protector was part of a chain. Another
man, whom you might have spotted, followed him. Another,
whom neither you nor your assailants could ever have seen,
followed the second. Behind the third or fourth man came a
small army, who could all be with you in less than – '
    'What happened when we were in the river? Raoul had to save
us.'
    Raoul, very pale and silent (he was not one for fights)
suddenly looked pleased with himself.
    'Raoul happened to be on the jetty, where he got a boat
launched. Anyway, they probably didn't fancy a cold swim; a
good fight on the other hand …'
    'And now?'
    'The Albanian has gone to pick up the abbé and his men.
There's to be a party at Montfaucon. Tonight. And we are all
invited.' He closed the curtain, firmly.
    Montfaucon?
    'Natalie! Wake up! Wake, I said! Oh, you are awake. Listen.
Where and what is Montfaucon?'
    'It's the great gibbet – outside Paris, to the north, on the grande
rue Saint-Denis.'
    'But surely there are more than enough places to hang
someone in Paris?'
    'Yes, but they don't leave them there, they take them out to
Montfaucon – '
    'And hang them again?'
    'Mostly they're already dead, but yes. And that's where they
leave them, for the crows to eat.'
    'So people are taken out there after they've been executed.'
    'Yes. Though not necessarily hanged. Beheaded. Boiled.
Anything. Then their bodies are hung up out there for the birds.'
    'But are people hanged there? Or only taken there afterwards.'
    'Oh, yes, people are hanged there all the time. Not women …'
    'Not women?'

'They don't like women's bodies hanging around, specially out there. The Church, you know. They bury the boiled ones, I think. And women caught stealing are buried alive.'

'Where?'

'In the cemetery of Les Innocents. I watched a woman being buried once when I went to the market.'

I knew. The huge cemetery where traders used tombs as stalls to display their shoes and clothes and sweets and trinkets while all around in vaulted charnel houses skulls and bones were piled high to make way for new-comers.

'And "a party at Montfaucon"? What's that?'

'Normally, it would be what it says. People go out there on holidays and have a picnic and talk and play. It's good for them. Especially children. An awful warning … But when my uncle says "a party at Montfaucon", he'll mean something else.'

'That he'll kill people. "Execute" them.'

'Yes. Then have a party.'

'Natalie … On the night your – master – was murdered, you left the house in the rue Saint-Pol.'

She shook her head. She was still dazed.

'You left with your aunt, Natalya, who is called Niniane. She was wearing a nun's habit. You were wearing a grey cloak with the hood up.'

'Ah. Yes.'

'Outside the house, your aunt stopped to help someone. You remember that?'

Slowly, she nodded. 'Yes. I was tired and cold. I wanted to go. She got angry. She said I was spoilt and needed a good beating. Me! She's the one who's spoilt. When was she last beaten? Anyway, the one you mean, she bent down and she picked him up. Just like that. I don't know how she could – he's horrible. No legs, no arms, no – no face, really. She picked him up and carried him all the way to the – to my other aunt's house.'

'And how long did you stay there?'

'Me?' This sleepiness was strange. She seemed half-drugged. 'Not long. I was worried – about my master.'

'Why?'

'I don't know. I was worried …'

'And who was there with your master when you and your aunt left?'

'No one.'

'The abbé?'

She stared at me, then nodded.

'Who else? The captain?'

'You know the captain?'

Now I nodded. Oh, I knew him.

'No one else?'

'No.'

'And what did you find when you went home?'

'My master was dead. You know that. There was blood everywhere. I ran for Jaquet, but …'

'You couldn't get past his mother.'

No smile.

'Why did you go to him, not back to your aunt at the Fille d'Or?'

'It was closer, and – and Jaquet is – we are …'

'I understand … Natalie, what were you doing today at the Hôtel-Dieu?'

'The Hôtel-Dieu?'

'Down in the cellar. You tried to kill a lay-sister called Lyse.'

She looked at me in horror. 'I've never been in the Hôtel-Dieu.'

She didn't remember, didn't know.

'Have you seen your mother?'

'My mother is dead. Oh. No, you said she's alive …?'

I felt the litter being set down. We were there.

27

Niniane examined the half-conscious Natalie.

Mireille sent one of the girls to fetch La Dame de Montrouge from the Paris residence of Olivier de Clisson, a long-time friend apparently of P'tit-Jean's.

I, meanwhile, insisted on talking to Disappearing Guilly.

'That disgusting creature?' protested Mireille, but she allowed me to go through to the kitchen.

There, for the first, but not the last - oh, not the last! - time, I came up against the redoubtable Seraphina?

'What do you want, girl? Sent you down for a beating, did they?' She took a long whippy rod down from a hook on the wall and flexed it between her hands, bending it double.

'No, of course not!'

'Least you're not all dressed up and prancing around like a lady, today.'

I looked down at myself. The old skirt Lyse had sent was torn and wet and muddy from the fight on the road and the blouse was hanging off one shoulder, most of my left breast on display. I looked back up at her, blushing.

'Mère Mireille's got no patience with whores what give themselves airs, and no more have I. Oh, have I got a rod in pickle for you!!'

'Listen, Seraphina, I've no idea what you're talking about. I just came through here to - '

'Oh, you haven't, eh? You've got no idea what I'm talking about, eh? And you're not a whore, never worked in a whorehouse, eh? Oh, and that's Mère Seraphina to the likes of you.'

What was the point? I tried to please Ferchard, I really did, but instead of seeming a lady I simply seemed a whore who dressed above her station and gave herself airs. Usually. Not even that today. 'Mère Seraphina, then. I came through here – '

'You haven't answered the questions I asked you.'

'All right, I do know what you're talking about and I have worked in a whorehouse. Now, please, can I see and speak to Disappearing Guilly?'

'How many whorehouses? Where? And for how long?'

'Two. One in Cuenca, in Spain, for two years. The other in Avignon, just for a couple of months.'

'And did you get beaten?'

'Yes.'

'Yes, Mère Seraphina.'

'Yes, Mère Seraphina.'

'Has anyone ever used a whip on you?'

Her eyes were on my breast, the livid welts left across it by the good abbé's whip.

'Yes, Mère Seraphina.'

'Right. Now we know where we are, don't we.' She bent the rod double again and looked me up and down with an evil leer on her face. Then pointed with the rod. 'It's through there.'

What was left of him was in a box on a bench in the kitchen. A small box. I thought at first he was sleeping. He had no lips, and the breath was whispering and rasping in and out between his teeth and through the hole where his nose had been. Around his gums the flesh had healed, and the base of his nose and the chin, if skull-like, were no longer raw. The left eye-socket, though, beneath its bandage, was still oozing blood and puss.

He was not asleep. The other eye was flickering as he peered out at me through long, thick, dark eyelashes. Let no one say that a man is his body. Most of Guilly had disappeared, but Guilly was still there.

'Bon soir, Guilly.'

'Soir, 'selle.'

Without lips there are various sounds you cannot make, such as B and F and M and P, but we were going to manage.

'I'm sorry about your eye.'

He gave a kind of smile. 'I can still see you.'

Was it so important that a woman be beautiful? Even to a man in that state?

'They shall not take your other eye.'

'Will take.'

'Tell me what you saw. Perhaps you saw something that makes your eye – and more to the point your tongue – dangerous to them.'

'Saw?'

He didn't know what I was here for. This had been One-legged Jack's idea.

'The night Madame Niniane brought you here …'

He nodded. 'La Fille d'Or, yes.'

The place he meant? Or the person? It didn't matter. 'You'd been left in the rue Saint-Pol, outside the miser's house.'

He nodded again.

'Who did you see go in? And who did you see come out? Think carefully. This may be very important.'

He thought. If he'd had any hands, any arms, he would have scratched his head.

'First, the witch.'

Witch? 'You mean the nun? Madame Niniane?'

He laughed. It wasn't horrible, or not as horrible as it might have been, because I kept my eyes on his one sparkling eye.

'Niniane no nun. Nor witch. She la Fille d'Or. Came later.'

'And the witch?'

Why didn't he speak?

'How long did she stay? The witch, I mean.'

He stared at me. 'Don't know.'

'You mean you slept? You missed some of the coming and

going?'

'Too cold to sleep. Was awake, waiting to die.'

'So…?'

'Was there, the witch.'

Still there. 'And who else was still there?'

'Montrouge …'

'Yes?'

'No. He'd left. The captain was there, and that abbé.'

'The captain?' But was it the captain, my captain? 'And the cabin-boy?'

'The captain alone that night. With the abbé.'

'And no one else came or went?'

'Dem'selle Natalie.'

I thanked him, asked if there was anything I could do for him: he wanted some water, which I gave to him, holding his head up so he could swallow it. Then I laid him down again, and – carefully avoiding Seraphina – returned to Niniane.

I had to talk to Natalie.

She was conscious, but Niniane took me out of the room. 'You must be careful with her. She's under some kind of enchantment.'

'What kind of enchantment?'

Niniane gazed at me. Then relaxed. 'We're going to have to work together here … Someone's trying to control her.'

'Trying? She attempted to kill a woman today, then afterwards remembered nothing.'

She looked shocked. 'Who?'

'A lay-sister at the Hotel-Dieu.'

'Her name?'

'Lyse. Of Strasbourg.'

'I don't know her. Is there anything special about her? Or does she happen to know something?'

Now it was my turn to gaze and wonder how far to take her into my confidence. 'There is something special about her,' I admitted.

'But you are not at liberty to tell me what. She may still be in danger.'

'She will be well protected by now.'

'Good ... Mariana, Natalie still has much of her own spirit.'

'Spirit?'

'But it is being drained out of her. We could lose her.'

'You mean her soul?'

'No. Her soul is her, is Natalie. We could find that again, we could reunite it with its body while that body is young and whole. But if the body-and-soul as one lack spirit, then it enters the world of the shades, without will, without hope, dead and yet not dead.'

Dead and yet not dead? Undead? The very word horrified me.

'The problem is that I have no idea who is trying to control her, trying to drain her spirit.'

'I know,' I said. 'It's the witch who was still … But there's also someone called Mère Athanasía. Which means, I suppose, that she's not French. Could she be Greek - or Albanian? She's not by any chance one of the seven sisters, is she?'

She smiled. 'She is, in fact, yes. Because she's me. Athanasía is a nom de guerre chosen to reflect my interest in … deathlessness. In immortality. I too, as you know, am in search of the Philosopher's Stone, but I have no great interest in earthly gold. What was that about a witch?'

'I don't know. But Natalie knows her.'

'I think I begin to understand.'

'Let me ask Natalie one question. Then I will tell you all I know.'

We went back to the pale girl lying on the bed, her face so thin-seeming suddenly, her eyes wide. 'Am I dying?'

Niniane took her hand. 'No. Someone's been trying to control you. Now we know, and she'll have Mariana and me to contend with as well, so you have nothing to fear. First, though, you must answer one or two questions for Mariana. And I suspect that if you'd answered those questions truthfully in the first place, much of this need never have happened.'

Tears welled up in her eyes, overflowed, ran down her cheeks, trickled down into her hair: a performance which, I had no doubt, always affected her doting "master", but made no impression at all on Niniane or me.

'Natalie,' I prodded pitilessly, 'who was in your "master's" house the night he died?'

'I told you – '

'Who was still there when you left with Niniane – when she picked up Disappearing Guilly. You told me the abbé was there, and the captain. But someone else was there, someone you haven't told me about. The one who really frightens you … Natalie, I've been in the hands of the abbé and the captain. I know what it is to be frightened.'

But Niniane interrupted: 'What happened, Mariana? With the abbé. I need to know.' She wanted me to tell that tale, give Natalie time to think – and something else to think about – or so I guessed.

I told them.

They both gazed at me raptly, then Niniane gently opened what was left of my blouse to see how the welts left by the whip stretched across both breasts.

When she took her hand away, I tried to cover myself up.

'Leave it,' she told me. 'I'll get you some other clothes in a minute.' She was upset by my story.

'And you really killed one of those men?' asked Natalie, clearly not troubled at all by the raping and beating, only impressed that I'd actually managed to kill someone without her help.

'I've been a slave and a prostitute for nearly twenty years now,' Niniane breathed, 'but nothing like that has ever happened to me.'

I looked at her. I couldn't see the point she was making.

'I mean that, unlike you, I've been asking for it. Have been in place for it. Like a lamb in a butcher's shop.'

I laughed. 'Any lamb that survives twenty years in a butcher's shop will live forever.'

'But you … you were so good, so innocent. So young.'

'So like a chicken, challenging the cooks. But as I see it, the abbé and the captain, although they were there and were quite capable of the deed, couldn't have been the ones who tortured Old Guillaume to death. They'd have taken him where they took me, tortured him there, in their own time, without risk of disturbance.'

'No. To the abbé – and this is how he would have portrayed you to anyone who enquired – you are a young woman who dresses as a boy, a whore and a foreigner, and quite without rights. Guillaume, on the contrary, would have to be dealt with through official channels, and by the Dominicans, presumably; he would slip out of the abbé's grasp.

'Listen,' Niniane went on. 'The abbé had arranged to meet Pierre that night at Guillaume's house. I turned up by chance, knowing nothing of this and anxious only to help Pierre – and spoilt things! Pierre was furious. He left. I begged him to take me with him, but …' She paused. 'If he had, he'd be alive now. The abbé said he and the captain would be staying for a while. They had things to discuss with Guillaume. I looked at Guillaume, but he simply nodded and said "You go, Natalya". Then he added: "And take Natalie with you." He seemed unusually serious. Natalie, who tended to argue with him, even boss him around (though she liked to pretend he was her "master"), for once gave in and obeyed without a murmur.'

I smiled at Natalie, who was blushing.

But then Niniane said: 'Natalie, who else was in the house? Someone was.'

There was a long silence while Natalie's eyes flicked

backwards and forwards between us.

    She wasn't going to say. She couldn't.

    I decided to take the lead. 'Natalie, I know who was there.'

    'You don't.'

    'I do. I want you to say it. Of your own free will.'

    'Tell me something - anything - just to prove that you know.'

    'There are witches and witches, witches whose motives are good, and witches whose motives are not good and whose methods are frequently evil.'

    'You do know. So why ...?'

    'Tell us, child,' urged Niniane.

    'It was the one called. She came first. She was in the laboratory with my master when the abbé and the captain arrived. She told me to take her to my room, where she could hide till they'd gone. But then Messire Pierre came. Then Tante Natalya - Niniane, here.'

    'And all that time this Mère Malina was in your little room, up in the attic?'

    She nodded.

    'You're certain?' I wanted to be certain.

    'No! How can I be certain? I was downstairs in the kitchen with Jaquet. But nobody else was let in or let out, so far as I know.'

    'And what do you know about this Mère Malina?'

    'Nothing. She frightens me.'

    'Tell me about her?'

    'She is … old, in a way; but tall, and very strong.'

    'How do you know that?'

    'She picked me up once by my hair - held me up in the air at arm's length.'

    'So she's been coming for years.'

    'Yes. No. Yes. But this happened recently. I was the same size I am now.'

    'I see. And how did it come about?'

'My master had told me not to admit anyone. Anyone at all.
He was indisposed. When she came to the door, I didn't know
what to do. D'accord, they were old friends. That didn't mean we
trusted her. He didn't, so I didn't. But when I told her he was
indisposed, she simply picked me up by my hair and carried me,
like that, all the way up to the laboratory.'

'You didn't fight? I saw you fight like a cat this very
afternoon.'

She shook her head.

'Why not?'

'I was like a rabbit in a dog's mouth. I was paralysed …'

'Well, we are a brave trio, aren't we?' sighed Niniane. 'A lamb,
a chicken, and now a rabbit. Natalie, I want you to lie here, on
the floor, in the middle of the room. You will be safer, believe
me. And you, Mariana, wait through there in the next room. I'll
take Natalie to the privy, then get her settled. I won't be a
moment. Oh, and I'll ask Mère Mireille to tell one of the girls to
bring you some clothes '

I walked up and down in the little red room, walked to the
window, peered out at the narrow street. Two of Mireille's girls
were outside tempting customers in, and Le Pitre was there,
sitting hunched up, his chin on his knees, in the doorway
opposite.

One was older than me and very elegantly dressed in a gown
fringed with white fur: too elegantly dressed. If one of the
sergeants saw her like that she'd be stripped and put in the pillory
in the nearby Place au Chats. And how could you turn a profit
when you could be stripped of your finery any time one of the
sergeants or a respectable citoyen – or citoyenne – decided to be
difficult? Spain was more civilised.

Of course, the sergeant may settle for a pleasant hour or two
instead.

The other, the young one, was Marie, the girl I'd met on my

first visit. She was dressed, by contrast, in a ragged old smock full of holes – rips that seemed to be natural but were in fact slits, artfully placed.

Catering for different tastes.

Mère Mireille would send me something like the first girl was wearing, I supposed. After all, she knew I was really a lady even if Seraphina didn't.

As I watched, a fat man stopped, said something abusive to the older girl, then took the young one's bare arm in his gloved hand and brought her into the house. Behind him, the older one made the universal gesture of castration then spoke to another, younger, man who had seen her and laughed.

I walked back across the room. Then back to the window. The man was touching her throat, her shoulder. She didn't push his hand away.

I walked back and forth again. They had disappeared. And now through the window I saw Mireille with another woman, richly dressed, and slightly taller and slimmer than herself.

Lule?

I waited.

A moment later, there came a sudden cry from the larger room next door. It was a cry of shock and pain, not one of joy, and it was not Natalie's voice, nor did it sound like Niniane. Then hushed voices, arguing. Then silence.

Still I waited.

Outside, it was getting dark.

Obviously they had forgotten me. I needed to go home, wash, change out of these clothes that had belonged to some poor woman I had never known. I needed to rest, to eat.

Niniane came in, closed the door behind her. 'She's unconscious.'

Lule? No, Natalie, of course. 'What happened?'

'She lapsed into a coma. It became too much for her.'

'What did?' But I knew what.

'She's dying.'

I stared.

'We have a few hours at the most.'

'And this Mère Malina: will she be too much for us?' How powerful was Niniane?

'She may be. A lot will depend on you, on your resources.'

My resources?

'Do you wear an effective amulet?'

'I have this.' I showed her the fish on a gold chain I sometimes wore, not at my neck but wound round my wrist. A talisman, but hardly an amulet. It was one of a pair, the other my twin brother Magnus had been wearing when he disappeared.

'And? You have something else. I can feel it.'

What could she mean? Ah, yes. I opened my pocket, took out the pendant Maître Pietri had made.

She held it and gazed at it. 'The Goddess. And the World. That is powerful.' She gave it back to me. 'Come through.'

'And my clothes?'

'Mère Mireille wasn't here, so I asked Seraphina. She told me to mind my own business. So I minded my own business. If you are wise,' she grinned, 'you will always do exactly as Seraphina tells you.' She put her hand out, brushed dried mud off my rags. 'You'll be all right. She'll just think you're dressed for the rough trade.'

She? Lule? La Dame de Montrouge?

Natalie was still lying on the floor where we had left her, and kneeling beside her was her mother: the woman from the portrait, still beautiful, and taller than Niniane when she stood up, but now her blonde hair was covered and the speedwell-blue eyes were filled with tears.

I realised I was staring. 'I'm sorry. I – '

Niniane interrupted me. 'You know us all so well that I forgot you've never actually met my other sister. Lule, this is Mariana, a friend of Natalie's friend Jaquet, and now of Natalie herself. You can trust her.'

She looked down her nose at me, her lips curling.

Was it the clothes? Or would she have known anyway?

'Please, don't concern yourself with me, Madame Lule. How is Natalie?'

'Worse. She's no longer here in her body.'

I looked at Niniane. Would she still take the lead? Yes. 'Then we shall go where she has gone and we shall bring - or send - her back.'

I looked at Lule. This was the one who hated and feared witchcraft and all things magic. 'We?' she said.

'I and Mariana. Yes, and you. For I shall need the help of both of you.'

There was a long pause, then Lule said, 'Whatever I can do, I will. Tell me.'

'First we must build up a ring of protection, a magic circle. Normally, I might prefer a pentagram, but now we are three, so: a triangle, a double triangle, the Seal of Solomon. And I will want it made of adamantine - which means: of steel. Mirela has sent someone to bring two lengths of steel chain. While we wait, will you finish your story, Mariana? You'd reached the point where Natalie attacked that poor woman, then fell into the icy river and was swept away. You never told me how she was rescued or about the attack on your litter.'

'How did you know about that?'

She smiled mysteriously. Then said, 'One of the bearers told me.'

Lule rolled her eyes.

I smiled, then described briefly how I had dived after Natalie and somehow held her up till we were rescued by Raoul. I had reached the attack on the litter by the abbé's men when Lule put her hand on mine. I thought she was going to say something like "Mariana, I know I can never repay you, or even thank you," but she didn't, she removed her hand as though it had touched something disgusting and turned her eyes away from me as though she couldn't bear to look at me.

Niniane, who had been watching this with a smirk, said, 'What matters here, what counts, is that Natalie owes her life to all three of us: is alive only because of us. You, Lule, gave her life. I saved her the night Guillaume was murdered. Both he and I scented death in the air. If she'd been with him still, she would have died. And Mariana saved her today.'

'She saved me once, too,' I said.

'How did that happen?'

'I was attacked unexpectedly, and overpowered. She had a dagger with her, a poignard, which she used, very expertly.' I looked at her, suddenly realising. 'Presumably the same poignard she used and lost today. Your brother was there. He arrived too late to intervene, but he threw it after her into the river. He said it was his sister's.'

Niniane said: 'It was. It was mine.'

'And you, not he, taught her how to use it.'

'Ah ha. So he thinks I am dead.'

'Presumably.'

'What is the point of all this about saving her life?' demanded Lule.

'Our lives, all three of us, are inextricably bound up with Natalie's. Now, Mariana, tell me about this attack. And tell me all you know of what is in my brother's mind.'

I described the attack, then said: 'Your brother intends to execute Abbé Soxxal and his men tonight, during the course of what he chooses to term a "party" at Montfaucon.'

'Ah! Now I see,' breathed Niniane.

'You know the place?' I asked.

'I've been there.'

'Everyone knows it,' said Lule. 'The bodies, hundreds of them, all swaying in the wind; the great birds, flapping away then alighting again as one of the children runs too close or throws a stone. You never forget it.'

'Who did you go with, madame? Did Maître Guillaume take you?'

'Guillaume?' She laughed. 'No. Such places horrified him. But it was he who first told me about it. He said that sorcerers in need of body parts buy them from the guards – can do so easily, with little or no risk. I was curious. And I thought it would be good for Natalie. So we went out there one day with a friend of mine.'

A friend? I let that go.

But Niniane was curious. 'And having seen the place, all those men hanging there in various stages of decomposition, what card did – do – you associate it with?'

There was a point to this question, I could tell.

Lule looked at her. Then at me.

I said: 'The Hanged Man?'

She almost laughed. 'Oh no. The Hanged Man doesn't symbolise death – something Pierre never understood – though it can symbolise the passing of time. Montfaucon I associate with the Judgement. I imagined the Last Trump, the heavens opening, and all those people coming back to life, being lowered to the ground ...'

'And led off to face judgement,' murmured Niniane.

Lule glared at her.

'And the other thing occupying your brother's mind must be the property of the Sire de Montrouge,' I said.

'Why? Anyway, there is almost no property,' said Lule bitterly.

Niniane just stared at me.

'It was your brother, madame,' I explained, 'who lent Pierre more and more and more and now holds the title to all Pierre's property.'

Now Niniane understood. 'Jean could appeal to the King,' she said. 'He would intervene.'

She meant she could persuade him to.

'He would not,' replied Lule. 'Remember Jean was an outlaw, a wanted man.'

I said: 'I've heard your brother tell his story. He had nothing against Pierre but his attack on you and your first-born child. It was all done for you, Madame Lule.'

'You mean …?'

I nodded.

'Does he know I'm alive?'

'I told him, madame.'

Niniane was gazing down at the unconscious girl. 'Lule, we must hurry. I'll see if the chains have come.'

Lule pressed her hand to Natalie's forehead. 'She seems stable.'

'She may seem stable, but she's not.' Niniane went, leaving Lule and me alone.

Lule was stroking Natalie's forehead and eyes. She looked up at me, pale blue eyes full of contempt. 'What makes you think my brother would hand over Jean's property to me?'

'I'm not sure he would. He might give it to Natalie.'

'Natalie?'

'Madame, he knows she's Pierre's daughter.'

'I see. Yes.'

'But I think it more likely that he would restore le Sire et la Dame de Montrouge to their former pomp – seeing as La Dame is his favourite sister and the only sister who in his eyes did no wrong.'

She stared at me. 'Do you have influence with him?' Light suddenly dawned. 'You're his personal whore!'

I laughed.

Lule was not one to join in another's laughter, but Niniane returned with the chains and, though she had no idea what I was laughing about, laughed with me, and carried on chuckling while she laid the chains out around Natalie in two equilateral

triangles, one superimposed on the other so that they formed a
star, the Star of David, the powerful Seal of Solomon.

When she had finished, she looked up me, those dark green
eyes shining now even if the worry lines were still there around
them. 'Laughter is good,' she said. 'It makes the circle that much
harder to break through. But before we start, I need someone
who can take a message to our brother at the Court of Miracles.'

'There's no one here, in this house?'

'No.'

'There's a girl at the Adriatica – Marie-Élise. She escorted me.
Mère Vèronique – '

'We're short of time now.'

'Then … there was a boy named le Pitre waiting outside.'

'He belongs to you? The girls have been asking about him.
They thought the poor mite was in love with one of them, but
hadn't a sou to ... '

'No, no. He's mine.'

We went outside, leaving Lule with Natalie.

'Le Pitre, I want you to go to the Court of Miracles of Saint-
Antoine. Don't be frightened. Ask to be taken to l'Albanien, or,
if he's not available, to le Grec. Say you bear a message of the
greatest possible urgency. Say it comes from his three sisters.
Listen: their names are Lule, Mirela and Natalya. Repeat that.'

He did so.

'When he hears that he will know it is genuine.'

'I'll say that you sent me, dem'selle, and that the message is
from them.'

'D'accord. But name them.'

'And the message is,' said Niniane, '"Perform the executions
only when you see one of your sisters. Be ready. Do it
immediately. But not under any circumstances until you see her."
All right? You have that?'

The boy repeated it, took the coins she held out to him, and
raced off down to the landing-stage.

We went back to Lule. Niniane asked her if she had her cards with her. She hadn't. 'No? I have a set somewhere. I've had it for years. Will you use them?'

'What do you want, exactly?'

'I want a card for each of us. Five cards.'

'Five?'

'You; Mariana; me, of course; Natalie; and Mère Malina. The cards will set us up for the evening. We shall know where we stand.'

'Who is this Mère Malina?'

Did she know her?

'An old friend of Guillaume's, apparently,' said Niniane. 'And a Wise Woman.'

'A witch? That's very strange. There was a Maalot, but she must be very old now – if not dead.'

'How old?' I ask.

'Ninety?' She is uncertain.

'Malina is forty, forty-something,' I told them.

'You're sure?'

'I saw her yesterday. With Mère Veronique, at the Adriatica. Which is owned by your brother.'

'We know that,' says Niniane, when Lule glares at me again. 'Did this Maalot have a daughter?' she asks Lule.

'Yes. Avice. Though I believe she was really her granddaughter.'

Avice?

'She wasn't a witch. She was a whore,' she shuddered, 'and simple-minded. Maalot used her, though, in her magic, or so Guillaume said. I never understood it. Guillaume was fond of Avice for some reason. He even paid them a pension so she didn't have to go on working as a whore, but of course Maalot just pocketed the money and sent Avice to work somewhere else without Guillaume knowing. Guillaume was a bit simple-minded too, in his own way.'

'Was it then she started working at the Adriatica, madame?'
'Yes, I think it was, in fact.'
Guillaume was not that simple-minded.
There is a moment's silence. Then Niniane sighs, and says:
'Please, Lule.'
'Very well. But first I shall need to spend some time alone
with the cards and my thoughts.'
Niniane smiles at me and goes to fetch the tarocchi cards.
Natalie is lying on her back, her head inside the apex of one
triangle, her feet inside the apex of the other, so that she is
enclosed within a trapezium, her hands extending towards its two
obtuse angles. Lule is kneeling at her head, on the corner.
Niniane returns and gives her the brightly-coloured cards.
Lule remains where she is, holding them just as they are, in
both hands, eyes closed.
Niniane takes me back into the red room, where we stand
together by the window.
'The way Madame Lule looks at me!'
'She can't stand being in the same room as a whore. The same
house even. That's why I was sent away as a child. But it wasn't
only her. My father and brother felt the same. When I was at
home I had to stay in this bothie out in a field right away from
the house. How old were you when people realised you were a
whore?'
'I don't know. Fourteen, I suppose.' I didn't like the thought
that I'd always been a whore, that everyone had known - surely
not! I liked to think it was something that happened to me, a
misfortune following my father's death, when I was kidnapped
and sold, but ... looking back and being honest, here with
Niniane, who was so open and honest and kind and good ... 'No,
I think my grandmother knew, long before that. And maybe my
teacher, the rabbi. It was - it was the way I behaved.'
'Of course. And don't tell me your father and grandfather
didn't know - and the men in your village.' She grinned

suddenly. 'But now, for a change, they need us as witches. Afterwards, they'll start treating us as whores again. Now, I know you've travelled to other worlds, but have you ever travelled successfully within this one?'

'I'm not sure. Sometimes, especially when I was child, but - they are more like dream worlds.'

'So I needn't ask whether you've ever appeared to people elsewhere in this world, in either ghostly or material form?'

I smile and shake my head.

'Then what we shall do is this …'

28

When we return to the other room, we are carrying three large candles in heavy, stable, candle-holders, Niniane in the lead with two of them, me following behind with the third.

Lule is still kneeling at Natalie's head, slowly shuffling the cards. She opens her eyes, watches as we place the three candles at the points of the second triangle.

Niniane lights them with a spill from the guttering, smoky lamp in the corner, then she blows the lamp out. She indicates that I should kneel at the corner to Natalie's right.

I do so.

She herself kneels at the corner to Natalie's left.

I realise that we're all facing in towards Natalie and each other. Surely in order to protect her we should be facing out? But Niniane seems to know what she's doing.

I wait.

Niniane's head is bowed in prayer, or meditation.

Suddenly Natalie stirs and speaks, making me jump. Then

there is silence again.

'What did she say?' I whisper to Niniane.

'That I should start with her,' Lule answers. 'Shall I, Natalya? Or is that Sitra Ahra speaking?'

Niniane says, 'Start with her anyway.'

Sitra Ahra: the power of the Other Side, the Left-hand Power. A chill runs up and down my spine. I'm beginning to seriously wish I was somewhere else. Somewhere like the river, where I had been in control.

No, I hadn't.

When had I last been in control of anything?

'Very well, then.' Lule gazes at Natalie, gives the cards one final shuffle, then lays the top card face up within the circle, by Natalie's head.

It is the World.

Lule says: 'The World is the most powerful of all the cards. She at least will survive this and be blessed.'

So the World is Natalie's card, not Strength. Interesting. But we could have done without that "at least".

'Why don't you put your amulet on now, Mariana?'

I take the beautiful silver pendant out of my purse and put it on, letting it hang outside my bodice, not hidden inside with the fish.

They both gaze at it, then Niniane says, 'That's you.'

I nod. I know, as they know, that this adds greatly to its power: power I shall need, for it links me ever more closely with Natalie. I do not tell them that the man who fashioned it died in a pool of blood shortly afterwards.

'And the fish?' I ask Niniane.

'No, keep that secret. Lule, you too should wear your amulet openly here.'

Niniane's bodice is cut low and I notice now that she's wearing a scarab on a gold chain. Why hadn't I noticed before?

Niniane misses nothing. 'It comes from Egypt,' she tells me. 'It protects those who journey outside time.'

Meanwhile, Lule has pulled out an amulet I know well: the
Hand of Fatima. She holds it for a moment before placing it on
her breast outside her bodice. 'My father – our father – gave me
this and told me to wear it always as protection against
witchcraft and magic.'

I know it only as protection against the Evil Eye: but perhaps
she is right.

'Who next?' Lule asks.

'You decide.'

'Then Mariana.' She leans towards me across Natalie,
extending the hand that holds the cards. 'Just touch the top card.'

I do so.

She lays it down beside the other. It is the Moon. Well, that's
a refreshing change from the Fool.

'Interpret them for us,' Niniane tells her.

'Mariana, you mustn't be frightened of the world that lies just
out of sight around the corner, the world where logic does not
reign; or of moonlight, thinking it will confuse you. The moon
will guide you; you will be astonished but you will not be lost.
Look at the crayfish, coming up out of the dark water into the
moonlight. And the dog and the wolf, which symbolise the two
extremes that call to you day and night: the tame and the wild;
the logical and the illogical.'

So. But she is right.

'Now my own is coming,' she says, and turns over the Star.
She lays it beside the Moon. She does not look impressed. But …
perhaps she is? I don't know her. I glance at Niniane: is that a
smile?

'I must stop hiding my head,' murmurs Lule. 'I must open my
eyes. There is light at the cave mouth: I must open my heart and
mind, which have been closed like a night-sky covered with
cloud.'

She takes another card off the top of the pack, plays with it, lays it on the floor face down, goes on playing with it, revolving it with her long tapering fingers and thumb.

I want to read that hand!

'Nininane?' she murmurs – and turns the card over. The Devil.

And now, for the first time, Niniane sounds upset. 'That's not me. It's Mère Malina.' The bitterness that lies between them is quite unbridgeable, I realise. Well, it would be.

'Let us pray that my card be a powerful one.' Niniane holds out her hand, ensuring that this next one will be her card.

Lule leans forward.

Niniane touches Natalie for a moment. Drawing strength? No, not that. Dedicating herself. Then touches the top card, as I did.

Lule smiles. She turns this one over: it is Justice.

Niniane's face is grim. For a moment she looks just like the figure on the card. 'A heavy burden.' Then she too smiles. 'Especially for a poupée like me.'

She means a pretty nothing, a doll, to be bought and sold. I am coming to know Niniane now.

'But,' the smile fades, 'I shall wield the sword.'

And with that she falls silent until, some time later, she says: 'We should turn round now, face out, and … prepare ourselves'

'I think I should remain facing in,' says Lule. 'I feel more comfortable like this, more secure. And what shall I do, how shall I guard Natalie, when you two are no longer with me?'

'As you like. But you, Mariana, prepare yourself.' She swivels round on her knees.

I follow suit, leaving Lule the only one now facing into the two triangles that form the magic circle.

Prepare yourself: before we came back into the room, she told me I must open a portal in my mind and wait for her: I imagine a door surrounded by roses, but it becomes one of a series of doors in a plastered wall. I do not like it.

Then I see the tunnel I used before.

I wait.

She said we would go to Montfaucon together, travelling outside time: by which I suppose she meant the journey would take no time. We shall be both here and there simultaneously. She will then appear to her brother. "And me?" I am simply to watch. Then when the men die, we shall seize their souls.

I don't quite like the sound of this: my uncle Rabbi Yacoub would not approve at all.

"I'll show you," she'd said. "You take one. I may take two or three; I may take just the abbé. We'll see." I'll take the cabin-boy, I decide. He won't harm me, dead or alive. But what use will he be? I must trust Niniane. Our motives are good – and I shall at least have something exciting to tell the Emperor Charles when I see him again. If I ever see him again. But on second thoughts, if he hears this story, he'll probably have me burnt. He's not a cabin-boy.

She is there, at the mouth of the tunnel. Reaching for me. She must have come along it.

I take her hand, step out into darkness – and see lights, hear voices ahead, and noise and music. Montfaucon. Row upon row of gibbets, of bodies slowly twirling. Around and among them, men and women drinking, dancing, laughing in groups, musicians and jugglers; people with trays of pies and sweets, and the occasional burst of light as a fire-eater passes by.

But the music seems strangely muted; I can hardly hear the voices, the laughter, the cries of the food and drink-vendors. I am invisible, too. And people not only look through me, they pass through me where I walk hand in hand with Niniane, as though I do not exist.

Niniane understands. For her, too, she says, everything is muted and unreal. She can make herself visible, but she is not really there: people walk round her, she says, 'but if anyone bumps into me they will pass through me as they pass through you. Look. Over there.'

A group of men in a tumbril. The prisoners. More men,

standing around the tumbril. The guards - the Albanian's men.
And the Albanian himself, with le Grec and some of his
henchmen, standing nearby, talking quietly.

'Choose your man,' she says.

'I have.'

'Go to him. Be with him when he dies. Then take him back to
the house, to Lule and Natalie. Wait for me there.'

'But what if he doesn't want to? What if - '

'No buts or what-ifs. Go straight back to Lule and wait there.
Do not wait for me here.'

'And if something should go wrong?'

'Then flee this place instantly, go on your own. Do not
concern yourself with me.'

We step forward.

The Albanian sees her.

Then he glances at me.

Does he see me?

A slight smile plays round his eyes.

She says: 'You took a sausage that he fed you. You took it
slowly, bit by bit. He's been in love with you ever since. He
cannot see you, but he knows you're here.'

The Albanian shouts orders.

'How do you know that?'

'I can read his mind, his memories - the open, obvious ones,
anyway. And the memory of his first meeting with you is like a
reflection in sunlight on the front of his mind.'

The tumbril is beneath a scaffold. The rope is placed about the
neck of a man I remember. They are all men who beat and raped
me.

That is why they are dying.

She is right.

The tumbril moves, the man screams and is jerked out and left
hanging there, legs kicking wildly.

'Go now,' she says. 'Go to your man. Let him know you are

here with him.'

'But what shall I say?'

'He will think you are dead. Let him think that, let him think you've come to meet him.'

The cabin-boy is behind the abbé, towering over him, taller than any of the others, but he is like a child: trusting still, yet bewildered and frightened.

The abbé is shouting that they cannot execute him, he is a religious, a priest. Even the Law, even the King, cannot execute him. They will be excommunicated. Their souls will burn in Hell.

I've heard that before.

I'm now beside the abbé. I look with his eyes at the Albanian, suddenly bright and real; hear the Albanian say, loudly, clearly: 'A real priest would be shriving the men around him, men about to die.'

'You mean – ?'

'I mean you will die last, and if you've given each one of them absolution, with no thought for yourself but only for the salvation of their souls, then I might …'

We look round desperately, grasp at the one who now has a noose round his neck. 'My son, do you repent of your sins?'

'I – '

'Misereatur tui omnipotens Deus et, dimissis peccatis tuis, perducat te ad vitam aeternam.'

'Get out of him! I must have him!' It is Niniane.

'I didn't mean to ...' I back out. He is absolving another man. 'But now he will not die.'

She laughs. 'You don't know my brother.'

And I realise. The first man died unshriven and her brother said "all".

'Exactly. Go to your man. This tall one here? You've chosen well, he is the only innocent. Now help him. Don't let him join in when the one they call the captain makes his bid for freedom.'

The captain's hands are loose. The Albanian knows. He will throw his knife, but not to kill.

I go to the cabin-boy.

And now I see the world through his eyes. He doesn't know I am there.

He wants his maman.

I come out again. Tears are streaming down his face.

I say, 'She cannot come to you, not now, not this time … But I am here.'

He looks straight at me, puzzled. The tears stop. A half-smile forms on his face; not the idiot-grin I know, but something. Then a noose lands on his shoulders, is jerked tight. He lunges round, huge and helpless, like a terrified horse. The tumbril moves, he is pulled backwards off his feet, knocking another man over – and the captain leaps.

But I know nothing of that, I am inside the cabin-boy, choking and jerking and leaping and dancing as he shits himself, writhes, leaps and twitches and dies, and I see his mother, his home, all gone now, burnt by skinners like those who burnt down Père Pierre's village of Saint Aubin, his mother burnt to make her tell them where her food was hidden in the forest, where what little silver she might have was buried. She died without saying, while he watched from the trees where she had sent him to hide.

And now he is calm … 'I didn't know you were dead,' he says. 'Did you die that night, beside the river?'

'No. But – '

'Then – I'm not dead?'

'You're dead. You have to leave your body now, it is no more use to you. You must come with me.'

'You? You'll look after me?'

'For a while.'

I need a portal, fast.

Imagine one – the same one you came through.

I glance back once at his motionless body; he does not. He

comes with me happily.

We emerge from the tunnel, see the three kneeling women before
and below us, the girl lying between them.
    'But that's you …'
    'Yes.'
    And now I'm in my own mind, my own body, again.
    'You're not dead?'
    'No.'
    'And me?'
    'You are.'
    'Then ... I have no body to go to?'
    'No.'
    'I can stay here with you in yours?'
    'No. Not that. But you can stay nearby. Be ready, should I
need you. And should you need me, I 'll be here.'
    'Then … I must live … outside?'
    'For now. Later, my friend and I will release you, set you free
to go wherever souls like yours – like you – do go.'
    'I shan't want that. I shan't – '
    'You will. By then, you will. For now, I have some tasks you
can perform, and so expiate the burden of guilt you bear for sins
against me and others like me. Wait.'
    I open my eyes.
    Blink.
    It's like waking up from sleep, except that I haven't been
dreaming. I remember when I woke up in Maître Herault's arms
on his horse; and that dreadful time when the bench crashed over
in the abbé's prison.
    I turn my head to let Lule know that I'm back. She is kneeling
as before, but her eyes are closed. I know at once that they are
not going to open. She is not dead: if she were, she would have
fallen forward over her knees, on top of Natalie. But she isn't
alive either, any more than Natalie herself is.

I begin to panic. Where is Niniane? Why doesn't she return? What if she can't return? Mère Malina … Horror courses through me. I can taste it. I remember a nightmare I had as a child, running headlong down the stairs with that same taste in my mouth and falling into my grandmother's arms, knocking her over so we both fell down and started laughing.

And now, with the memory, I find I can stand back and examine myself and my panic, watch as the other me argues that all will be well for I drew the Moon, and Natalie drew the World: and Niniane herself drew Justice and will even now be wreaking it.

Still fighting the fear (is it my own fear, or a fear imposed on me from outside?) I glance again at Lule. She drew the Star: now she is face to face with reality as she has never been before; but she will not be lost. No more shall I, for the world I am about to face is the world the crayfish faces as it comes up out of the waters of Maya, of illusion, into the light of the moon where all is revealed.

'Don't be frightened, dem'selle. When you are frightened, I too ...'

The cabin-boy. I'd forgotten about him. 'It was nothing – '

'Dem'selle!'

'What is it? Oh …'

Niniane. And with her, like a trapped hell-cat, a black ball of fury, the abbé.

Back in her body, Niniane glances at her sister, then looks at me. 'He knows who she is, this Malina, and where she is.'

'She is not who she is!' he screams. 'Nor is she where she is! You will never find her!'

Niniane ignores him.

I say: 'He must mean she is not who she seems to be – '

'Quite. And neither is she where she seems to be.'

'Like you this evening, when you appeared to your brother.'

'Not exactly, for I appeared as myself. And more real, for she can touch and be touched, speak and be heard. The one we seek exists, only she is not the figure Natalie and Guillaume, and the Flamels, and Soxxal here, know.'

'But in that case, why is she so concerned with Natalie? If Natalie cannot identify her …' Then I realise. 'She thinks Natalie may yet find Guillaume's papers.'

'That would be good news for us. What is not so good is that she is likely to be in possession of Natalie when it happens. Abbé!'

There were no more sparks flying off him. He gave the impression, now, of hand-wringing. I focused for a moment on the cabin-boy, who had been keeping in the background, and the abbé immediately became aware of his presence.

'You! What are you doing here?' The fury had not abated.

'He's mine,' I say.

'He's not. He's mine. As you should have been – almost were – would have been if I hadn't listened to you!'

'I warned you what would happen when the Albanian caught up with you. You wouldn't listen.'

'You will take us to Mère Malina, Abbé,' Niniane said.

Who did she mean? The real Mère Malina? Or ... who? Who was it? And suddenly it came to me. 'The one we want is not Mère Malina,' I said, 'as the abbé knows very well – for she is not who she seems to be, and nor is she where she seems to be. The one we want is an old woman, bed-ridden for years: one Mère Maalot, of Saint Aubin on the Island of Jersey.'

'Tell me. But be quick.'

'Natalie said – you heard her – that Guillaume knew Mère Malina well, like old friends. She also (but this was at the beginning, and I didn't realise the significance of it) mentioned a woman who could control the virgin-stone. So can Mère Malina. Maalot's granddaughter is called Avice. So is the mother of a university lecturer I know. And his grandmother, or great-grandmother, is bed-ridden. They come from Saint Aubin on the

Island of Jersey. So did Guillaume and his brothers.'

'I see. And you think this Maalot may have been Guillaume's original teacher – may be a more powerful sorcerer than he ever was, only she does not have the secret of the Philosopher's Stone.'

I nodded. 'But is she really unable to leave her bed? If she is …'

'There's only one way to find out: take Soxxal, and see.'

'You do that,' I told her. 'I prefer to go on foot and have my body with me where I can look after it.'

'Picture the house for me.'

I did so: the street, the front door, the interior so far as I remembered. Then, when she had it, I said, 'But what about Natalie and Lule?'

'There's nothing we can do for them. Not yet. Now we must attack.'

'I'll leave the cabin-boy with them.'

'The cabin-boy?'

'I'm a great believer in the power of innocence.'

29

Gesturing to le Pitre to keep out of sight, I knock at the door —
which is opened, after a long moment, by a woman of fifty or so.
The same tall woman. She was beautiful once: still is, though her
hair is white and her blue eyes a little empty-looking.

Avice. Philippe's mother. Also known as Mère Malina.

Will she remember me? No — because she is not Mère Malina.

'Bonsoir, madame. I am so sorry to disturb you at this time.
My name is Mariana de la Mar. I am a friend of your son's — of
Philippe's.'

'Philippe?' She looks vague. Trying to think. 'Philippe's not
here. He will be, soon.'

'I should like to talk to Philippe when he returns, but my
business tonight — and it is urgent business — is with his
grandmother. Or rather your grandmother.'

'Oh, you can't see her. She's bad tonight.'

She gazes, frightened now; is about to close the door on me. I
could hardly blame her. I followed her gaze as it took it my rags,
my bare breast, the marks of the whip.

But she, too, had been for many years a whore.

'Philippe would not like it if you shut me out.'

'Philippe …? No. No, of course not …' She stands aside for
me to enter the house, then leads me into the room where Raoul
and I spoke to Philippe on our earlier visit.

She seems uncertain what to do next.

I say: 'Where were you when you heard me knock? In here?'

'Oh no. I was in the kitchen.'

'Then let's go to the kitchen.'

She is not too sure about this either, at first, but once we are in
the kitchen she relaxes, and smiles at me for the first time.

'What were you doing?'

'This.' She touches a large mortar and picks up the pestle she laid down to answer the door. 'It's grain. I'm kibbling it to make frumenty for him tomorrow.'

'And what will you serve it with?'

'I have a rabbit. I shall cook it sweet and sour.'

'Sweer and sour?'

'Oh yes. I learnt that when we were with the army.'

'You were with the army?'

'Mm. The English army. Before we came to Paris. You cook it with raisins and onions and wine and vinegar and whatever spices you've got: I have some ginger and some canel.'

Canel? That is cinnamon, I know. I smile. 'It sounds delicious. Does Philippe eat again in the evening when he comes in late?'

'Oh no. If he's hungry, he eats in a tavern somewhere with his friends. Or with a friend.' She smiles. In the French it was "une amie" – a woman friend.

'So your grandmother is bad this evening? That's a problem because I do have to see her – and quickly. How bad is she?'

'When she's like this, she's not here. Not awake, not – you know?'

I know. Not conscious. And yet conscious perhaps of some quite other world or reality.

'And she hasn't been here, hasn't been awake, for hours,' the poor woman went on, 'not since yesterday. That's longer than ever. And she hasn't eaten or drunk …'

'Can you take me up to her? I should like to see …'

'I don't know. I don't think … She doesn't – '

'I must see Mère Maalot now. I really can't wait till Philippe comes home.'

I think it is my use of the name Maalot that does it. She leads me back out of the kitchen and through to the staircase. 'Up there. The first door on the left.'

Sending me up alone.

She is afraid of everything: afraid to take me up, afraid of offending Philippe. Most afraid of her grandmother.

I share her fear. From half way up the stairs, I look back down.

She has gone.

Then the stairs turn and lead up to the landing and the bedroom doors. It is dark, but not dirty. Avice is a good housekeeper.

The first door on the left.

I raise my hand to knock. Lower it again. She probably wouldn't hear me. And if she did – why give her time to compose herself?

I open the door.

I can see nothing. There is absolutely no light whatsoever. No light. No sound. A smell, though. The smell of age and of approaching death. Then my eyes adjust to the very slight light coming in from the landing behind me.

A curtained bed. A window, also heavily curtained.

I step in. Approach the bed. Put my hand to the black – black – drapes. Change my mind. Cross to what must be a window hidden behind those other curtains.

I draw the curtains aside.

It is night outside, but the moon is shining. The Moon.

I open the window (a real, glass window), breathe in the moonlight, let myself relax.

I turn back to the bed. Very cautiously, I pull aside the curtain.

I can see only her head. Her eyes are open. I am horrified; then realise they can see nothing.

Her cap has fallen aside: she has almost no hair – no eyebrows, no eyelashes. And she is tiny. She is like a doll, a tiny, ancient doll.

I want to protect her.

I do not trust this feeling.

I ought to want to kill her.

I should have to do it quickly. Instantaneously. If I give her time to return, if I smother her with that pillow, she will return and I shall not be able to handle her.

I peer round in the darkness.

And see, on top of the chest, a hand, holding a candle. I know it at once. It is the Hand of Glory: a dead hand, cut from the body of a hanged man. They used to make them at the House of the Two Fish in Cuenca, "curing" the hands, rendering the fat from the body to make the candles.

The hands add evil to already evil spells, and are very powerful.

Beside it lies a poignard, just such a poignard as Natalie lost in the river. But not that one? Forgetting the Hand of Glory (but now, surely, under its spell) I pick up the poignard and turn back to the head on the pillow.

Where does one pierce a head? The temple?

I nerve myself, steel myself to do it. Hesitate.

This is murder.

It wasn't supposed to be me who wielded the sword.

I dither. Begin to panic again.

Something is happening.

Should I do it now, fast?

But she hasn't stirred. It isn't her. It is Niniane. Niniane is here with me.

And then I see her, visible in the darkness.

'No, not that,' she says. 'If you had done that, Lule and I would truly have been lost. My body is closed to me now, just as Lule's is. Only Lule is trapped inside hers, and it is paralysed. And this would have taken over Natalie's body, possessed it, for ever.'

How much better to do nothing than to do the wrong thing. The beginning of wisdom. I vow never again to kill, at least in cold blood, never again to let myself be tempted to become the instrument of justice.

'Powerful witches like us never simply die. That is why they burn us. They think they have to. That if they hang us, we get up and walk away, undead. That if they cut off our heads, the heads go on thinking, go on casting spells. Whereas in fact what we do, given the chance, is leave one body and take up residence in another, younger one. The body is dead, but the witch is not. She has simply moved on.'

Like us? 'And that's what she wanted to do here. Take up residence in Natalie's body.'

'Précisément. If she'd settled for Avice's body, a body she had used so often, but this time on a permanent basis, no one would ever have been any the wiser; but she made a bid for someone younger and stronger, someone much more beautiful.'

Natalie. Yes.

'So what can we do? To prevent her from leaving her body and taking over – if not Natalie now, then some other defenceless girl or woman?'

'Seal her in.'

Seal her in?

But at that moment Philippe appears in the open doorway.

'Mariana? Is that you?' He peers in. 'Are you all right?' He comes in, glances at the bed, takes me in his arms. 'But what – what are you doing here? Have you any idea how dangerous …? And who were you talking to? She's not – '

'Philippe, listen.' I explain the situation, briefly. He doesn't argue or disagree. Finally, I say: 'Philippe, does she use your mother's body? Is Mère Malina your mother Avice's body and Maalot's soul?'

He nods. 'Yes. "Soul" I'm not sure about, but yes, that's what happens. Always she has ruled and dominated my mother. When I was a child, I didn't see, I didn't understand. I worshipped her, thought my mother a fool. Oh, she was beautiful, my mother, when she was young, but I knew that that wasn't … She gave her to the village priest on the island, to keep him sweet, to have him on her side when people started saying she - Maalot, my great-grandmother - was a witch … I'm that priest's son. It worked for a while, then Avice - my mother - was accused of living in concubinage with a priest. It was a way of getting at Maalot, but … they were tried in the bishop's court. He was ordered to fast on bread and water for a month. She was sentenced to nine strokes of the birch in the church yard on nine market days. Then they turned on Maalot again, and this time she had no protector; she brought us across to France.'

'How old were you then?'

'I was one.' He smiles. 'I have no memories of the island, of Saint Aubin. It's all a dream. My mother's dream.'

'And your great-grandmother? Does she still dream of Jersey?'

'She goes there. She makes their lives a misery. She's much more powerful now than she used to be … We followed the English army for a year and a half. Two full fighting seasons, and we wintered with them on the coast somewhere. She told fortunes, and sold amulets and potions. She put my mother to work as a whore. They were both very popular, from what I hear.'

'Who speaks of it?'

'Maalot. At least, she used to. She enjoyed being on her travels. She has - she had - great zest for life. At other people's expense, of course.'

'Of course. And she longs to enjoy life again.'

He nods.

'In this room with us is one we will call Sister Athanasía. Are you aware of her?'

He peers round. Then: 'Yes, I think so.'

Niniane makes herself more visible. She is not dressed at all like a nun.

I smile, I can't help it. 'Perhaps on second thoughts we will refer to her simply as Niniane.'

'Niniane. Yes.'

'She is a force for good.'

'I - I'm sure she is. Je suis enchanté, Dem'selle Niniane.'

I don't want him "enchanté". But perhaps Niniane does; it might be easier that way.

'Philippe,' I say, 'your great-grandmother needs to die.'

He drags his eyes from Niniane, and stares at me. 'We can't kill her.'

'No. But that wasn't what I said. She is ready to die. She should be dead. She keeps herself alive by means of sorcery, and at your mother's, and others', expense. It must be stopped.'

'I … D'accord. Yes. But how? She is very powerful. Very dangerous.'

'So are we,' says Niniane.

He looks back at her. Can he hear her?

'Niniane says we are too.'

'I understood. I heard her in my mind.'

'Good. So - Niniane?'

'We must build a magic circle around her, one even she cannot penetrate.'

'But she penetrated our other one.'

'No, this will be different. Simpler. The trouble there was that she was already both inside the circle, in possession of Natalie, and outside it, attacking Lule and me, and struggling with your cabin-boy. Natalie knows where the gold is.'

'She does?'

'Maalot helped her think, made her focus on the problem. Now they both know. However, she cannot take Natalie through the magic circle, which is guarded by the cabin-boy. Also, if she attempted to do so, Lule and I would be released and her hold on the cabin-boy would be lost. So you see, we must bring her back here. I suggest we smother her with a pillow.'

'Smother her?' Philippe looked shocked.

'Yes, but gently, carefully. She must panic, must think she is dying, must come rushing back here.'

'We shall have to leave a gap in the magic circle for her to enter, then close it.'

'Yes.'

'But how shall we build the circle? And with what?'

'I told you. It will be the simplest one, and in many ways the most effective. The three of us will surround her, holding hands.'

'And that will be enough?'

'With the cabin-boy and the abbé, yes.'

'Soxxal?'

'He is here, with me.'

I could neither see nor sense him.

'And Philippe is her own blood and wants her dead: that is the condemnation.'

'I don't understand.'

'Philippe is not motivated by self-interest.'

'Ah.'

'Philippe, stand here. Hold my hand. Can you?'

'I – yes! I feel you!'

'Now, Mariana. Press that pillow to her face – and as soon as she returns, take our hands, close the circle.'

I have just vowed ... But this is not killing. I am simply going to pretend to kill her in order to frighten her. I pick up the pillow, put it down squarely over the wizened little face and head, and press.

In seconds, she convulses.

I panic and hold the pillow down, tight – then remember that I am supposed to drop the pillow and grab their hands. I drop it, grab Niniane, then Philippe, but as I do so Maalot rears up, eyes wide, fighting to free her hands from the blanket that covered her.

She falls back again, glares up at us. At me. 'You ...'

Suddenly I realise we have no protection. We are the protection.

Her gaze shifts to Niniane: 'And you ... You will never re-enter your body.'

Then she realises that Niniane is not alone. 'You?' The abbé. Soxxal. She tries to conceal it, but she is shocked.

Till now she has not deigned to glance at Philippe, but with the first stirrings of doubt she turns to him. And it is his weakness she focuses on, not his kindness. Know yourself, they say; but you must also know and understand others.

His hand tightens on mine.

With a harsh coughing snarl like that of a savage cat, her mouth opens and we stare as, from the black hole between the drawn-back lips, there springs an imp, a tiny black devil, spitting and rasping.

It flies straight at Philippe's face.

He jerks back, tugging his hands free to defend himself, but I hold on to him and somehow Niniane does too.

The imp ceases to be.

Her second mistake. If she had launched the imp at me, I would have thrown up my hands and Philippe would have let me.

But now, Soxxal is talking to Niniane. 'When she is dead, shall I be free?'

'You will.'

'Swear it.'

I hear, but still do not see him.

'I swear.'

'By? You believe in nothing.'

'I believe in things you cannot dream of.'

'Then?'

'I swear by the lives of my sisters.'

'Agreed.'

And at last I see him, a faint outline as he spreads himself out above and between us, capping the small circle that we have formed around the old witch.

Then there is silence.

We wait.

'Water. I need water.'

We wait.

'Will no one give an old woman a cup of water?'

I am the weak link, not Philippe. He could be frightened, once; he cannot be appealed to. She fills him with horror.

Niniane? Hardly. Niniane herself is at stake, as well as her sister and Natalie.

And the abbé is a claustrophobic cloud of rage weighing down on her. Does he blame her for his predicament? We can feel some of it, but only the fringes.

Another croak which means something, then: '… an old woman thirst on her … bed?'

I feel Niniane tighten her grip on me. She knows.

'Did you notice the pause before "bed" …? Tell her you might, for one on her deathbed.'

'I might, Mère Maalot, for one on her deathbed.'

Suddenly, the floor shook - the whole building shuddered - swayed -

I screamed. I had been in an earthquake before, in Granada.

I was being held tight by Philippe now, as well as Niniane.

The tremors subsided.

They had felt nothing. It wasn't the building - or the earth. It was me. She had control of my mind. Through my sympathy. That urge to protect I had felt when I first beheld her.

Right.

I glanced down, looking for Pietri's pendant, but I had slipped it inside when I put on my cloak and forgotten to take it out again. There was nothing I could do about it now.

The cabin-boy said, 'I can take it out.'

'You? What are you doing here? What about Natalie?'

'She's recovered. She's looking after her mother. And Madame Niniane - her body … There's no danger there. The danger's here.'

He was right.

'Very well,' I said.

Still he hesitated. He was shy. I laughed – and so did he, remembering how he had once cradled me naked in his arms. I felt nothing, but suddenly the pendant was outside my bodice and seeming to glow, to shine silver in the darkness. She could touch me no more.

'Join me,' the abbé told the cabin-boy. 'Help me press.'

And the cabin-boy, long used to obedience, joined his weight to that of the abbé. It was not physical pressure. The old woman did not groan, did not show any reaction.

I was beginning to admire her. I wanted to stop him. I could have: he was mine, now, not the abbé's. But I did not.

We waited.

'Let me go back to Jersey, die there.'

We all heard the word "die".

'Now … a little water … for a poor old woman on her … deathbed.'

Was Philippe weakening?

We waited.

She was sleeping, her breath no longer rasping, just the faintest hiss … hiss … hiss …

'Take my place,' Niniane told the cabin-boy.

I felt nothing when he took my hand, but I knew he was there.

Niniane, inside the circle, was completely visible now, as solid-seeming as if she were really in the room with us.

She sat on the bed, gazed down at the dying woman.

'Maalot, do you hear me?'

She did.

'I am closing your body, Maalot.'

'No!'

'I am confining your soul, I am sealing you in.'
     From the little finger – the Mercury finger – of her left hand,
she took a ring I hadn't seen before, and placed it on the middle
finger of her right hand, the Saturn finger, but on the tip, and
back to front, so that the silver ring was outside, across the nail,
and the black stone underneath on the soft pad that forms the top
digit. A dull black stone, like nothing so much as a small black
pebble.
     'I seal each orifice – '
     'No! Do not bare me before the boy!'
     Niniane, her left hand on the edge of the blanket at the old
woman's neck, hesitated – then removed the hand. 'Bare you? I
do not need to bare you. This sealing, as you well know, would
work were I not in the room at all, but lying unconscious in some
other room on the other side of the city. There would be – there
is – nothing you can do, Maalot.'
     And with that, she extended her middle finger, the other
fingers raised like wings to each side of it, and touched Maalot
through the blanket. 'In the name of the All-powerful, the Ever-
open, I seal you, Maalot: I seal you here … and here … and here
…' She came to the head, the mouth: 'Have you anything you
wish to say before I seal your lips?'
     'Yes! Satan's curse on – '
     Niniane did not let her finish. She put the black stone to the
in-drawn lips, and said softly, calmly, 'I seal your mouth … I seal
this ear … and this ear.' Then she put the stone on the bridge of
the old woman's nose and with her index and ring fingers she
pressed the sides of the nose, sealing the nostrils. Finally, still
without another word, she placed the stone on the woman's
forehead, pressing it to the third eye, and held it there in silence
while the woman stared up at her, stared, only her eyes now open
... till Niniane closed them with her two fingers and held them
there.
     After a moment, she relaxed, returned the ring to the little

finger of her left hand, and said: 'Abbé, as soon as she is dead, you are free. And you, too, Mariana - wait here till the end, if you will. Farewell, Philippe.'

'But - !' Philippe and I cried simultaneously.

No buts, no what-ifs. She had gone.

30

I refused to get up the next morning. Yet I couldn't sleep. It was like wanting to forget a nightmare and at the same time trying to recall every detail.

Yahia was in the room. How long had he been there? He was the only one who never knocked. Why did he have that privilege? Because as they saw it, he was not a person: he was a thing. And in a sense, they were right. When you eunuched a man he was no longer a man, and he certainly wasn't a woman.

Foolish thoughts. Yahia was as important to me as any person in the world - and a great deal more important than any thing.

He had something to tell me. Something not urgent enough to warrant disturbing me, or even speaking first; nevertheless, he needed to say it.

'What is it, Yahia?'

'Lalla Natalie is here.'

It wasn't over.

'Bring her up.'

While Yahia washed and dressed me, and Natalie watched wide-eyed, she told me Niniane had disappeared early that morning, no one knew where to or when she'd be back. And her Aunt Mireille wanted to hear no more of the affair.

'What do you mean, disappeared?'

'I don't know. She took her nun's habit with her, and Tante

Mireille says she's always gone for weeks or months when she does that.

'She goes to a convent? On retreat?'

Natalie burst out laughing. 'Niniane? She uses it as a disguise. I thought you knew that.'

Silly me.

'And your mother?'

'She's talking to my uncle. He arrived early this morning and demanded to see her. He's very funny. He pretended he didn't know Tante Mireille: so she pretended right back – said it was a respectable house and they didn't entertain men of his type there. Then it was time they started, he said. He would send her a hundred men to entertain this evening – men of his type – and another hundred as soon as the girls recovered. I was shocked. I've never heard him speak like that.'

I laughed. 'And Mireille? Was she shocked?'

'Nothing shocks Tante Mireille. She was sure she could accommodate everyone, and would; she had her reputation to think of. Everyone except him. Now would he please state his business and get out.'

'And his business was?'

'Simply to talk to my mother, whom he does still recognise as his sister. But of course she'd gone back to the Montrouge residence. Still, he's right, isn't he. My mother is a lady.'

'She certainly is. So, what brings you here this morning?'

'Niniane left my – you know – the astrolabe that belonged to my – my – '

'Say it: say father. She gave you your father's astrolabe.'

'Yes. And – '

'Say it!'

'All right! She left me my father's astrolabe! I brought it with me because – '

'You brought it?' I raised my eyebrows at Yahia, remembered he could not follow our conversation, and asked him in Arabic.

'Yes, it's downstairs, Lalla Maryam.'

'Fetch it. And bring me – bring us – up some breakfast. Did Niniane say anything else, Natalie?'

'I didn't see her. But Tante Mireille told me Niniane had put a curse on whoever should further harm Disappearing Guilly. And she'd left him in my care! I was to see he was looked after! But when I went to check on him he said he didn't want to be looked after, to let them finish him. He could see I was disgusted. And it would be better to finish him! Tante Mireille's disgusted by him, too. She told me that even as a child, Niniane was always bringing home dying birds and animals and attempting to revive them. And getting beaten for it. I said, "Pity she doesn't get beaten for it still. Then I wouldn't be stuck with that creature." She smiled and said, "Oh, Seraphina's got a rod in pickle for her, too, when she returns."'

I did not like that "too". And with a sudden sinking feeling wondered what else Mireille – or Seraphina! – had told her. But she was still talking.

Very fond of her own voice this one was.

'I couldn't believe it! Niniane? But Maman said the other girls all get to taste Seraphina's rod if they annoy Tante Mireille, so why not Niniane? ... You know, when I was young, I wanted to be like Niniane when I grew up.'

When she was young?

I noticed suddenly that she who had blushed so easily no longer blushed at all. Ever.

She'd gone from being hardly more than a child to being this opinionated young adult overnight.

If she was rich, she'd be unbearable. No, she wouldn't, she'd be perfect.

'And now?' I ask.

'Now?'

'Who do you want to be like now?'

'Like Maman, of course. A lady. And hard ... I understand

finally - about Niniane, I mean - well, I have for a while - that
apart from her witchcraft - which is not something to be proud
of, is it? - she's just another feather-brained whore. Oh, she's
gorgeous - gorgeous enough to catch, and keep for a long time, a
King - but she hasn't a shred of common sense. I mean, consider:
she hasn't got two sous to rub together! After being for years the
mistress of a King! Where are the purses of gold and the jewels?
Maman says Pierre Montrouge took everything. Then after he
sold her to Tante Mireille, Mireille took everything. Of course.
And quite right. Mireille's not stupid.'

Mireille owns Niniane? 'But if Mireille owns Niniane, how is
it she's allowed to just disappear whenever she feels like it?'

'That's what I said. Disappearing like that without permission
would be running away - a crime. "She isn't allowed to," said
Mireille, "of course she's not." But Mireille's soft with her,
Maman says, she always has been; she takes advantage because
she knows Mireille won't declare her a fugitive. Maman believes
Mireille should. She says if Niniane belonged to her, then she
would.'

'And you?' I ask, curious.

She thinks about it. 'I don't know. Maman knows best about
such things, though, so yes. If she's a whore and belongs to
Mireille then she should behave accordingly. And if she doesn't
behave, she should be treated accordingly. Which, of course,
she's going to be from now on, at least by Seraphina.'

This second mention of the redoubtable Seraphina had the
same effect on me as the first mention, and this time Natalie
didn't miss it.

I found myself dropping my gaze.

'The good abbé did nothing wrong using his whip on you - at
least, that's what Maman says.'

I glanced back up and saw the smirk of triumph on her
beautiful face as she said, 'Mireille agrees. So does everyone.'

At that moment, Yahia came back with the astrolabe, put it on

the table and placed a piece of fresh bread and a sweet-smelling
tisane in front of each of us. Then carried on brushing my hair.
    I picked up the tisane and sipped at it. Yahia had saved me.
But no:
    'Maman finds you disgusting.'
    Right.
    I raised my eyes back up to hers: 'Like Disappearing Guilly.'
    She laughed. 'You know what I mean. I've spent a lot of time
at Tante Mireille's house over the years and I'm used to being
with prostitutes, talking with them, laughing at their stories and
complaints about all the different kinds of men they have to deal
with and commiserating with them when they're sobbing their
hearts out because some man's spanked them or Seraphina's
beaten them for being silly or thrashed them with that rod of hers
if they've been really naughty. I know their lives and I know
them. And I know that they're dirty, that they smell. No matter
how hard they try to keep clean, and some do try very hard, poor
things, a lady can tell at once if she's breathing the same air as a
prostitute.'
    I had lowered my gaze again when she mentioned Seraphina's
rod, desperate to hide the effect it had on me and the fear in my
eyes, and my embarrassment, and prayed that what Seraphina
told me had not, in fact, reached the ears of this new Natalie.
Now I looked up at her again.
    'You're right,' I said.
    'You know from experience.'
    'Oh, yes. I'm sure all but the most closeted ladies do.'
    'Well, obviously. I was thinking more of your experience of
being the one emitting the offensive odour. You certainly were
last night. As I say, I'm used to being among prostitutes, and
perhaps to some extent inured to the smell, and I'd never been
quite sure with you before, but yesterday I noticed even though I
was ill. Poor Maman found it quite overpowering.'
    'I was wearing someone's old clothes all afternoon and

evening – after jumping into the river to save you! Perhaps they smelt.'

'Ah yes. Maman and Mireille talked to me about that. I felt I owed you my life, but Mireille laughed and Maman said I was naïve, that prostitutes are always on the lookout for a chance to make a few sous. A rich girl in the river was a golden opportunity to one who could swim. I said they were being unkind, that you loved me.'

'I do.'

'So we organised a kind of test. If you had done it out of love for me, you would never mention it again, and be embarrassed if I did. If, on the other hand, you brought it up, it would prove to me that you expected gratitude, that you expected payment.'

Yahia, who is more sensitive to such things than any man, must have been aware of the animosity between us. I would have expected him by now to have offered, in Arabic, to throw the offending guest out. However, Yahia, too, is very fond of Natalie. Has been ever since that night she saved my life then stayed here at our house.

I sighed. I'd had more than enough of this conversation. And more than enough of Natalie for one morning, much as I loved her. 'Yahia, stop that and pass me the astrolabe.'

He set the astrolabe down between us and we both looked at it.

Why had Niniane taken it to Mère Mireille's house? For safe keeping? In that case, for some reason, she considered it important.

And she was right. It was. That was what had been nagging at the back of my mind. The astrolabe which had not been there.

'Maman says the real Lady Marian MacElpin lives in London.'

'What?'

'In a place called South-work.'

'That's nonsense!'

'My mother is a lady – a great lady, La Dame de Montrouge –

and she doesn't talk nonsense. You should be very careful what you say.'

I swallowed my anger. Moved my fingers in their own little dance as my grandmother had taught me so long ago: when the fingers say one thing and the face and the voice say quite another.

'Yes, of course. I'm sorry. Now can we get on with what is important?'

She laughed delightedly. 'Oh, please! If you're finally ready. Really, you're worse than Niniane. I must warn Mireille and Seraphina.'

Our eyes met.

Did she decide she'd teased me enough? She turned her gaze back to the astrolabe.

'The World is my card,' she said.

There was little doubt about that!

And mine was the Moon. Let her take the lead from now on.

'Do you think there might be something inside it?' she wondered. 'I don't want to break it. Anyway, it's not heavy. There can't be any gold there.'

'No, but …' I'd thought of that, and weighed it in my hands, when I first saw it in Maître Guillaume's laboratory. But if it did open, there might be papers in it. I remembered that ibn Khaldoun had had one in Granada, but I'd never seen him do more than fiddle with it and gaze at it. 'Yahia, did you ever see your master, Sidi Abd-el-rahman, open his astrolabe? Did it open?'

'Oh yes, lalla.'

'And do you remember how he did it?'

'Oh yes. I did it. You need big hands.' He carried on brushing my hair – one of his favourite tasks, and not to be abandoned without a struggle.

'Then do you think you could possibly open this one for us? Without breaking it.'

'Yes, yes, of course. Just let me finish – '

'Now, Yahia!'

He undid a brass screw at the top and spread one great hand out over the front and the other over the back, and twisted. For a second, nothing happened, then it began to undo, to unscrew, all round the edge.

He gave it a few more turns and there it was, in two halves, lying on his palms. And inside it was a small sheet of paper, folded in half.

I nodded to Natalie.

She picked it up, unfolded it, gazed at it – and passed it to me.

Greetings, little mermaid. Mermaid whom I never met. Search now beneath the Serbian guard.

The Serbian guard? Chuvar? But we have! We already have!

I tell Natalie what it says, watching sympathetically for the tears of frustration to start, but the superior smile she's been wearing all the time we talked, or rather she talked, does not fade.

'Shall we go back and try again?' I say.

She shrugs. We both know the compartment below the snake contained only papers.

'Do you trust your father?'

She nods.

'He had become neither crazed nor stupid with age?'

She laughs. 'Oh no. Anyway, he wasn't old.'

'You believe that as a general rule he will know more than you do – than we do?'

She shrugs again. Nods again.

'Then let's go.'

The secret compartment was now empty. Someone had been there, removed every scrap of paper.

The abbé?

Could there, though, be another, even more secret,

compartment? I tried to compare the sizes inside and out. There didn't seem to be.

Natalie watched me. 'If there's a secret compartment, it's empty – or it contains only more papers.' She tilted the box, then picked the whole thing up easily, and set it down again. 'No gold in there.'

She took something from around her neck.

It was Niniane's gold scarab.

'Niniane left me this. Tante Mireille said Niniane thought it might come in useful.'

I couldn't see how, unless Niniane expected Natalie too to undergo out-of-the body experiences. Which seemed unlikely. But I did see, suddenly, how Maalot had gained such complete control over this very intelligent and very headstrong girl. It had been that blood.

'Natalie, how did you come to be on the Île de la Cité yesterday?'

'I wanted to go home and search once more. You'd told me it was all mine now, and …'

'Did you ever get there?'

'I met Mère Malina and we were talking about what happened and I knew – and she knew I knew – and … Then somehow we locked eyes and I don't remember anything after that. I remember being in the river and you coming and then nothing else.'

'You told me your father took some blood from your finger that night, just before he died.'

'That's right. Yes! And you think – ?'

'I know that in the wrong hands … When she sent you to kill Lyse, it was a test – at least partly so. Oh, she wanted Lyse silenced. Lyse knew that your father's first love was with him that night – and I knew that Avice was Maître Guillaume's first love.'

'Avice?'

'Malina's real name. She is Mère Maalot's granddaughter.

Your mother knew Maalot and Avice, but by the time you came
to know "Mère Malina" years later, you'd forgotten all about
Maalot and Avice.'

'And Avice was my father's first love? Really?'

'On the island of Jersey, yes, when they were young. And her
grandmother, Maalot, was his first teacher.'

'I see …'

She was holding the scarab by its chain now, letting it dangle.

'She wanted Lyse silenced but, as I say, it was also a test and a
confirmation. If you shed blood at her bidding, you were hers.'

'Ugh ... You're good at that kind of thing, aren't you. So like
Niniane.'

The scarab was swinging from side to side now as if it had a
mind of its own. She held it over the wooden box. It began to
swing round and round in a circle, sunwise. Just as my little
silver fish had, all those years ago in Pedro's boat!

She was good at this kind of thing, too.

She stepped away from the box. Almost at once, the scarab
changed to a backward-forward swing.

It was swinging towards the box, I noticed. I gestured to her
to move round the box a little.

Still the scarab swung towards the box. Wherever she stood, it
swung towards the box. Again, she held it over the box. Again, it
swung round in a circle.

'Move the box,' she ordered. 'Over there.'

I took the whole box right out of the way. And now, even
when held over the box, the scarab swung towards the spot
where the box had stood; and when she held it over that spot
where the box had been, it swung round and round with no sign
of ever slowing down or stopping. And it was doing this for her.

'Did your father always keep the box in this same place?'

She nodded.

We both gazed down at the floor. There was no sign of a
break or an opening. We went to where the floorboards ended up

against the wall. Nothing. At the opposite end, the boards went under a cupboard.

We looked at each other. She opened the cupboard, got down, peered in. I jumped – for suddenly the floor beneath my feet had moved, two boards swivelling apart and opening a long narrow space between them. Where the box had stood were two bags of gold. Gold pellets, exactly as Pietri had described them.

She took one out and handed it to me.

I looked at her. She wasn't smirking. She was serious. The rich girl paying off a debt to whore. 'Maman will say I'm mad, that it's far too much, but grace à Dieu it's your lucky day, just as it is mine.' When I didn't take it, she laughed and said, 'Don't be frightened, I won't let her send men to beat you and get it back. I'll tell her it wasn't just for saving me from the river, it was for helping me here, too, and for everything. So. Your lucky day? All right?' She pressed the heavy nugget into my hand and closed my reluctant fingers over it. 'Talking about my lucky day, Mireille told me this morning that when she dies La Fille d'Or will belong to me.'

I was stunned. It must have shown.

'Hey! You don't look very happy for me!'

And so will poor Niniane had been my first thought. But now I smiled and said, 'I'm delighted! Of course I am! The Wheel of Fortune has turned, and after being so sad and so lonely for so long, you deserve all the happiness and good fortune there is.'

'Jaquet hasn't actually met my mother yet, but when he does, he'll adore her, and he'll want me to be just like her. He won't want me involved and mixing with prostitutes, let alone actually running the place like Mireille does. Of course, she's not a whore like Niniane, but then neither is she a lady. So it will probably be best to leave everything to Seraphina, let her sort you all out. She's good at that. Well, what do you think?'

'I think ... ' I thought I didn't want to hear why she'd said "sort you all out". I thought I didn't want to hear about Seraphina at all.

I thought the Three Weird Sisters had been busy and a future
very different from the one I had planned was coming up now in
the stars and on our hands and in the cards.

'I think that whatever you do, from now on you at least will be
happy, really happy.'

'Mm, I'm sure I will. Here, carry this for me.' She handed me
one of the bags of gold pellets.

'Ouf! They're heavy.'

She laughed. 'You're right, they are. You can carry them both.'
She pointed to the other one on the floor.

'Oui, dem'selle.' I put my own pellet in my purse, and picked
the second bag up.

'I notice you pocketed that nugget I gave you.'

'Yes. I ... '

'Whores are not gracious but according to Seraphina they can
be taught to be polite, and it would be polite to say something
like "Merci, Dem'selle Natalie".'

I'd been being sarcastic when I called her "dem'selle", but
she'd obviously missed that. Now though, it was only the
mention of Seraphina that stopped me throwing the pellet – and
her two bags! – through the open window. And the fact that I still
loved her, loved and liked the new Natalie.

'Merci, Dem'selle Natalie.'

'That's better. Much better. Now do come along.' And she
strutted out of the room.

I looked around.

And the papers? The real papers? Maître le Grec had left his
remaining gold to Natalie, and rightly so, but the real papers, the
secret, had not been meant for her, or for "the mermaid".

Who had they been meant for? Maître Nicolas? I doubted it.
Natalya – Niniane des Sept Soeurs, also known as Mère
Athanasía (and as Soeur Marie Saint-Pierre)? And as a feckless
whore? Or someone quite other? And had she – I was sure it was
a she – received them?

Perhaps I would never know.

When I got home, a footman from the palace was awaiting me
with a note from the Emperor. It read: I am permitted to invite
you, dear Mariana, to be my companion on the excursion to
Vincennes for a farewell pique-nique at Beauté-sur-Marne on
Sunday. Do please try to look after your nose and all other
vulnerable parts at least until then. Charles.

                          END